STORIES OF
SHEER PURE GRACE

Jan, 2019
Marian,
may God fill
you with fresh
grace for
the journey.
Nancy

N A N C Y   L.   N E L S O N

FOREWORD BY STEVE MOORE · EXECUTIVE DIRECTOR OF THE M.J. MURDOCK TRUST

Cover photograph by Makoto Fujimura: makotofujimura.com
Cover design by Jason Pearson: pearpod.com
Book design by Kris Hull: KR15.com
Set in Adobe Garamond & Proxima Nova

First Edition: November 2017
Printed in the USA

Dedicated
to
my loving husband, Stan,
who has been a conduit of
God's sheer pure grace and
has helped me become more
whole in Jesus.

ENDORSEMENTS

"Nancy's stories share firsthand her experience of God's grace in a way that is fully authentic and real. Read this book to those you love, out loud and around a campfire, and draw closer to each other and to God."

Ed McDowell, Executive Director
Warm Beach Camp
Stanwood, Washington

"Reading through *Stories of Sheer Pure Grace* is sheer, pure joy. Every chapter is marked by engaging stories of answered prayer, and profound insights into the character of God. If you're like me, you'll not only come away from reading this book with a greater appreciation for God's grace, but with a deeper inspiration to pray to the One who wants you to experience His grace!"

Joshua Brooks, Lead Pastor
Warm Beach Free Methodist Church
Stanwood, Washington

"Nancy Nelson's *Stories of Sheer Pure Grace* is a first person account of an extraordinary God at work in an ordinary life. How often we long for evidence of God at work in a frequently cruel and confusing world! Through Nancy's stories we see that God is always there, and if we are willing, He will use us to be the conduit for his unfailing love."

Joan Wallace
Wallace Properties, Inc.

"Nancy Nelson's book, *Stories of Sheer Pure Grace*, invites us into the power and generosity of our God's grace. Story after story reminds us that God calls us beloved and is present moment by moment in the subterranean sanctuary of our souls. You will laugh, cry, and be over-whelmed by joy as you read these stories of how the Triune God of the Universe cares about us individually, mindful of the smallest detail of our needs and desires. You will be encouraged and your hearts lifted, causing you to experience hunger for this amazing grace that is the rich presence of God indwelling in us lavishly and bringing transformation."

Rita Nussli
Spiritual Director
SoulFormation

"I have a deep yearning to see the activity of God around me, and to hear the stories of God's faithful provision, guidance and movement! Reading these stories has illuminated for me the wonderful diversity of ways in which the Triune God moves, speaks and reveals more and more to those who seek to be awake to that activity. If you seek, as I do, to hear about God's movement around us and to be encouraged, bless-ed, challenged and refreshed then this book is for you. Immerse yourself in God's activity through these stories, and maybe you will begin to see where God is at work around you as well."

Rev. Samuel C. Schaar
Senior Pastor, Real Family Church
San Jose, California

"Nancy's heart is warm and welcoming to the spirit of God. This is evi-denced by the humorous and captivating way she unfolds her life's jour-ney within the pages of this book, and in the way she conducts herself. Dedicated to prayer and devouring scripture, she has found her voice in God's grand story of sheer pure grace, inviting us into the same. Her delight is contagious and in her efforts to be ordinary, she offers an ex-traordinary gift here--the promise of answered prayer and a reminder to be intimate with the One who loves us the most."

Nancy Murphy
Executive Director
Northwest Family Life Learning & Counseling Center

"*Stories of Sheer Pure Grace* is a running account of real experiences of grace and guidance in lives committed to following Jesus Christ. It is stirring, inspirational, honest, uplifting, and just plain delightful. My privilege was to work alongside the author for at least half of these stories during my term as Executive Director of Warm Beach Christian Camps & Conference Center. I saw the growing fruits of faith, joy, and results in the Nelsons' lives along with a good sprinkling of the miraculous. Read carefully. You might find yourself challenged on some of these pages. Prepare to be prodded!"

Bob McDowell
Executive Director (retired)
Warm Beach Christian Camps/Conference Center

"The Nancy Johnson that I knew from our mid-1960's senior high school youth group at Trinity Lutheran Church of Minnehaha Falls in Minneapolis was quiet, shy, and reserved. The Nancy Johnson Nelson I met when we reconnected a few years ago after a forty year interlude, and have since come to know more deeply, is an outgoing, disciplined, highly competent leader and communicator. Each of her *Stories of Sheer Pure Grace* shines additional light on the attitudes, influences, experiences and decisions underlying that striking transformation. At its core is her rock-solid faith in Christ and strong reliance on prayer."

Gary Alfson
Senior High Youth Director, Trinity Lutheran, 1965–1967;
National Youth Director,
Lutheran Evangelistic Movement, 1967–1971

If you want to understand the power of prayer, this book is for you. Through delightful storytelling, Nancy Nelson gracefully reminds us that it doesn't matter if we're praying for what seem like earthly things (cars, motel rooms, lost dogs) or deeply personal things (our child to read, our parents to enter Heaven NOW!), the Lover of our Souls hears our cries and answers in His way and His time. This book drew me to the warm, listening heart of the Father, and inspired me to leave a legacy of prayer in my life, as Nancy has in hers.

Heather Tuininga
Guest Commentator – The Eternity Portfolio Illuminated
Speaker, Writer, and Principal of 10|10 Strategies

"What an amazing book! This collection of fifty inspiring stories ignites HOPE that God does immeasurably more than all we can ask or even imagine! Nancy writes simply yet profoundly and moves our hearts to listen to HIS voice, trust Him, and obey Him! As you read, you will hear the music of God's good future coming your way, and by faith you will begin to dance to it NOW! I believe God will use these stories of sheer pure grace to launch a mighty prayer movement in families, churches, and ministries across our nation! After reading this book I am convinced once again that God releases his power in response to the prayers of his people! Thank you Nancy!"

Dr. Jason Hubbard, Executive Director
The Light of the World Prayer Center, Bellingham WA

FOREWORD

Sometimes the way to catch the best picture of something is indirectly, at the edge of our vision. Maybe it's wildlife while we are on a walk in the woods. Maybe it's a shooting star in the night sky. Maybe it's a gentle expression of love being shared by a long-married couple.

Stories of grace are just that. It's hard sometimes to describe, to capture, to envision grace in a way that fully represents this uniquely divine expression of God's generous and undeserved favor and love. Perhaps one of the best-suited ways for that to take shape in the human imagination is through stories: stories of God breaking through; stories of God overcoming; stories of laugh-out-loud, take-a-breath, you've-got-to-be-kidding-me kinds of experiences that remind us that we are not only finite beings, but we are also fragile and in great need of God's grace more than we can ever imagine. In fact, He is at work in ways all around us whether we realize it or not! If our hearts, minds, and senses were more attuned to it, we would be even more amazed than we are at how He is at work and where He is moving!

Nancy Nelson is one of those people whose passion is to pay attention in just those ways. And she would like it, thank you very much, if all of us would pay attention too! She provides for us, in this collection of stories, beautiful glimpses of God breaking through. But she also models for us someone who is paying attention.

I have sometimes said that gratitude is much more than good manners; it's a spiritual practice. G. K. Chesterton said it better: "Gratitude is happiness doubled by wonder!"

There are several threads that run through these stories Nancy has carefully crafted and remembered. One thread is gratitude, one is grace, but most certainly other threads include wonder, joy, and the belief that God desires to meet us not just at the point of our need, but at the point of His calling in our lives. He has created us for a purpose and wants to shape and mold us to the fullness of who He made us to be so that we can be fully the ambassadors of His kingdom come, on earth as it is in heaven.

As you read these stories, you'll catch a glimpse, many glimpses of grace—shooting stars in such a time and place as this. Pay attention, with eyes wide open to the mercies of God.

Steve Moore
M.J. Murdock Charitable Trust
Fall 2017

ACKNOWLEDGEMENTS

Writing a book is a lot like birthing a baby and parenting that child into adulthood. Those of us who have become parents have had no idea what lay ahead; otherwise, we might have been too afraid to attempt the journey. We soon found out that it really does take a village to raise a child. Likewise, it takes a massive support system to bring a book to completion.

This book would never have become a reality if it were not for Leigh Wilson, trusted friend and editor, who worked hard to save my writer's voice while skillfully dissecting every sentence. I joke that Leigh eats grammar books for breakfast. And then there are the three "J's" who so carefully critiqued the manuscript with suggestions for the editor: Judy Lang, Joanie Yonker, and Joan Husby.

The beautiful picture on the cover, Charis-Kairos (The Tears of Christ, 2017), was gifted for that purpose by Makoto Fujimura, artist and founder of the International Arts Movement. Thank you to Makoto for allowing us to use one of his images for the cover of this book. The original is Japanese Nihonga art (mineral pigments and gold on Belgium linen). Makoto Fujimura can be contacted at _MakotoFujimura.com_ and is represented by Claire Ho, Artrue International (_Claire@Artrue.asia_). Makoto, thank you also for encouraging me to write down these stories to be shared.

Jason Pearson, graphic artist and owner of Pearpod in San Clemente, California, so graciously designed the cover as a whole. Trish Beagle, owner of Trish B Photography, with patience and expertise commandeered a wiggly group of grandkids for the back cover picture taken in our favorite spot in front of Warm Beach Camp overlooking Port Susan Bay on Puget Sound.

I would also like to thank Scott Brownson (A.K.A. "Mr. Montana"), Development Director at Clydehurst Christian Ranch in Montana, for his song entitled "Grace Upon Grace" that so appropriately wraps up this book.

From start to finish three people read the raw unedited copy and cheered me along: Gary Alfson, my former youth pastor; Jonathon Anderson, the Lutheran Evangelistic Movement historian; and my former pastor at Warm Beach Free Methodist Church, Pastor Sam Schaar, who is now the senior pastor at Real Family Church in San Jose, California.

Steve Moore, Executive Director of the M.J. Murdock Trust, allowed me to use the Murdock Trust's name in many of the stories and then agreed to write the Forward to the book.

A huge thank-you goes to Warm Beach Camp's Executive Director, Ed McDowell, and the Camp's Board for granting me a two-month sabbatical to finish the first draft of these stories.

And then there's my dear family and multitude of friends who have allowed their parts in the stories to be shared in print. Without their scrutiny and permission, the book would lack authenticity.

After four years of the birthing process, just when I was near exhaustion, Kris Hull, of KR15 Creative Services, coached me through the final grand design push to bring this book to press. The professional look of the book's interior is entirely due to Kris' expertise.

And finally, I am eternally thankful for the army of warriors who prayed me through this birthing process, including the Soul Crafter's Sunday School Class at the Warm Beach Free Methodist Church in Stanwood, Washington; Art and Martha Smelser, Chairmen of the Warm Beach Camp's prayer team; and Pastor Larry Wersen, founder of His Place Church in Burlington, Washington.

My heart is filled with gratitude for you all!

INTRODUCTION

I originally began this book, a collection of fifty stories, to leave a written record of my husband's and my life's journey for our family, including the future generations that we will never have the opportunity to meet. Since my husband, Stan, and I have spent almost forty years working at Warm Beach Christian Camps and Conference Center (WBC), the book also began to take on a historical perspective of the Camp's ministry during our time on staff. Because we raised our family while living on the campgrounds for seventeen years, some of the stories about our family thus have the Camp as the backdrop. As it turns out, the following pages interweave our family's history with that of Warm Beach Camp, and this book tells both our personal story and significant portions of the Camp's story as well.

While I recounted these memories primarily for our family, we aren't keeping them to ourselves; you can take a peek too. So that you don't get lost, here are the main characters besides Stan and me: our son, Thad Johan, and wife, Abby, and children, Julie, Clara, and the wee baby, Johan, on the way; and our daughter, Cherith Joy Lee and husband, Chad, and sons, Preston and Eli. Oh, and I mustn't forget the granddogs: Latte, our son's family's beloved chocolate lab, and EZ, the Lee's gentle plott hound.

It won't take you long to uncover that I love Eugene Peterson's paraphrase of the Bible, *The Message*. After reading Peterson's *Eat This Book*, explaining why he produced *The Message* for plain folks like me who don't have a grasp of theology nor of the Hebrew and Greek languages, I realized that I took his advice: I have meditated, chewed, and prayed my way through *The Message* many times—especially key passages. I will forever be grateful to Eugene for his paraphrase. I love to pray *The Message* because it's more like the way I talk. Praying *The Message* has gotten me through the last twenty years raising resources for WBC in the Development Department, a task that will always be impossible in our human strength alone.

In June of 2017, Stan and I had the awesome privilege of spending time with Eugene and Jan Peterson in their lovely home on Flathead Lake in Montana. At that meeting I showed him my tattered, torn copy of *The Message* that literally has pages falling out of it. I exclaimed to Eugene that I had taken his advice and "eaten the book!" He threw back his head while laughing heartily.

By far my favorite passage to pray from *The Message* is Matthew 11:25-30, parts of which are woven through some of these stories. It begins, "Abruptly Jesus broke into prayer: 'Thank you, Father, Lord of Heaven and earth. You've concealed your ways from sophisticates and know-it-alls, but spelled them out clearly to ordinary people. Yes, Father, that's the way you like to work.'..." So many times I have thanked the Lord that we are plain and ordinary, and that He is willing to reveal His ways to us. As Eugene concludes in his introduction to I and II Samuel: "...As we submit our lives to what we read, we find that we are not being led to see God in our stories but to see our stories in God's. God is the larger context and plot in which our stories find themselves." And like I and II Samuel, these *Stories of Sheer Pure Grace* are all framed by someone praying.

I have tried to place these fifty narratives in chronological order. While each is written to stand on its own, it's perhaps best to read them in the order they appear. Make certain to start with the first story, "The Revealing Wordsmith," to discover how the book came into being. While it has taken me four years, I have tried to contact everyone named in each account to make certain that my memory is correct, and to obtain their permission to be included by name in the book. If I have somehow missed you, please forgive me.

All profits from this book will go toward the Special Friends camping program at Warm Beach Camp, a program that serves people with disabilities.

Life in God is really all about grace, sheer and pure, and the very title from this book was taken from passages in *The Message:* sheer grace is found in Jude verse 4, and pure grace comes from Ephesians 6:24. Perhaps the title of the song by Scott Brownson found at the end of the book summarizes it best: we each live in *Grace upon Grace*. Enjoy these fifty *Stories of Sheer Pure Grace*, each one an answer to someone in prayer, and each one bringing out a characteristic of our God, who while we may humanly try to describe Him, is infinitely indescribable!

STORIES OF
SHEER PURE GRACE

1: THE REVEALING WORDSMITH

This collection of fifty stories that you are reading is actually a long answer to a prayer that I began consistently praying sixteen years ago, a prayer that God can't resist answering. As a matter of fact, God, who is not confined to time or space, was answering the prayer before I even began to pray it! Paul prayed this same prayer often for the Christ-followers in Ephesus and he recorded it in his letter to them in Ephesians 1:17-21 (NIV). My personalized version begins like this:

"God, give me 'a spirit of wisdom and revelation' that I might know you better…"

The very thought that the God of the Universe is willing to have an intimate relationship with us human beings is beyond my comprehension. Because mankind had made such a mess of things, God took on human form in Jesus and experienced everything we humans do. Eugene Peterson paraphrases Romans 8:4 this way in *The Message*: "In His son, Jesus, he personally took on the human condition and entered the disordered mess of struggling humanity in order to set it right once and for all." Jesus gave his life so that in knowing him we could be covered with his blood and he could present us righteous before his Father. As Peterson paraphrases in Romans 5:20, "… sin didn't and doesn't have a chance in competition with the aggressive forgiveness we call *grace*." We can have a relationship with God, not because of anything we do, but because of what Jesus did for us in becoming the sacrifice for our sins.

God began revealing his answer to my prayer "for a spirit of wisdom and revelation to know Him better" in a unique way as I began collecting stories that were all answers to someone praying. Each story revealed a characteristic of God and how He was revealing Himself to me. I began to ponder compiling a book of these stories, especially since I had dreamed of writing a book since childhood. Books held a lot of wonder for me because I didn't begin to read until fifth grade.

While I have told many of these stories often, I thought that writing them down, along with the conclusions I drew from them, would be reserved for my private worship of God, praising Him for who He was revealing Himself to be. But that all changed in December, 2013, when I had a brief encounter with an artist and educator, Makoto Fujimura, the visiting scholar at the M.J. Murdock Trust (The Trust).

Makoto and I were both at a reception before the Christian Leadership Conference sponsored by The Trust and the Stewardship Foundation. The conference was about to begin the next day at the Hilton Hotel in Vancouver, Washington. When Makoto asked what I did as a career, I explained that I was the development director in charge of raising resources for Warm Beach Camp and also on the faculty for The Trust's Essentials of Development Program. During our extended conversation I shared that it was delightful to raise money for Camp since God had opened up so many exciting streams of ministry to the marginalized.

After telling Makoto the story of how God changed the culture at Camp through the Special Friends Program for people with disabilities, I found that he was intrigued. After hearing that I had many tales like the one I had just shared, Makoto asked, "Have you ever thought of writing a book?" I responded that I had been praying about it but my concern was whether my stories should be shared in print since this collection was used in my private worship of God to praise Him for who HE is. Makoto emphatically said, "No, these stories are a sacred trust from God. They are not to be kept to yourself but have been given to you to be shared."

After the dinner that followed the reception, Makoto, who is the founder of the International Arts Movement, found me and handed me a copy of the introduction to his next book, *On Becoming GENERATIVE, An Introduction to Culture Care.*

After college, as a young artist Makoto taught in a special education school, and the story I had shared with him earlier in the day came from the trenches. The story (titled *"The Culture Changer"* in this book) was a practical illustration of the thesis of Makoto's next book. It was a perfect example of what it would look like to bring beauty into culture. Over time these special people with disabilities have mysteriously and tenderly changed our Camp's culture, bringing out the "special" in all of us.

I went home from the conference and looked up Makoto's website and was amazed at his gallery, the result of using an ancient Japanese technique of painting involving precious metals. As I scrolled through the art work I came upon a collection entitled, "Images of Grace." One painting in particular caught my eye: "Charis" was made with layers of pure gold that "create space that is both flat and spatial." Like this beautiful painting, each of my fifty stories, in a tiny finite way, would also magnify a layer of God's infinite character.

Within days, I started writing one story at a time without concern as to the order that they would eventually take. This collection is the result of sitting at the keyboard each morning for two months and praying, "Holy Spirit, wordsmith through me these stories so that they bring honor and glory to God." And throughout my many days of writing, two words stayed before me like the Star of Bethlehem in days of old: "sheer" and "grace." The title of this book, *Stories of Sheer Pure Grace*, was confirmed in my spirit by Makoto's artwork and my sense of God's limitless love for us all.

The word "sheer" has two definitions upon which I relied when writing. The word first means utter, complete, absolute, total, and pure. It also can mean, in reference to fabric, diaphanous, thin, gauzy, and transparent. And so, it seems, that God's grace for us is indeed "sheer." Not only is it absolute and pure, but like a thin garment it surrounds us and is wrapped around our very souls, simply waiting for our invitation for it to enter the fabric of our lives.

Over and over again, grace is emphasized by the authors when beginning and ending the letters that are recorded in the New Testament of the Bible. A typical example is found at the beginning of Galatians in verse three: "GRACE and peace to you from God our Father and the Lord Jesus Christ…" (NIV). My all-time favorite usage is found in Ephesians 6:24 in *The Message*, where Paul writes: "Goodbye, friends. Love mixed with faith be yours from God the Father and from the Master Jesus Christ. PURE GRACE and nothing but GRACE be with all who love the Master, Jesus Christ."

God is **THE REVEALING WORDSMITH**. He not only called the world and everything that exists into being with His word, He wrote the best seller of all time, *The Holy Bible*, through some of his devout followers. God's storyline is restoration which depends solely on trusting in HIS sheer pure grace. And He is willing to intimately reveal Himself to anyone who sincerely asks for "a spirit of wisdom and revelation to know Him better," for He is the "Word who became flesh and dwelt among us." (John 1:14)

2: THE WAY MAKER

Little did I realize what a blessing it was to be part of Trinity Lutheran Church of Minnehaha Falls throughout my entire childhood. This was a "thin place" where Heaven overlapped earth and the Kingdom of God was at hand. Trinity provided an amazing community of faith with a rich history of prayer and altar calls at the end of services.

The camping movement was also a huge part of Trinity's heritage. Every summer, the Spirit moved mightily at camp! I remember experiencing the grace of Jesus upon committing my life to the Lord at Camp Emmaus in fifth grade. After renting Camp Emmaus for years, while I was in high school the church purchased land up in northern Minnesota and built Camp Patmos with all-volunteer labor. Out of Trinity sprang the Lutheran Evangelistic Movement, the World Mission Prayer League, and the Lutheran Colportage Mission. Stories have been passed down about two of Trinity's pastors, Rev. Conrad and Rev. Force, which affirm that they were mighty prayer warriors.

In 1950 Pastor Force felt the call of God to leave Trinity to begin a two-year Bible school, California Lutheran Bible School. It was quite common for graduating seniors at Trinity to attend this non-accredited school in the heart of Los Angeles before beginning college. A lot of our camp counselors had gone to CLBS, including Jan Bays, an influential person in my journey. At the beginning of my senior year, along with others in the youth group, I had my eyes set on leaving home after graduation for an adventurous couple of years. However, my parents opposed this plan as they had dreams of a college degree for me and had saved to help make it possible.

I scheduled a meeting with Gary Alfson, our Youth Director, to get advice and hopefully gain his support. Gary himself had gone to CLBS and surely would override my parents. I was not, however, pleased to hear this man's advice: "If God wants you to attend CLBS, He will make a way. You are not to go without your parents' blessing." Looking back now, I marvel at the wisdom Gary displayed at only twenty-three years of age. So, we began to pray. There was a prayer mantle over Trinity, and it extended to the youth as well. Prayer was the answer to everything.

One day in the spring of 1967 my mom and I were shopping. I saw a pair of winter boots on sale and pointed them out to her. I was shocked by her response: "You won't need them if you are in California next winter." From that point forward it was just accepted that I would be going with the gang to study God's Word, in-depth. I was afraid to ask what had changed her mind and wouldn't find out until years later how God had opened the way.

Upon my promise that I would complete my college education after Bible school, my parents very graciously paid half of my tuition for CLBS along with part of the living expenses for an apartment in the inner-city slums of L.A. During those two years, I not only learned about the Bible, I learned about life…simple things, like paying bills on time, buying groceries and fixing meals, cleaning the toilet, getting along with roommates, and doing my own laundry.

CLBS students went to school in the morning and held down part-time jobs in the afternoon. I was the assistant to the professor of actuarial math at Occidental Life Insurance Company, doing tasks like correcting math tests and filing. I marvel at God's protection as it was not a safe neighborhood. We were within walking distance of MacArthur Park, where someone was stabbed or raped every couple of months.

This wasn't the only time that God made a way in my life for a major move. After finishing school at CLBS, I returned home and registered at the University of Minnesota, where I completed my freshman year in 1970. That summer, my future husband, Stan, was in Minneapolis painting houses with his former CLBS roommate, Sid Featherstone. I still remember a particular Saturday in August as if it were yesterday. In order for Stan to finish a house by Lake Nokomis, I was helping him paint so that we could go waterskiing the next week. My painting experience was almost non-existent, and I was covered with paint from head to toe. We were taking a break for lunch, sitting on a blanket by the lake. While I was eating a peanut butter sandwich, Stan asked me to marry him. It wasn't the way I had imagined a marriage proposal would be, so I thought he was kidding. I made Stan ask me three times until it was evident that he was serious.

My folks loved Stan and could see that he was the man for me. Yet, they were concerned that I finish college, so I assured them that we were planning to wait three more years until I had my B.S. degree from the University of Minnesota. In September, Stan returned to Sacramento to continue his education at American River Junior College.

With a diamond ring on my finger, we began a massive letter-writing campaign—almost one a day. Before emails or texting, our letters would cross in the mail and sometimes contain the same Bible verse for each other. While this was an extremely "safe" way to have a relationship, it was even less romantic than "kissing through the screen door." Our theme song quickly became "Leaving on a Jet Plane." It was like a part of me was missing, and after being together at Christmas time it was even more difficult. I would often cry in secret while washing the glassware as an assistant in the Nutrition Lab.

Sensing my distress, one night in January my parents came upstairs and gathered around my bed on their knees and said it was time to ask God for wisdom. My folks were not used to praying out loud, and the only prayer I had ever heard them pray was a memorized grace before meals. I had no idea that my mom was a secret-closet prayer warrior! That night I heard my Dad pray for the first time in my life, a simple but earnest prayer, asking God to show us what to do about the timing of my marriage. After he finished praying, he said words that I will never forget: "Your mom and I have been talking. If you and Stan want to get married before you graduate, we will continue to pay half of your tuition and books." This was unbelievable to me as they had not done this for my sister, Peggy. She was financially on her own to finish college after she and her first husband got married.

Stan was speechless on the phone when I called the next day to inquire, "What are you doing for Easter vacation?" Without giving him a chance to answer, I added, "Why don't we get married?!" Everything was pushed into high gear: there were only three months to plan a wedding! We got married on a Tuesday night, April 6, in the middle of Stan's spring break so that he could be back in class at American River College in Sacramento the following Monday.

I sat out spring quarter before starting at the University of California, Davis in the fall of 1971. Instead, I found a job managing a department at a brand new Penny's store after applying at fifty-six places. By jamming each quarter with extra classes, I graduated with the rest of my class in June of 1973, with such a high GPA that I was able to get into an all-expense-paid, government-funded dietetic internship including a master's degree program in Public Health at UCLA. My folks proudly attended both of my college graduations. I had more than fulfilled my promise to them, and graduated debt-free by working part-time.

Years later I would learn that my promise to finish college wasn't the only promise fulfilled. When I was in graduate school, I began experiencing pains in my left arm—probably from carrying too many books! While talking with my mom about it by phone, she revealed a long-kept family secret. When I was six months old I had surgery to remove a cancerous tumor under my left arm. The surgery was not news to me as I had been told that my huge scar was due to the removal of a fatty tissue, but I had not known it was cancer and I was shocked. Because I was working with cancer patients during my hospital internship rotation at the VA, this sudden revelation sent me into a deep depression which was termed an extreme "anxiety reaction."

Long after I had recovered from the two-year depression, I asked my mom whatever had changed her mind back in 1967 to let me go to Bible School before college. Her explanation gave me a deep appreciation for this woman's commitment to me and to God. After the cancer surgery in my infancy, the doctor told my parents that he felt they had gotten all the cancer because the tumor appeared to be encapsulated. Since the medical team did not recommend any treatment for such a wee baby, I would be pronounced "cancer free" if the cancer did not return within five years. My mom took to the prayer closet and begged God during those five years to heal me completely. She made a promise that if God would save my life, HE could have me for HIS purposes.

Seventeen years later, the Lord reminded my mom of her promise. HE made a way for me to attend CLBS, just like HE made a way for me to marry Stan before I finished college. HE is **THE WAY MAKER**, orchestrating the details behind the scenes in the unseen realm!

3: THE ULTIMATE MATCH MAKER

During the early spring of 1968, while I was completing my first year at California Lutheran Bible School (CLBS), my former youth pastor from Trinity Lutheran Church in Minneapolis, Gary Alfson, appeared in Los Angeles to reconnect with a bunch of his former high school youth group members. As the newly appointed National Youth Director for the Lutheran Evangelistic Movement (LEM), this now-twenty-four-year-old visionary was putting together groups of young adults to travel throughout the United States on Gospel Crusader Teams in order to share the grace of Jesus with the younger generation. Gary was ahead of the pack, and after witnessing how effective youth were at reaching their peers, was about to bring his God-inspired vision to reality.

Since coming to CLBS, I had enjoyed touring southern California with a six-member gospel-folk group called The Coruscation Singers. To "coruscate" means to give off light, and our purpose as a group was to reflect the light of Jesus as we represented the Bible school in the most interesting places. Gary had hoped to recruit the entire Coruscation Singers group for a summer of ministry. But while the group had experienced tremendous blessing and had enjoyed times of sharing the Good News of Jesus, after much prayer we decided to disband for the summer.

The team's decision left me as an eighteen-year-old desperately praying for God's guidance as to whether or not I should attempt a summer strumming my guitar while traveling on a Crusader Team. Within hours of the moment when Gary needed a decision, I heard Pastor Maynard Force, president of CLBS, preach a sermon on one verse, I Kings 17:7, which described the time when Elijah was camping near the Brook of Cherith (some translations spell it Kerith). When the brook of Cherith dried up, Elijah was forced to move on to find another water source. The familiar Bible account then unfolds as Elijah moves on to the victory on Mount Carmel, where he dueled with the prophets of Baal. Pastor Force shared his interpretation that sometimes God allowed things that were once huge blessings to dry up so that we had to move on into His bigger plans for our lives. At that moment, the Lord confirmed in my spirit that God was calling me to volunteer for the summer on a Gospel Crusader Team.

Months later, on a hot, sticky day in late June, fifty-three of us young adults were training at a church in Thompson, Iowa. I was placed on the Midwest Crusader Team that would travel a five-state area ministering at churches and camps. We were trained in drama, music, and leading others to a saving knowledge of Jesus. Accompanied by Marlene (a fine piano player) and me on my guitar, this eight-member team was affectionately dubbed "Dick and His Disabilities" (after our fearless nineteen-year-old leader, Dick Egolf). We were squished into an old station wagon accompanied by a trailer full of our gear to begin an unforgettable summer of adventure.

It didn't take long to discover that only two of us could ride facing backwards in the station wagon's jump seat without getting car sick. Those two were Stan Nelson and me. After traveling miles on the Midwestern roads and discussing every imaginable topic, within two months' time Stan and I were deeply bonded even though we had not had an official date. Mid-summer, while playing horse-shoes with Stan at Camp Bird in Michigan, I had this wild thought: "Wouldn't it be wonderful to be married to someone like Stan, so that I could just completely be myself?!"

How and when this mysterious bonding happened I am not exactly sure, but I do know when I suddenly became aware of it. When the five Crusader teams reunited in Minneapolis for a final grand rally at the end of the summer, I saw Stan get back together with his long-time girlfriend who had been traveling with the New York Team. We all assumed Stan would marry his sweetheart after two years of dating at CLBS. Upon witnessing their reunion, my heart felt ripped out and I fled to a bathroom to cry in secret.

Stan's girlfriend was a good friend of mine. As a second-year student at CLBS, she had been assigned to be my "Big Sis" during the first weeks of school to help me transition. Other than knowing that Stan was her special guy, my only inter-action with Stan before Crusades happened when we would often be the finalists facing off in the round-robin ping-pong tournaments played every day during the morning breaks at CLBS (Incidentally, we still differ as to who usually won those games!). But there was no doubt in our minds that summer of 1968: Stan clearly was committed to someone else.

What a dilemma to be in after the summer was over! The only other human being I told was Patty Agrimson (now Madison) who had traveled on our Cru-sader team. Both Patty and I were returning to CLBS for our second year so we committed to pray together. Five days a week we met early in the morning near the CLBS classrooms to pray in the big Angelica Church sanctuary where God seemed so near. For months, Patty supported me in my prayers, as we asked God that if these feelings for Stan were not from Him, that He would take them away. Stan had graduated from CLBS with his two-year degree in Bible and returned to Sacramento, eight hours away, to begin college. Strangely, my feelings for Stan only got stronger in the months of his absence. He had no idea that I missed him so, that I was longing to renew our deep soul friendship.

One Saturday in the early spring of 1969, a year after Gary had recruited us to join the Crusades, the course of our lives changed forever. The second group of Coruscations Singers, which included me once again, was meeting to make a recording that would soon be released. That morning, while having my devotions I read Psalm 20:4-5: "May he give you the desire of your heart and make all your plans succeed. We will shout for joy when you are victorious and will lift up our banners in the name of our God. May the Lord grant all your requests." The words of the psalm blessed me so that I tucked the verses into my pocket to share with the other singers. I was confident that it meant the Lord would hear our group's prayers and that our record would bless a lot of people.

Much to my surprise, when I got to the CLBS parking lot, there was Stan, standing in front of the school! He had come with his dad, who was on the CLBS Board and had arrived for its annual meeting. I knew right then that someday, somehow, even though miles separated us I would marry Stan Nelson. A few months later I would learn the *real* purpose of Stan's trek to Los Angeles. He and his long-time girlfriend had broken up and he was on a mission to discover if there was any possibility that I would be interested in coming to visit his family in Sacramento during spring vacation. After seeing some of the molehills on which we had skied in Minnesota, Stan used to tease me on Crusades that someday he would show me a real mountain! And he did: our first "official" date was skiing at the beautiful Squaw Valley Ski Resort.

While there were many additional chapters to our romance, during the following two years we were soon separated by 2,000 miles in order to continue our college educations. We did manage to be together during school vacations. If you were to add all the vacations together it would total three months and a lot of air miles between California and Minnesota. We were at last married on a Tuesday night, April 6, 1971, in the beautiful sanctuary of Trinity Lutheran Church of Minnehaha Falls in Minneapolis, surrounded by family and friends.

There wasn't time for a real honeymoon as Stan needed to be back to college in a few days. Just being together after such a long separation seemed like heaven on earth. So, with all of our wedding presents in a trailer loaned to us by some friends, we drove back to Sacramento to begin a new life together. Little did we realize the adventure that God had in store for us in years to come, which would include four major moves around the state of California to complete our college degrees, a relocation to Washington to work at Warm Beach Camp, and the joy of raising our family of two children on the campgrounds.

Our son, Thad Johan, was born in 1980, two years after we arrived at Warm Beach Camp. After being married for almost nine years we were thrilled to have this energetic bundle of joy. And even before we were married, I had promised that if God ever blessed us with a daughter, we would name her Cherith. Thirteen years after we were married, Stan held up our second child in the hospital delivery room and exclaimed, "It's Cherith Joy!"

While it has been forty-nine years ago that Stan and I rode facing backwards in that station wagon, we are still traveling through life together in the ministry of Christian camping! It's really true that opposites attract. Stan and I always end up scoring as extreme opposites in every category on various personality inventory tests. But God, **THE ULTIMATE MATCHMAKER**, has given us everything we need to serve Him and has uniquely bonded us together by His sheer pure grace.

4: THE MASTER PLANNER

It was the beginning of 1971 and the Vietnam War was raging. The U.S. had moved troops into Cambodia while I was embarking on my winter quarter at the University of Minnesota, majoring in nutrition and dietetics. It was a scary time. Many students and professors were protesting this expansion of the war by demonstrating and going on strike. Arm bands indicating an intention to strike were worn by many people and could be seen throughout the campus, including the one proudly displayed on the arm of my biology professor.

Since my major had a strong science emphasis, it was imperative that I take Biology 101 that particular quarter or it would add an extra year to my college experience. I marched into my professor's office and declared that his stance as a striker must be illegal, since I had paid my tuition and needed his class to graduate on time. He quickly responded that I could do an independent study for Biology 101 entitled "The Study of Evolution." Fresh from a two-year Bible school course, I retorted as a feisty twenty-one-year old lacking diplomatic finesse, "Fine! I will do an independent study of 'The Christian's View of Evolution'!" The professor's shocked look told me that he thought I was one crazy sophomore!

A few days later, upon coming to grips with my moment of insanity, I was sharing with a friend from my church (Trinity Lutheran Church of Minnehaha Falls in Minneapolis) the huge dilemma that I had just created for myself. In a few short weeks I would need to produce a well-thought out research paper. My friend responded with just the solution: "You need to talk to our new choir director, Neal Thorpe. He is the Dean of Biology at Augsburg College and just finished teaching our adult Sunday School class an eight-week course on "The Christian's View of Evolution."

The next Sunday my friend connected me with Dr. Thorpe after he descended from the choir loft. He very calmly and graciously agreed to help me. A week later, Dr. Thorpe handed over a box of books after giving me a few tips on how to approach the topic so I would not be laughed completely out of the scientific community. He commissioned me to study these books and footnote everything.

I followed his instructions and turned in my independent study paper at the end of the quarter, just a week before Stan and I were to be married on April 6th. After returning Dr. Thorpe's books I was off to begin a new life in Sacramento, California, and would be transferring to the University of California, Davis, to finish the last two years of my undergraduate degree. While Biology 101 was the furthest thing from my mind as a new bride, I was delighted when I opened the mail one day to find an "A" in Biology 101 on my final transcript from the University of Minnesota!

Upon completing my Master's Degree in Public Health at UCLA, I often marveled at the fact that during the course of five years of college education, the

Lord made certain that I was provided an alternative to taking Biology 101 at a secular campus. Since my major required a track of hard-core sciences every year, all the way from organic chemistry to biochemistry, the Lord had arranged for me to have a different lens through which to ponder creation.

But that's not the end of the story. Somewhere in our attic is that precious research paper that launched me into a much bigger "God-story." Years later, in 1998, as the brand new Director of Development at Warm Beach Camp, I was sitting in a grant seeker's forum in Seattle listening to the executive director/trustee of the M.J. Murdock Trust present on one of the largest private foundations in the Pacific Northwest—one which awards millions of dollars in grants each year to nonprofits. I recognized his soothing voice, his wavy hair. After putting his face and name through every possible sieve of acquaintances that I had made on the west coast in the last twenty years, I read his bio in the Trust's brochure. Amazingly, the trustee was Dr. Thorpe, the former Dean of Augsburg College's Biology Department who had come to my rescue for Biology 101!

Upon returning to camp I quickly typed Dr. Neal Thorpe a letter thanking him for helping me to get an "A" in my independent study of Biology 101, and more importantly, for giving me a firm foundation for the rest of my college studies. I brought him up to date on the journey that Stan and I had taken into the camping ministry, which had started for me back in high school when I had cooked for the volunteer crews that helped build our church's Camp Patmos in northern Minnesota. Later, I would learn that Dr. Thorpe's family held cherished memories from Camp Patmos. Within a few days, I had a letter back from Dr. Thorpe inviting me to stop and see him at the trust office the next time I was in his "neck of the woods" in Vancouver, Washington.

Four months before Jack Murdock died on May 16, 1971, and before the M.J. Murdock Trust was established in 1975 with his life fortune, God had master-planned for me to connect with a future trustee. I took Dr. Thorpe up on his invitation and the rest is history. That meeting began a long and fruitful journey for our Camp with the M.J. Murdock Trust. To kick off the journey, two of the Camp's board members, Roger Hancuff and Frank Cranston, and I attended the "Essentials of Development" course offered by the Trust, right as the Camp was taxiing down the runway for the first major $6.5 million "Journey of Faith" campaign. If you had told me in 1998 as a "scared-to-death" new development director that thirteen years later I would be on the M. J. Murdock Trust's faculty for this same "Essentials of Development" course, I would have never believed you. God really can do "far more than you could ever imagine or guess or request in your wildest dreams!" as Eugene Peterson paraphrases Ephesians 3:20 in *The Message.*

For years my good friend, Rita Nussli, Warm Beach Camp Director Ed McDowell, and I have prayed for an "angel donor" for Warm Beach Camp, a donor who would donate one million dollars. One day, as I was wondering why God was taking so long to answer our prayers, I decided to add together all the grants that the M.J. Murdock Trust had given to the Camp thus far, including a $320,000 grant for the waste water treatment plant and a $490,000 grant for the Cedar Lodge renovation project. The total was just over a million dollars! While I don't have a clue in my finiteness how this works, the Sovereign Lord of the Universe is not bound by our finite time/space dimensions. He was master-planning the answer to our prayers when I was a college sophomore and long before the three of us had even begun to pray as well.

God is **THE MASTER PLANNER**, and He is infinitely way ahead of us!

5: THE "WOOER"

The end was in sight. After four years of college spread between Minnesota and California, I had one quarter left before graduation. My major, Dietetics and Nutrition, was rigorous with a heavy load of science and math courses in addition to the food service administration and diet therapy classes that were required. Because I took a break from college in the spring of 1971 after Stan and I got married, the following quarters were packed with extra courses in order for me to be able to graduate with my class. In the past, when I did have room for an elective, I had chosen anthropology classes as we were planning on overseas work with other cultures, but electives were a rarity as I finished my college career.

In the spring of 1973, I was therefore thrilled to be able to take a three-credit elective class— something that really interested me—that wasn't required except for fulfilling the grand total of credits necessary for a B.S. degree. To my delight, as I scanned the class schedule, I found a course entitled The Bible as Literature which would miraculously fit into my last quarter. Since I had previously attended a two-year intensive Bible school, I reasoned that it would be an incredible gift to receive college credit for reading the Good Book.

Due to my attention deficit disorder, the first day of class I plunked myself down near the front so as to not get easily distracted. Sitting near the front also gave me better access to the professor to ask detailed questions. Four years of college had taught me how to be an excellent "test-taker;" at times I was even able to predict what the questions would be on the final exams. I remember one biochemistry exam on which I received and "A+," not because I deserved it, but because I guessed that the professor, in order to correct the exam quickly, had simply reversed the numbers for the glycogen storage disease enzymes.

As I nestled into my chair for the first session of The Bible as Literature I did not expect the introduction to the course that came from a wiry looking, middle-aged man. He had taught at a mainline seminary until he admitted to himself and everyone else that he didn't believe in God or the Jesus who was in the Bible. We were here to study the Bible strictly as literature. He warned us Christians who actually believed that he would be challenging our faith. There would be no exams in his class. Our grade would depend solely on one assignment: we were required to select and follow a topic through the entire Bible and write a term paper on our findings.

What I thought was going to be a "snap" class ended up being the toughest class in my four years of undergraduate studies—even harder than physics or statistics. And it wasn't just the time involved. The class turned into an experience that expanded my mind, causing me to ponder, pray, question, and to once again take the leap of faith in Jesus and the grace he provides.

For three hours a week we would listen to this professor tear apart scripture as he pointed out all the inconsistencies and what he was certain were the many fallacies that we had been taught in Sunday School. No one could miss his critical analysis of the Word. He must have done his dissertation on the Book of Job, for we spent a lot of time listening to his interpretations of that book and hearing his final conclusion that Job did, in fact, curse God.

I would leave each class session sick to my stomach and working on a headache as my brain did somersaults. It felt like the very foundation of my life was being shaken. I spent considerable time in Pastor Terry Oliver's office at Good Shepherd Lutheran Church in Sacramento. Not only was I working through anger at not being better prepared for this challenge through my two years of Bible school in Los Angeles, but in my naiveté, I was also wondering if Pastor Terry had ever confronted this stuff. He sure didn't preach or teach as if he had any doubts about the authority of Scripture or the redeeming grace of Jesus!

Having been through seminary training and ordination in the American Lutheran Church, Pastor Terry confirmed my suspicion that he was familiar with the highly critical approach to the Bible that I was experiencing in my college course. When I asked him what he did with all that he had been taught, he smiled and walked over to a file cabinet and, while pulling out a drawer, he answered, "I keep it filed away for times like these!" Then we would begin to study together.

Thankfully, in addition to having a working knowledge of the Bible, I also had personal experiences that confirmed that the God of the Universe had become flesh and dwelt among us. Coming from my home church I had a rich heritage of prayer and had seen how the Lord worked in our lives. The Spirit of the Lord had led Stan and me through a host of situations—too many to just be "coincidental." In my late teens and early twenties he and I had been "wooed" into going deeper with the Spirit, the third person in the Trinity.

Upon finishing the two-year Bible school in Los Angeles I had returned home to Minneapolis to live with my parents and begin college at the University of Minnesota. I craved "real Christianity," seeing the Spirit move like He did in Acts. I didn't want to just "play church;" I wanted to be involved in a wave of Kingdom activity. After attending my home church for a while, I was then asked by Rev. Al Hendrickson and his wife, Judy, to help with the youth group at their Lutheran church in the suburbs. It was just the beginning of the 70's when the charismatic movement was sweeping though many denominations.

Al and Judy were strategically placed in my life to begin leading me into a more intimate relationship with the Holy Spirit. They were well-grounded in the Word, stable, humble, and mature. Also, at this time I began attending mid-week meetings at a "home church" with Pastor Fred Herzog. I began to feel that the Spirit was "wooing me," and could work deeper within if I invited Him to do so. My introduction to more of the Spirit was quiet and gentle, but ever so real. When Stan and I were married at my home church in April, 1971, it was two very Spirit-filled pastors, Al and Fred, who took part in the service.

Having experienced this taste of the Spirit, Stan and I continued our journey with the Lord through Pastor Terry at Good Shepherd Church—Stan's home church in Sacramento. Pastor Terry was one of the first Lutheran pastors who joined the Charismatic Renewal Movement in the early 70's. There was a small group of people who were interested in the Spirit who met regularly for a Bible study at Pastor Terry's home. Before Stan received his "Greetings from the President of the United States" draft notice, we had joined this group in order to go deeper in the Spirit. It was a sweet time.

In addition, when Good Shepherd Church hosted Life in the Spirit seminars, Stan and I eagerly signed up for the journey. In the last session, Stan and I prayed for the infilling of the Holy Spirit. We saw the best in the Spirit movement as it began to blow through other denominations as well. The Full Gospel Business Men and Women's Aglow organizations began to tie denominations together in advancing the Kingdom of God.

With this backdrop of experience I decided to do my term paper for The Bible as Literature on the Holy Spirit and to follow the third person of the Trinity through the Bible, beginning in Genesis 1:2 where "the Spirit of the Lord was hovering over the waters." This was before the days of computerization, so without a quick way to scan the scriptures, it required intensive research.

As I worked my way through the Old Testament I was amazed to see that the Spirit had been actively working among mankind all along! He didn't just show up in Acts when the wind blew through the upper room. The Spirit of the Lord fell on the prophets of old, commissioning them to be a voice to their generation and causing them to forecast the future.

By the time I got to Acts and Pentecost, I was better acquainted with the activity of the Holy Spirit. Beside the fact that that He was able to hover and woo, He was all-knowing and all-wise. In Acts it was obvious that the Spirit was also all-powerful. Confidence returned and began to fill my sails! My fingers hit the old-fashioned typewriter keys, spelling out what I had discovered while tracing the movement of the Spirit through the Bible. It was before the days of word processing, but we were delighted to have erasable typing paper.

After staying up most of the night to finish the term paper for The Bible as Literature class, I proudly displayed it on the little round counter in our tiny house nestled in the olive orchard off of Winding Way. Within a short time I would be jumping into our little VW Bug and driving to UC Davis, just 30 minutes away, to turn in the paper. Then, the unthinkable happened. While hurrying, I accidentally bumped my cup of coffee on the counter and it spilled over part of my paper. This was 1973, and there was no stored copy on the computer to access, no button to magically print off another copy.

Without any other option in sight, I set up the ironing board and began ironing my precious paper on the Holy Spirit. The hot iron quickly dried the pages of the erasable paper, leaving it with a turn-of-the-century look, like a scroll with tarnished edges. But it was still readable, even though it looked like it had been "baptized with the Holy Spirit." I turned it in with a note of explanation attached, apologizing to my professor. Even if the professor knocked off points for its deplorable condition, hopefully the term paper would still retrieve a passing grade for graduation.

We were packing up all of our earthly belongings to move to Los Angeles for my internship when I received my final quarter grades in the mail. To my disbelief, there was an "A" next to the line that read, The Bible as Literature, granted by a professor who no longer believed in the Creator of the Universe who through HIS spirit "hovered over the waters" and spoke the world into being.

The "A" represented far more to me than a passing grade for my B.S. degree. It was the result of an exciting journey through the Bible in which I began observing more closely the third person of the Trinity, with whom we were about to become more personally acquainted ourselves. Without our knowing it, the Lord was setting the stage for our life work that was going to require a more intimate relationship with Him through the Holy Spirit, the "Breath of Life."

When we arrived in the Los Angeles area, upon the recommendation of Pastor Terry we began attending Loving Shepherd Lutheran Church in Gardena. For the next fifteen months we would be involved with the ministry of Pastor Don Ausland, a very Spirit-directed man whom God used mightily in our lives. This quiet, humble man was one of the first Lutheran pastors to be swept into the wave of the Charismatic Renewal Movement in the 1970's. Stan is sure that the Lord sent us to Los Angeles for my internship so that we would be connected with Pastor Ausland and his wife, who ministered by his side. Loving Shepherd lived up to its name, welcoming us two college students into their fellowship.

It has been many years since our college days, but we continue to often sing the chorus, "Breathe on me Breath of God," and over time I have expanded my prayer of Matthew 11 in *The Message* translation to include, "Abba, take me in your arms, pull me close, I want to feel your heartbeat, I want to smell your breath as we dance together to your unforced rhythms of grace." I often pray Ephesians 1:17-21, asking the Lord to give us a "Spirit of wisdom and revelation..." When interceding, I have come to believe that one of the most powerful things we can pray for others is Ephesians 3:20, as stated in *The Message:* "God, you can do anything...far more than I could ever imagine or guess or request in my wildest dreams! You do it not by pushing us around but by working within us. Holy Spirit, work deeply and gently in *name the person.*"

Somewhere in our attic is that term paper acknowledging that the Spirit is "**THE WOOER**," who woos Abba's children into a relationship with Him through the grace of Jesus. The Spirit continues to woo His children into more dependency, more wisdom and revelation, and more grace upon grace. He won't force himself into our lives, but He is delighted when we call out for Him to "breathe in us afresh" and to "take us by the hand and lead us."

6: THE STAGE DIRECTOR

Suspense was in the air at the University of California, Davis, that spring of 1973. Nervous dietetic/nutrition majors were waiting to see if they were chosen for an American Dietetic Association approved internship. Graduating seniors were only allowed to apply for two internships, and the day had finally arrived for the notification calls. Within twenty-four hours, all the spots would be filled. Fortunately for me, married students had just been allowed to apply.

When selecting where to apply, I went down the list to see which California-based internships paid the most money. Stan had received his AA degree in horticulture and had decided to pursue his B.S. in agriculture. Before transferring to a university for his two final years, Stan still had at least a full year of science and math prerequisites to complete which could be taken at any junior college in California where the tuition was free. This meant that I was looking for an internship near a junior college which would also pay me as much as possible. Most of the internships did not pay anything, so that quickly narrowed it to two choices: a twelve-month program at the San Francisco Medical Center or a fifteen-month experience at the Wadsworth VA Hospital that was coordinated with a Master's degree program in Public Health at U.C.L.A.

While I had no intentions of getting a master's degree, the government-funded internship at Wadsworth VA Hospital paid an amazing amount of money that would more than cover my tuition and books at graduate school in addition to all of our living expenses. Stan would not have to work while going to school. Since I had two years of working part-time in the Sacramento Mercy Hospital Dietary Department and a very high GPA, along with references from the head dietitian at work and from my professors, I was awarded both internships. Without a second thought, I chose the fifteen-month program because it paid the most money.

Upon Stan's return from active-duty reserve training, we had become involved as youth workers with Pastor Terry Oliver at The Lutheran Church of the Good Shepherd in Sacramento where Stan had attended his entire life. We were very close to Pastor Terry and his family. It was no doubt God's response to the Olivers' prayers that brought Stan home a few days early from active duty in order for us to become godparents for their second child, Todd, on Easter Sunday of 1972.

In June of 1973, after saying goodbye to our church family and our landlords on the olive-orchard estates where we were living, we loaded our entire belongings into the old ¾ ton blue truck that Stan had used for his landscaping business. We looked like the Beverly Hillbillies moving to L.A. when we parked in front of our new home, a one-bedroom apartment in Mar Vista, just three blocks from Venice Beach and about twenty minutes from the hospital and college. It was as close as we could afford, as the campus sat perched near Brentwood where some of the movie stars resided. Stan had secured a month's free rent by agreeing to paint the entire apartment during those summer months.

Truth be told, I was sick of studying and exhausted from trying to keep a 3.8 GPA at UCD. Thankfully, graduate school didn't start at UCLA until September, and it was a relief that my first three months in L.A. were spent working in the Food Services Department and wards of the V.A. hospital.

It was the middle of July when Pastor Terry called to inquire if there was any possibility that we could join the youth group on a week-long missions trip to Tijuana, Mexico, to work at the Lutheran Baja California Mission (LBCM) which included a church, clinic and school. Stan was needed to direct the youth group as they painted the director's home. Pastor Terry wanted me to coordinate and oversee the meals for the group of twenty teens. While I suspected there would be little chance of getting free from my training, we prayed, asking God to clear the way. Back in Sacramento, the youth group and Pastor Terry were also interceding. Much to our surprise and delight, the internship director, Miss White, thought this would be an excellent experience for an intern studying dietetics and nutrition.

In August, Stan and I met the Loving Shepherd group at the border in our old truck bulging with food and supplies. After a week of hard work in the heat, the youth group felt very proud when the Mexican pastor and wife who directed the mission returned from vacation to a freshly painted house.

Toward the end of the week, Rev. Gussick, the American director, came from the LBCM headquarters in San Diego to inspect our work and express thanks. When Rev. Gussick heard that I was about to enter a degree program in public health, he declared that I should do my master's project at the mission in Tijuana since they were working with the poorest-of-the-poor who lived in cardboard shacks built in the dry river bed on the outskirts of town. These people had moved to Tijuana thinking that there would be a better life, only to find that the living costs were high and good paying jobs were not to be found. Babies were dying of malnutrition and intestinal diseases, largely because the formula companies were enticing the babies' moms to put their infants on formula instead of breast feeding. This was a nutritional travesty that had reached a crisis point, and Rev. Gussick pleaded with me to come.

Miss White just smiled when I thanked her for allowing me the amazing experience of being totally in charge of the missions dining service provided from the back of our truck. But she was even more excited about Rev. Gussick's proposal. God was setting the stage for the research needed, and secretly auditioning the players to complete the project.

In September, I left my white dietitian uniforms in the closet to begin the master's degree classes at UCLA. These courses turned out to be mostly a review of the hard-core sciences that I'd had in my undergraduate studies while competing with pre-med students. Compared to the other four students in the internship, I had a stellar preparation for the classes and hardly had to study. I loved the international public health classes taught by world-renowned Dr. Derrick Jelliffe. And after struggling with weight issues my entire life, I was interested in how to change people's eating behavior, so I also added a behavioral modification class to my already rigorous schedule.

In the summer of 1974, with a small travel trailer in tow, Stan and I returned to Tijuana. Stan was in charge of all the American youth groups who came down during those six weeks to work on maintenance projects at the mission. Meanwhile, the pastor's wife and I were combing the neighborhood conducting a nutritional survey of all the infants less than a year old. With my limited Spanish from high school and college, using memorized questions, I took diet histories to find out what the moms were feeding their babies.

The pastor's wife was a very trusted soul among the river-bed population. When we appeared in their yards, the moms quickly called off their barking dogs used for protection. I had a small tape recorder that we used to record the surveys. Thankfully, the beloved pastor's wife took over when my limited Spanish failed. At night, I would sit with an interpreter provided by the mission to help me sift through and record the survey answers.

Plunging into the riverbed neighborhood was my first experience with deep poverty. I had never seen a starving child. Because these families couldn't afford infant formula, they would dilute it, often leaving the remainder at 100+ degree temperatures because they had no refrigeration. Babies were literally starving to death or dying from bacterial infections. One baby, at the point of death, died before we returned the following day. It became apparent to me that training "stay-at-home" moms to simply breast-feed their babies and put what little money their husbands were earning into food for themselves would help decrease the infant death rate that was spinning out of control in this cardboard community.

After returning to the States, I wrote up my research with the required statistical analysis of the data, and quickly found someone to help make educational flip charts in Spanish. These colorful books simply outlined for expectant mothers the importance of breast-feeding their babies and eating nourishing foods themselves. The LBCM hired trusted aides from the community to cover the riverbed neighborhood, targeting pregnant women. Armed with this simple training tool, the aides declared war on the infant formula companies' advertising that could be seen on billboards lining the Tijuana streets.

Rev. Gussick was respected by government officials in Mexico City for his work in public health. He had my research paper translated into Spanish, and by the grace of God, before I graduated the research was placed in the right hands and published in the Mexican Journal of Nutrition, drawing attention to the tragedy in Tijuana along with its educational solution.

Armed with an old-fashioned slide show depicting all phases of the project, in the spring of 1975 I faced the PhDs of the Public Health Department at UCLA. I was so nervous! Something as simple and practical as urging moms to breastfeed their babies might not be considered worthy of receiving a master's degree.

After my hour-long presentation came the dreaded question period that I'd heard about from former interns. My advisor asked for questions. The faculty just sat there staring at me. There were a few simple questions and comments, and although it seemed like an eternity, the session was finished ahead of schedule. The PhD committee thanked me as they left the room.

I asked my advisor if she thought I had passed. While the faculty had not officially voted, she assured me that my project would capture a degree. I will never forget her comment: "Nancy, some of these professionals have worked in the field for years and not been able to accomplish what you did in six weeks because of the trust already established in the riverbed community by the pastor's wife and aides." She went on to explain that some could only dream of being published in a foreign country as I had been.

God is **THE STAGE DIRECTOR**, working behind the scenes, moving the characters onto the stage to accomplish what HE wants done. His heart beats for the marginalized and HE responds to the prayers of mothers crying out for their unborn children. When the "prayer bowls in the Heavenlies" are about to overflow, HE is ready for the grand finale, even if it's as simple as using the natural ability HE designed for mothers of mammal species to nurse their young. And HE is even able to get the U.S. government to fund the stage production!

7: THE HIJACKER

It was 1975 and we had just moved to Paradise, California so that Stan could finish his education at Chico State University. Paradise was located on a hill, and a sign beside the road said, "You are now ascending into Paradise." We would joke whenever we left town that "we were descending down the hill," and craving fellowship, one day we did just that and drove to Pastor Terry Oliver's home in Sacramento to attend a Bible study there. Stan was about to park when Pastor Terry and several others pulled away in a car. Soon we were in hot pursuit, hoping to catch up to see where they were going. Apparently, there had been a change in plans and we were not in the loop.

When we got to a stop light, Stan jumped out and ran to Pastor Terry's car and knocked on his window. Stan found out that everyone in the car was headed downtown to Bethel Temple to attend a special service with the "Happy Hunters." Since we had driven a hundred miles to join this group we decided to go with them. I had never heard of Bethel Temple or the "Happy Hunters." Trusting Pastor Terry, we were game for anything.

Upon entering the massive Assembly of God church, which looked more like a movie theater than a house of worship, we were ushered down to the very front row. The service had already started and these ringside seats were the only ones left. The "Happy Hunters" lived up to their name. A middle-aged couple, ministering side-by-side with incredible energy and faith, they began to call different groups of people up to the front to receive prayer for healing and/or deliverance.

I had never seen or heard of anyone being "slain in the Spirit." Growing up in a Lutheran church, I had no intellectual category into which I could place the array of events that was unfolding in front of my very eyes. I certainly would have never signed up to attend, much less have parked myself in a front-row seat at a service such as this. There was no way to escape, even if I tried.

The Hunters would finish with one group and then call out another group. I remember calls for people needing certain kinds of physical healing, and for others who needed a touch from God to overcome specific addictions. The Hunters would lay hands on each individual and they would fall to the floor and lie there, peacefully rejoicing in the Spirit. Many were worshipping the Lord all around us, and I heard people "speaking in tongues." Pretty soon the lines around the altar were three-deep as people waited for their turn. We were so close that some participants even fell towards us.

This intrigued and scared me at the same time. Why in the world had the Lord hijacked us and taken us on a wild-goose chase that ended up by placing us in a front-row seat to observe a phenomenon called "being slain in the Spirit"? It was as if people were drunk, but enjoying it more. I sensed that they could get up at any moment, but didn't want to come back to reality. Had they momentarily been "kidnapped" and transported to the Heavenlies?

Towards the very end of the service the Hunters called for people to come forward who would like to be prayed over for their marriages, especially those couples who wanted to be used in Kingdom work. Stan and I both felt the Spirit wooing us out of our seats. Before I knew it we were standing on the stage ourselves with the Hunters laying hands on us! Within seconds I felt myself crumbling to the ground. Strong hands reached out to break the fall. Stan was lying right next to me. Being "slain in the Spirit" was the most intoxicatingly amazing feeling, and it is beyond description. I had no desire to get up, and wishing that this would last forever, I could have pitched my tent and displayed a "season pass" over my body.

Finally, it was time to arise and try to go on with normal life again, but that feeling didn't go away for days. It was as if I was high on something. Several days after being "slain in the Spirit," I boarded a flight to San Diego to give a summary of my master's project to the Lutheran Baja California Mission's Board. I remember thinking, "Who needs a plane? I could fly down there myself!" While sitting in the plane I continued to talk about Jesus to anyone who was willing to listen. It was like I had been plugged into an electrical circuit and there was power running through my body.

Within a few weeks, however, the feelings of ecstasy had vanished, and I was left pondering the entire experience. Every time I thought about it, more and more questions would arise. For years I tried to come up with the answers. Perhaps the Lord wanted us to be familiar with this phenomenon since He knew that we would be ministering to multiple denominations in the ministry of Christian camping. Yet while it had been an electrifying experience, it seemed to serve no purpose in the times that followed. Surely it would be foolish to hop around continuing to search for such a spiritual "high" again. Little did I know that seventeen years later, the Lord would begin unrolling some of his strategic master plans for me.

Stan finished his education and we went to work at Hartland Christian Camp and then landed at Warm Beach Camp. In 1980, right after our son, Thad, was born, we found out that my sister, Peggy, had a very aggressive form of breast cancer and was on chemotherapy. While the cancer temporarily went into remission, two years later the medical profession determined that the end was in sight; her cancer had come back with a vengeance. Our pastor urged me to visit Peggy before she was confined to bed so that we could have quality time together.

My sister and I did not have a very close relationship. I always felt guilty because she got all the bad genes and the tragic breaks. Peggy's life was filled with diseases such as diabetes and cancer. Her first marriage didn't make it when her husband, a Navy pilot, spent long periods of time overseas. Their baby boy had died in her womb, two months before its due date. When she and her second husband were at last approved for adoption, her cancer made it impossible to take on a child.

Peggy had not had the same wonderful experience at our home church as I. While going through confirmation, she had not bonded with the other students. Originally, there had been a commitment on her part to follow Jesus, but she had not received discipleship or been part of a community of faith that provided for growth to occur. Talking with Peggy about my relationship with Jesus and Stan's and my Christian camping ministry was always forced and awkward. But oh, how Stan and I would pray for her, asking the Lord to touch her life in a special way!

About a year before she died, Peggy was brought by the Lord into a saving knowledge of Jesus. A fellow computer programmer where she worked witnessed to her after hearing news of her cancer. Peggy was eager to learn all she could and wanted to be plugged into a church. Her second husband, Phil, had grown up as a Catholic so Peggy let him pick a nearby Catholic church. The very first Sunday they attended someone from their neighborhood recognized them and invited them to a home Bible study.

A few months before Peggy died I flew into Minneapolis to spend a few days with her. She asked if I wanted to go with Phil and her to the last "Life in the Spirit" seminar that they were attending at their church, and I readily agreed. As I entered their fellowship I realized that the Lord had arranged for Peggy to land in a Catholic charismatic church! The priest started the meeting and reviewed what the group had covered in the previous sessions. Since Stan and I had attended a "Life in the Spirit" seminar at Stan's home church a few years prior, I knew what was about to happen this last session. The priest said that before being given the opportunity to be prayed over for the "in-filling" of the Holy Spirit, he would like anyone who had never given a public confession of their faith to have an opportunity to do so.

Peggy was the first one to jump to her feet. I was overwhelmed that the Lord had arranged for me to hear my sister's one and only confession of her faith in Jesus as her Savior! After she sat down, Phil was the next to stand and give testimony to the saving grace of Jesus that he had personally received. When the time of confessions was complete, the priest then asked for those wanting to receive the "baptism of the Holy Spirit" to come forward, and both Peggy and Phil went to the altar. As in the tradition of the Catholic Church, the priest sprinkled them with holy water and laid hands on them. It is a memory that I will cherish forever.

Unless the Lord decided to miraculously intervene, her doctors had determined that Peggy's remaining time on earth would be less than six months. One day during those last months I received a surprise phone call from her. I hardly recognized her voice; it was full of energy and joy as she was talking fast. She told me that since she was just lying in a hospital bed that she might as well pray for me, for Stan, for Thad, and the Camp. Was there anything specific I needed her to pray for? Our conversation was unbelievable, because all of this had been off-limits before. Due to her tragic life, we had never talked about anything other than her cancer. Her baby had died; ours had lived. I had a job that was fulfilling, while Peggy had to quit her career when cancer had taken over her life. Stan and I were happily married, but Peggy's first marriage had ended in divorce. Her second marriage to her loving husband, Phil, while still very new, had been plagued by her cancer. When the disease struck, I had been afraid to talk about my life with her because I thought that it would be too painful for her.

I honestly couldn't believe that I was talking with my sister. Someone must have hijacked her and done a complete transformation! Hoping I wouldn't think she was crazy, she filled me in. Their home Bible study group had begged Peggy to come to a special healing service that the priest was having at their church. Peggy had been prayed over so many times that, while she appreciated the group's love and concern, she was "done" with such attempts. But upon their insistence, she relented and went to the service. When the priest called for those wanting healing to come forward, Peggy said something drew her out of her seat. As she walked down to the front she told the Lord, "You don't have to heal me. I want what you want for me." It was an act of total surrender to the Lord.

After she knelt at the front, the priest sprinkled holy water and laid hands on her while praying for healing. She was unable to stay kneeling and was "slain in the Spirit." She didn't have vocabulary for this experience as it was just as foreign to this former Lutheran gal as it had been for me. Peggy excitedly told me that it was like God took fire and burned out all the unresolved emotional distress that she had been carrying around for years. She felt free at last! Peggy went on to explain that she felt like she was high on drugs, and that she might not even need her pain medication from that point on. Finally, she wrapped up the experience by saying, "I think I could fly without an airplane!"

At that moment in time, some seventeen years after my own encounter with the Spirit, I realized why God had hijacked me for the same incredible experience that Peggy had just undergone. I assured Peggy that she wasn't crazy, and that the Lord had allowed HIS Spirit to do an amazing inner healing. We rejoiced together at the awesomeness of God. Little did I realize that it would be my last conversation with my sister. They had placed her in the hospital to do a special infusion of chemo right into her liver. Something went wrong, she grew worse, and we soon received a call to come quickly to Minneapolis. Peggy was dying.

After dropping Thad off at "Aunty Thayla's," we jumped on the first flight we could get to Minneapolis. As the jet shot through the darkness, I wondered what Peggy must have thought of the last letter I had sent her, which included the verse Jeremiah 29:11. What had prompted me to send that particular passage?

While we were mid-way to Minnesota, Peggy took her last breath. While we did not make it in time, at least I had the memories of our visit a few months earlier. The funeral was conducted by the priest who was very close to Peggy, and who had walked her through extensive counseling toward the end of her life. The casket was a plain, simple, cloth-covered box and contained the earthly body of someone I had loved who had just received an awesome inner healing. The Lord hadn't had much time left, and HE did it HIS way, in a quick, miraculous fashion as HE was preparing to take my sister home to eternity where there was no disease, and where she would be whole and completely restored in body, soul, and spirit.

When the Priest delivered the message at the funeral he stated that he wished to share verses that had been very meaningful to Peggy in her last days. And then he read Jeremiah 29:11 from her Bible, which she had underlined:

"For I know the plans I have for you, declares the Lord, plans to prosper you and not to harm you, plans to give you a hope and a future."

After Peggy's death, whenever I thought about being "slain in the Spirit" those many years before I would thank God for arranging that event so as to prepare me for my sister's end of life. When we had joined the staff at Warm Beach Camp, Stan and I had tucked away these charismatic experiences, as they seemed out of place. The Free Methodists had not been a part of the wave of the Spirit that swept through congregations during the 70's. We had also seen what happened to the movement when very immature believers, not grounded in the Word, had risen to leadership. Things got very messy. What had been a blessing in the beginning was now ripping apart churches as pride rose up and disagreements began over different gifts of the Spirit. To be honest, I had been glad to take a break from it all, and often pondered why the things of the Spirit had caused such devastation in the Body of Christ.

In the early 2000's I noticed a blurb in our church's announcements about a "Holy Spirit Conference "at the Everett Free Methodist Church. Rev. Dr. David Carr, a Free Methodist pastor from the United Kingdom who had formerly been ordained in the Pentecostal denomination, was coming to conduct a three-day meeting. Needless to say, I was interested. I learned many things at that conference, including that the Lutheran church was one of the first denominations to be involved in the charismatic renewal of the 1970's. Some of the history of the Free Methodist Church revealed that it too had at one time had the Spirit fall afresh on the denomination in astounding ways. As I participated in the conference I watched the English pastor pray over people as they were called up by groups. There were many people slain in the spirit there.

The next year, Superintendent Steve Fitch from the California Conference conducted the second "Holy Spirit Conference" for the Pacific Northwest Free Methodists at the Lakeview Free Methodist Church. I attended, still in wonderment about it all. Part of the conference included a "Holy Spirit Clinic," where as a body of believers we prayed for people, and Superintendent Fitch explained what was happening at that moment. When a person was overcome by the Spirit and lying on the floor, Superintendent Fitch noted what was happening with the man's twitching eyelids and stated that he could get up if he wanted to, but he was probably enjoying the experience too much to even consider ending it. Then he said something that I processed for weeks: "We don't really know what is happening. The Lord is doing some deep work in him. He will probably never know himself, but the Spirit knows."

I left the conference with more questions and continued to ponder the Spirit who, like the mysterious wind, seems to "blow where He wills." Because of my sister's inner healing, I had quit asking the Lord why I had been "slain in the Spirit" so many years previous: our common experience had created a loving, Godly bond. But there was still a feeling of mystery deep inside my consciousness. Months after that second Holy Spirit Conference, as I was walking across the lobby of our church after Sunday morning service, the thought hit me: "The Lord did something deep inside me when he slew me with His Spirit. I will never know what, but He knows why it was important for me." Up until that moment,

I had only applied my understanding to the experience with my sister. But the Lord doesn't waste anything and is constantly multi-tasking.

The Lord is **THE HIJACKER**. He sometimes has to intervene to get us where He wants us. For He does know the future, and He makes certain that we are prepared for it, even if we don't know what He's up to! His ways really are higher than ours and He is full of holy surprises!

8: THE DREAM GIVER

Upon finishing my internship in Los Angeles, we ascended into Paradise, California, so Stan could commute down the hill every day to attend Chico State University. After much research Stan had chosen this college to finish his degree in agriculture, in order to be prepared for international work on the mission field.

But as we were just midway through my two-year clinical depression, it was becoming clearer that going overseas was not a good choice. After many prayer sessions with Pastor Don Ausland and his wife at Loving Shepherd Church in Gardena, California, they challenged us to reexamine our call to make certain that it was from God. Just the thought of being able to break the pledge I made by raising my hand at Camp Patmos as a young child caused a peek-hole of light to come into the darkness. I was raised at a church that had begun the World Mission Prayer League, and missions were lifted high. Somehow, in my childhood I had connected foreign mission service to salvation, and from that point on I didn't think there was any other choice.

Stan and I were pondering the future one day while soaking up the sun with my sister, Peggy, on the beach by Lake Oroville. An aimless feeling had set in because we didn't know how to prepare for whatever lay ahead; furthermore, Stan was struggling in his agriculture classes. My sister simply asked a pointed question: "Why do you always think God wants you to do something you don't want to do?" Before we could answer, she followed with, "What's the funnest thing you could ever dream of doing?"

Stan immediately sat up straight on the blanket and declared, "Work at a camp!" I laughed and added, "Well, I could run the food services." While God was closing the door on our original plan, HE was opening a window and the light was starting to punch holes in the darkness. We began to plan for our imaginary camp, chatting often about what we would do.

 A Christian couple who had befriended us was in the same situation as we were, and we wives were both fulfilling the "brunette scholarship" plan. We were working hard at Butte County Mental Health Services to put our hubbies, both named Stan, through school. The "other Stan" was majoring in Recreation Administration. When he heard of our camping dream he encouraged Stan to switch his major and join him in the Recreation Department.

Stan did change his major to Recreation Administration, and at the end of his junior year he was required to do a survey for his Land Usage Management class. He decided to survey Christian camps in California to see how they acquired their land while also asking a host of other questions that would fulfill the assignment requirements. At the college library Stan found a little mimeographed directory from Christian Camping International (CCI), now called Christian Camps and Conference Association (CCCA), that listed all their member camps in the United States, and he and I went to work.

Using our old clunky typewriter, I helped type the survey. At the last minute Stan added this final question: "If you could change anything about your camp, what would it be?" After licking about fifty envelopes and depositing them at the post office, a few weeks later Stan began to receive a record number of responses. Without any warning we were about to be swept into the camping stream when we read the survey from Dan Neufeld, the Director of Hartland Christian Camp. His answer to the bonus question stated, "We need a cook and an all-around camp worker."

After considerable prayer, Stan contacted Dan Neufeld to see if he could take a seven-month "work-learn experience" that would count for college credit through a newly created government program. Dan proposed that we would come in January and work through the summer season. But just before Dan's invitation for an interview, Chico State contacted me to see if I would apply for an entry-level professorship to teach nutrition classes. This had been my goal, and I had been doing everything possible to make myself known to them. I was in a dilemma, but we still went forward with our visit to Hartland Camp.

After touring Hartland and being interviewed by their Mennonite board, I made my decision and informed the head of the Chico State Nutrition Department that we had decided to experience camping at a small camp tucked away near the giant sequoias in the Sierras. There was just one problem: the camp had no staff housing available. After many moves we had finally worked our way into a two-bedroom rental house in Paradise, and so I pleaded with God, asking that He provide us with a two-bedroom place at Hartland. For all I knew, we would land in one of Hartland's old hotel rooms without even a kitchen.

Days before our move the phone rang and the director excitedly informed us that they had purchased one of the nearby lease-lot cabins for us, and it had two-bedrooms! Those two words ringing in my ears were the final confirmation! What he didn't tell us was that this was a summer cabin, yet to be winterized and hooked up to camp water, and with septic leach lines so plugged that flushing a toilet was not possible. In addition, when we arrived in the middle of winter with two feet of snow gracing the ground around the cabin, we discovered that the two bedrooms were so tiny that we had to lie on our double bed to provide enough room to get the dresser drawer open. It still makes us laugh. God indeed has a sense of humor!

We boiled the creek water until Stan could dig a ditch and bring the clean camp water to the cabin. The old pot belly stove in the kitchen and the fireplace in the living room kept us warm until electric floor board heaters were installed. Stan learned about plumbing as he quickly cleared the way for us to use our toilet. After I spent our first two months crying myself to sleep, our little cabin by the creek began to feel like home. We felt like pioneers, without any television or radio reception and no possibility of getting a private phone line. Hartland was our boot camp, and we began to experience what it would be like to work in Christian camping.

By the summer, my deep depression had completely lifted. Those long, hard fifteen-hour days of physical labor while cooking and managing the camp's food services were just the medicine I needed. Stan loved camp work so much he decided to finish his degree at Fresno State University, just two hours down the mountainside. Since weekends were the busy time at camp, he was able to go to college part-time and still work four days a week. We discovered that camping was similar to the hard work of running a family farm, and we were made for this community lifestyle.

After surviving my first year as food service manager, I was asked to give a workshop on "Training Food Service Personnel" at the sectional CCI conference at Camp Sugar Pine, near the entrance to Yosemite. Looking back now we realize that Bob McDowell, the director of Warm Beach Camp where Stan and I now work, was playing the piano for the general conference worship. And unbeknownst to me, a lady recorded my workshop and sent the tape to the national CCI headquarters.

A few months later, as probably the first registered dietitian to work full-time in the field of Christian camping, I was asked to give three workshops at the 1977 International CCI Convention in Banff, Canada. At that conference I met Sam Johnson, the editor of the CCI Journal, and became a contributing editor, writing articles about food service administration. Throughout the years I remained involved in that field, and one of my biggest joys has been teaching seminars around the United States and Canada for Christian Camping International, now known as the Christian Camps and Conference Association (CCCA).

And, incidentally, when we were praying for housing before coming to Warm Beach Camp, I informed the Lord that one bedroom would be just fine, but gently suggested to Him that, if possible, it would be nice to have a little extra room to open the dresser drawers without lying on the bed!

God is **THE DREAMGIVER**! He has prepared good works for us before the creation of the universe and He has an infinite number of mission fields out there, one uniquely designed for each of us. He won't stuff us into anybody else's box.

9: THE CONNECTOR

As the bus was on its final leg of the journey from the Calgary airport to the beautiful Banff Springs Hotel in the fall of 1977, I was having a very private conversation with God that no one else could hear, including Stan. In my mind I was putting up a fuss over my husband's idea to relocate to Washington State when he finished the spring quarter at Fresno State University, about two hours from where we were currently working at Hartland Christian Camp in California.

Stan had a list of camp directors that he hoped to meet at the Christian Camping International (CCI) convention that was to begin in a matter of hours. In order to receive his BS in Recreation Administration, Stan needed a three month internship. At the very top of his list was Bob McDowell, the director of the largest Christian camp in the Pacific Northwest. Since Warm Beach was the farthest camp from where we were nestled in the Sierra Mountains, Stan figured that it would be important to connect with this director at Banff in order to save time and mileage.

At Hartland, I had finally learned how to make spaghetti for 200 campers and had passed the Mennonite test of preparing everything from scratch. Our tiny cabin by the creek had been winterized and the starched yellow gingham curtains fit our country décor. After many moves to collect all of our college degrees, I had "nested" and wasn't happy with the possibility of yet another relocation. Besides, I worried that there wouldn't be a job for me in my field and I would probably end up being the craft director for a mob of campers with glue and sequins on their sticky fingers. There was little doubt that Stan's mind was made up. He could see that Hartland was too isolated to raise the family that we hoped to have someday. And Stan's adventurous side was seeking a new horizon to test out his education in the field of recreation.

Just as the bus pulled up to the luxurious hotel, I heard the Lord whisper in my spirit, "What are your options? Are you going to follow your husband?" My less-than-enthusiastic response was, "Yes, Lord, even if I have to be the craft director!"

The CCI convention started with a fancy dinner in the Banff Springs Hotel's elegant dining room. There was excitement at each table. Many camping folks were still eating off of tin trays back home, so the long-stemmed glassware and multiple choices of forks and spoons were electrifying! Over 1,000 camping leaders from all over the world begin to fill the chairs. We quickly introduced ourselves to a couple who were about to sit down directly across from us. The gentleman, noticing the yellow ribbon hanging from my name tag that advertised I would be a presenter, asked what seminars I would be teaching. I proudly exclaimed that I would be giving three workshops on food service administration. He quickly responded that they sure needed someone at their camp to administrate the food services. They had a fantastic chef but he liked to stick to the kitchen and not get involved with their four dining rooms.

Then this man looked in Stan's direction and asked what he did at Hartland. Stan summarized by saying that he had done just about everything possible in the last two years and that he needed an internship in recreation administration to finish his degree. Stan's eyes got real big as this man proceeded to tell about all the recreational options that they had at their camp…swimming pools, horses, mini-golf, tennis courts, etc. All of a sudden both Stan and I focused on the couple's nametags and realized that within the first few minutes of the convention, God had connected us to Bob and Muriel McDowell from Warm Beach Camp in Stanwood, Washington!

By the end of that meal all four of us knew that Stan and I were going to Warm Beach Camp. No formal jobs were offered, but we didn't contact anyone else on Stan's list. Bob and Muriel went back to Camp to begin the process of developing two positions in our career fields. We went back to our room and lay awake all night, too excited to sleep. Furthermore, I think we were afraid that if we went to sleep, in the morning we would awake to realize that it had all just been a dream!

A few months later, in January, we drove up to Stanwood, an hour north of Seattle, to have official interviews. We had never heard of the Free Methodist denomination, so we had a number of doctrinal questions as well as questions about the camp itself. After a tour of the huge campus which, at that time, was really a conference center with two satellite camps, we were set for an interview with three board members: Chairman Bud Hansen, Frank Cranston, and Jeannie Matthews. Since we were the first non-Free Methodists that would be hired for year-round positions, it was important to all of us that this was a right fit. I could see from inspecting the kitchen that it needed a lot of updating and renovation. The camp was still using old brick ovens that had come out of a steam ship. The tiny mixers were not adequate to make large batches of anything. The counters were made out of wood, which was impossible to sanitize. And to my disbelief, they didn't even have a meat slicer to cut meat in order to serve up to 800 people! I felt a strange tug to help this kitchen become equipped for the 20th century.

After everyone's inquiries were answered, we were offered the newly created positions. I didn't realize it at the time, but I would be the first full-time salaried woman to join the staff. We returned to California with the secret that in May we would be migrating north to begin a new life at Warm Beach. As May drew nearer we gave adequate notice at Hartland and began to prepare for the adventure ahead.

Thirty-nine years later I can still remember the excitement that we felt after connecting with Bob and Muriel McDowell. We know **THE CONNECTOR**, and HE can cause anyone, anywhere to be connected through HIS sovereignty. I also learned that day in October, 1977, that the prayer God loves to both hear and answer is, "YES, LORD!

10: THE REMODELER

Before leaving Hartland Camp I had written my first article, a centerfold complete with pictures on "Convectional Cookery," for *The Journal of Christian Camping*. Under the direction of John Drake, head of the Equipment Sales Division at the S.E. Rykoff Company, I had secretly begun to do the research needed to replace the existing ovens at Warm Beach Camp. Upon arrival at Warm Beach as their new food services director, I hoped to see that the old brick ovens, which took eight hours to preheat, would be replaced with new convection ovens that would be ready in fifteen minutes.

Armed with the ordering number and price for the exact convection oven model that I had picked out, I was soon to learn the definition of "limited funds." This was an entirely different experience than my first several years in camp food service. When I had inquired about the food budget at Hartland I was served up an unbelievable food service director's dream on a silver platter: "Just make the food good, whatever it takes!" The Hartland kitchen was full of new, shiny stainless steel equipment with all the latest features.

But things were different at Warm Beach. It was impossible to hide the $20,000 needed for new convection ovens in the "Repair and Replacement" line of the Warm Beach Food Service budget. That giant amount stuck out like a sore thumb and was quickly removed from the bulging budget the first two times I presented it. The second time I even placed an asterisk by my request, footnoting at the bottom of the page, "Just ask about our Cremation Plan; why not memorialize an oven!" The head chef, Jerry Bussard, and I used to joke about being able to cremate people in the three eight-foot long oven cavities. Just in case anyone inquired, we even had a humorous plan worked out for how much a cremation would cost, with a discount if you were willing to be cremated in between the biscuits as opposed to requiring an entire oven to yourself. But just as we were about to begin in jest to design proposed memorial plaques that would be attached to the new convection ovens, we received yet another "not this year" from the "powers-that-be."

To be honest, I was beginning to get a really stinky attitude. As a matter of fact, I was so discouraged that I was about to infect the rest of the staff with my bitterness. How could camp leadership not see that we were wasting electricity with these ovens that were heated up on May 1 and left running until October 1? Furthermore, due to the ovens the kitchen was over ninety degrees for a large part of the summer, which was a clear detriment to the staff. And then God intervened, and I can still tell you my exact location in the downstairs hallway of Cedar Lodge, right before the staff dining room, when the Lord impressed these words into my spirit: "Do the best with what you have and I will trust you with more!"

It was as if someone had snuck up behind me and whacked me with a 2 x 4! God instantly had my attention and I suddenly became creative, thinking about all the additional things that we could bake in those large oven cavities that were running twenty-four hours a day. The Mennonite cooks had trained me to bake everything from scratch at Hartland including French bread, dinner rolls of every variety, cakes, cookies, and their famous cinnamon rolls. Why not start an evening shift of baking and manufacture everything from scratch?

I approached Director Bob McDowell with my latest baking brain storm that would require the addition of an eighty-quart mixer, which we needed anyway. The small twenty-quart mixer was already overworked and insufficient for our needs. Because of the mixer's size, we had to make five batches of mashed potatoes to feed a full dining room. This was a huge process of dumping the batches into big, stainless steel dishpans. While this strengthened my arm muscles, I knew that if we were going to bake in the evening we would need a huge mixer with a big dough hook to make home-made bread. When Bob inquired about the cost of an eighty-quart mixer, I told him we could buy a used one for $1,000. I simply pulled that number out of thin air, knowing that if it were larger, the idea would be dead before I walked out of his office.

Upon receiving the green light, I put the word out to all the used equipment dealers in the Puget Sound area along with our food service vendors that I was looking for a used eighty-quart mixing bowl with attachments for a grand total of $1,000. Needless to say, I was met with comments like, "Are you kidding?!" We started praying for a mixer, and I started hiring the additional college-age summer staff that would be our second shift of bakers. I had trained many kids to bake at Hartland, complete with the introductory class on the "Food Chemistry of Bread Baking." In my mind I could smell the scent of baking bread, yet we had no mixer.

About two weeks before the busy summer season was to begin, I received a phone call from our Bargreen's salesman, Jim. He was wondering if we still needed that eighty-quart mixer. While he had been taking an order from a bakery in Port Townsend he noticed a second mixer pushed up against the wall. He quickly asked if they would be willing to sell it, saying that he knew a lady who would pay $1,000 for it with attachments. Since the bakery had closed down a program to teach baking to the town's special needs population, the old mixer had been sitting and was taking up needed space. Within a few days, Danny Cook, the business manager at Warm Beach, and I were on the ferry going to fetch the mixer. After we carefully moved "Big Bertha Thuderbuzit" (the name affectionately given to her) from the bakery's dock down its ramp and into our truck (using small pipes to roll the mixer along), the owner of the bakery generously threw in two big mixing bowls. We were soon on our way to begin a new chapter in the Camp kitchen.

Danny and I arrived back at Camp with just enough time for Les Sargent, a volunteer electrician, to wire the three-phase mixer into the kitchen. In no time at all the smell of freshly baked bread wafted through the lobby. Baking was occurring late into the evenings, with yummy treats ready for the next day.

In the following spring of 1981, while chasing after one-year old Thad I heard an announcement on the radio for an evening "Grant Proposal Writing Class" offered at a neighboring junior college. My career in fund-raising was about to begin when I mustered up all the courage I could find to march into Bob Mc-Dowell's office and propose my latest scheme to fund the needed ovens.

While I was sure the answer would be "NO," I blurted out, "I have a deal for you. If you will send me to this quarter-long class on work time in a camp car and let the camp pay the tuition, I will try to get grants to pay for the needed convection ovens." After a long silence he said, "On one condition: that you let me decide what projects you will write grants for." Amazed and grateful, I walked out of his office and into a new career path that had just unfolded before me. No one signs up for fund-raising on purpose. But passion for a cause will motivate an individual to do things never considered before the need arises.

I soon learned that most foundations were not interested in funding ovens in the early 1980's, no matter how badly the Camp needed them. Still, Bob and I made a fantastic partnership in the grantsmanship process. I did the research and ghost writing of the proposals after he had visited the foundation representative to see what they were interested in funding. Grants started pouring into Camp, but none of them were for replacing the old ovens!

Meanwhile, the smell of bread baking was enticing some of the women from the Camp auxiliary to come and see what was happening in the bakeshop. The women flew into action with their "women power!" They put the need for re-placement ovens before the women at retreats, and soon most of the $20,000 was in the bank. Finally, a foundation gave a grant for the last $3,000 and the ovens were installed!

That first set of four convection ovens was ultimately replaced after about twenty-five years of use. A foundation funded a $30,000 grant for a second set of new units because we serve so many at-risk innercity kids. Later, that same foundation would fund more kitchen equipment, including stoves, and a shiny stainless steel tilting skillet, something I never imagined the Camp would be able to have.

And today, if you walk downstairs in Cedar Lodge you will encounter the complete remodel of the food service operations due to many generous donors, including the M.J. Murdock Trust. Not only have a brand new walk-in cooler and freezer been installed that are twice the size of the old ones, but new offices and storerooms have also been created to re-direct the flow of inventory when the delivery trucks arrive. No longer do the food supplies have to cross the kitchen during busy preparation hours. Deliveries can come right from the trucks and down the remodeled hallway directly into the refrigeration or dry storage areas.

In 2002, I had the pleasure of teaching a seminar on grantsmanship with Bart Hadder, a program officer for the M.J. Murdock Trust, at the Christian Camping International Convention in Vancouver, British Columbia. He gave the grant-makers' portion, while I presented the grant-seekers' half. After telling the story of my famous deal with Bob McDowell and explaining that over a million dollars of grants had been funded to date, I looked to see Bob in the front row and laughed as he said, "That deal sure paid off!"

GOD is **THE REMODELER**. He knows our needs and hears our heart's cry. He is able to do more than we can ever imagine in our wildest dreams, even if it takes a complete remodel of Cedar Lodge and one food service director's attitude!

11: GOD'S EXPANDABLE FAMILY

In our excitement to join the Warm Beach Camp staff in a faraway place called Stanwood, Washington, neither Stan nor I realized how hard it would be to have our families so far away. Stan's clan was in California; mine spread throughout the Midwest.

To complicate matters further, in the fall of 1978, even though Stan appealed to three levels of leadership at Fresno State, the administration ruled that Stan could not take his recreation administration internship out-of-state. So, reluctantly putting aside the amazing program that Director Bob McDowell had designed at Warm Beach Camp in Washington, after much prayer Stan went home to live with his parents in Auburn, California, to take his internship at the neighboring town's Recreation Department.

Our first summer at Warm Beach Camp, except for time spent sleeping, we both had worked around the clock. After my college-age staff returned to school, I realized that when Stan's little yellow Capri took off for California I really didn't know anyone else at Warm Beach. The first Sunday after Stan left, I ran out of church during the closing hymn weeping uncontrollably. As I passed through the lobby I felt someone envelop me in her arms, but couldn't see who it was through my stream of tears. To this day, I have no idea of the identity of this "angel" who comforted me.

Questioning God's purpose for yet another separation, I asked God to help me get through the next three months without Stan. I organized the "Lonely Hearts' Club," inviting people on the Camp staff who I determined might be lonely. The newly formed intergenerational group included both sexes. There was Darlene Wiley, head accountant, whose husband was an evangelist and on the road most of the time. Dick Klein, the new Guest Services Director, was roughing it as his wife was an hour away finishing her teaching contract. Al Cowin, an older gentleman who had never married, was working in the Accommodations Department. Brenda Maples (now Russie), the young single registrar, lived in the apartment below us. Jean Snodgrass, the new receptionist, had lost her husband in a tragic accident a few years before. This unique combination of folks tackled many joyous outings together. I was beginning to experience how reaching out to others could help extinguish the pangs of loneliness.

Stan finished his internship and returned to Washington with his B.S. diploma ready for display on the wall. While my deep loneliness subsided upon Stan's return, it would still rear up in full force during holidays and birthdays. We were both from big families who loved to celebrate with lots of aunts, uncles, and cousins. So, to brighten things up, I decided to throw a surprise "family" birthday party for Stan. I contacted people who reminded me of Stan's parents, sisters, nieces, nephews, aunts, and uncles. Before they arrived I provided each of them a nametag with detailed facts glued to the back about the relative whom they would be impersonating. Darlene and Forrest would play Stan's parents as their personalities and looks were a perfect match. Thayla Smith and her kids would play Stan's sister, Priscilla, and our niece and nephews, Kim, Greg, and Josh. Fran Jones would play "Sister Cindy." The planning went on and on, as I carefully plotted to get all Stan's family members represented. Excitement was in the air, and for the first time I found myself not dreading an upcoming birthday.

The day of his birthday, I left Stan's favorite carrot cake with cream cheese frosting in sight on the counter. Stan didn't suspect a thing; everyone had done an incredible job of keeping the secret. Unbeknownst to me, Stan had invited the Camp's volunteer electrician, Les Sargent, to come by in the evening to help devour his special treat.

After dinner, Stan was shocked when his whole family began to arrive for the celebration. Everyone played their part to the hilt, including Al Cowin, who was "Uncle Arnt" from Alaska, the one who often drank too much. Al showed up with a flask covered with bear skin hanging around his neck. He apologized for being late, explaining that his dog sled had broken down on the way to the Anchorage Airport.

In the midst of the celebration, long-lost relatives begin hugging, some who didn't even know each other! We made quite a family and, upon the insistence of "Aunty Gladys," we even had a family photo taken before the end of the evening. Stan was amazed that I had found someone to play every member of his family, except "Uncle Johnny" from L.A., whom I had somehow forgotten. Just then there was a knock on the door and there stood Les Sargent, ready to enjoy a piece of cake. I threw open the door while everyone screamed in unison, "Uncle Johnny, you made it after all!" Les had no idea what was going on as the crowd began to hug him, but he played right along anyway. What a wonderful evening we had!

That experience gave us a "whiff of grace" that comes from being part of the family of God. But I still dreaded holidays, and wished that they didn't exist. One day, while I was whining to Danny Cook, the business manager, he said words that propelled Stan and me into another chapter in our lives: "There is no need to be lonely. Just find other lonely people and invite them into your family. Look around; there are plenty of lonely people out there!" That began our adventure of putting together a family for each holiday. In the beginning, to get the hang of it, we joined Danny and Glenda Cook and Rod and Kathy Brown for holidays.

I remember one Christmas in particular, right before our Thad was born. We got a call that the Browns wouldn't be with us for Christmas dinner as Kathy had just gone into labor. Danny and Glenda were caring for Rod and Kathy's first born, Zach, during the event, and after eating a delicious Christmas dinner with the Cooks, we all traipsed into Arlington Hospital to meet Timothy Robert (later nicknamed T-Bob), the Brown's second son, who was born on Christmas Day. A few years later we would meet their daughter, Katy, on Christmas Eve.

After the Cooks left for the mission field in Haiti with Compassion International, we carried on the tradition of the holiday family. While there were some standard members like "Grandma Liz" from the senior community next door, and "Auntie Janer" from the Camp staff, the rest of the family changed each year depending on who was able to be with their families of origin and who was not. If my mom and dad were visiting, they became everyone's parents.

I recall a very large Easter celebration held the year that our daughter, Cherith, was about three. There were so many who needed a family that year that we had to move our celebration from our camp house to one of the Camp's satellite locations, W-Bar-B Ranch's multi-purpose room. Close to sixty people posed for the traditional family picture. Facundo Gomez, dressed in a bunny suit, surprised all of our children during the traditional Easter egg hunt. The celebration was a massive effort, and after working hard all day, I fell exhausted into a big chair with a less than grace-filled attitude. But God had a future reminder for me of the importance of the sense of family that we provided at holidays.

Years after that day, one of the grown "Camp kids," James Daniels, who was then pastoring a church in the Midwest, wrote a blog about the first time he realized, as a ten-year old, that there was an "Expandable Family of God." In detail, he outlined that very Easter event that had so exhausted me, where Cheryl Vlach, the wife of Accommodations Manager Dwight Vlach, had won the "Name the Family Contest" with her entry, "THE EGGSPANDABLE EASTER FAMILY." Her name fit our celebration beautifully.

While we now have our own adult children along with our precious grandkids close by for holidays, our family through the years always expands to include our "adopted son," Doug, a staff member who is all alone in the Pacific Northwest. A couple of Christmas Eves ago, we opened our hearts to include a lady who, like Dorothy in the Wizard of Oz, "clicked her heels" and appeared out of nowhere to volunteer for the entire *The Lights of Christmas.* And when the holiday is at one of our children's homes, they often carry on the tradition by inviting people to join.

After soaking the holidays in prayer for many years, the Nelson family's definition of hospitality has become, "when the Spirit of God mysteriously connects with two or more human spirits and the transfer of grace happens back and forth." We are made in God's image, and our Heavenly Father has a huge, **EXPANDABLE FAMILY**. Through His Spirit, He woos all of us to join that family, and there's always room for one more!

12: THE GOD OF THE IMPOSSIBLE

It was mid-April of 1980 and I had just returned to work after a two-month maternity leave. Our first child, Thad Johan, was being cared for by a neighbor on the campgrounds. I sat at my desk pondering how I would ever be able to direct the huge Food Service Department with a nursing baby. The Camp director, Bob McDowell, honored my request to condense my full-time job into a part-time position. Now I just had to figure out how to make this happen!

A year before, I had proposed the idea of a Food Services Management Internship to Bob. We had advertised the position in the national CCI (Christian Camping International) *Journal of Christian Camping*, but hadn't had any applicants who really wanted to make camp food service a career. With the need for professionally trained camp food service personnel so great, I abandoned the idea at the time when we couldn't find anyone with intentions of staying in the field upon graduation from the program.

As I sat pondering the challenge facing me as a brand new mom, the dream of training food service personnel resurfaced, and an excitement began brewing in me that I tried to dismiss as ridiculous. How would anyone even know the potential program existed? It hadn't been advertised in a year. The Spirit quietly whispered, "Someone will read it in an old *CCI Journal*."

I returned home for lunch and spotted a letter sitting on the old buffet we had purchased at a thrift store to match the rest of our newly-married furnishings. The letter was from Lynn McKay, a soon-to-graduate senior from Brier Crest College in Ontario, Canada. She had read an ad in an old *CCI Journal* and wanted to apply for the Food Service Management Internship Program! There was no doubt in my mind that this was the answer God had designed. Lynn McKay would be our first intern to pilot the program.

Upon returning to the office, I called the US Immigration Department in Seattle to see what would be needed to get a visa for this Canadian woman. When the receptionist heard that we needed the visa by June 1, just six weeks away, she declared in a strong voice, "What you are asking is IMPOSSIBLE!" In my mind, I instantly disagreed: "But we *know* the GOD OF THE IMPOSSIBLE!" Hoping that this rushed government worker wouldn't hang up, I kept talking and coaxing her until she finally agreed to mail the H-3 Training Visa application forms to me.

After the phone call, I marched into the kitchen to inform our head chef, Jerry Bussard, that the Lord was at last sending our first food service intern from Canada and that we needed to pray that we could obtain the required visa for her. Jerry excitedly shared with me that his father-in-law had just retired from the US Immigration Office in Seattle, and he could quite possibly be of help!

Much to my dismay when the forms arrived, the H-3 Training Visa application required us to outline how every hour of the fifteen month internship would be spent. Late one night, after the baby was sleeping, I made a grid and divided it into five three-month sections. Then I listed categories on the left-hand side, including: on-the-job floor training, classes, reading assignments, management training tapes, and written assignments. I quickly laid out all the workshop materials I had taught around the country at conventions, along with all the text books that had been required during my college food service management classes. And my plan came together. The intern would rotate around the department, filling in all the floor hours that I could no longer work. In addition, future interns would finish standardizing all the recipes and procedures that still needed to be organized. And, at any minute, the intern would play health inspector by pulling a surprise sanitation inspection.

Within the week I met with our chef's father-in-law in his Seattle home. With a red pen in hand he reviewed the visa application. After a few slight changes in wording, he declared, "There! Now it won't get hung up on anyone's desk while they investigate what your real meaning is."

What a victory for the Lord! Within a few weeks we had the H-3 Training Visa issued from the U.S. Immigration Office and Lynn McKay was on her way. Stan and I met her at SeaTac Airport with four-month-old Thad in our arms. She started work on June 1, only six weeks after the phone call to the Immigration Office.

Lynn did an outstanding job as the first of five food service interns. Not only did these amazing interns learn how to manage a real food service, they gave me the opportunity to work part-time. When Lynn returned to Canada she became the food service manager of a large Christian camp in Ontario and taught Food Service Administration workshops at Canada's CCI conventions. Following that experience, Lynn was called by the Lord to be the food service director at the Wycliffe Training Center in Central America for several years.

After the pilot internship program had finished at Camp, Bob McDowell advised me to get it connected with Seattle Pacific University. I met with Sam Dunn, who at that time was the Dean of Professional and Graduate Studies at SPU, and after careful consideration the internship became accredited. I thus became an adjunct professor and thereby fulfilled my desire to someday teach at the college level, for all six interns were college graduates before entering the internship. One of the interns, Lorna Martin, took my position as food service director when I moved on to other roles at Camp. Just this past year, I had the privilege of writing recommendations for two of my former interns who were pursuing new positions in the food service field.

Every December when I unwrap the shiny Christmas teddy bear ornament with the inscription, "Thad, 1980," and hang it on our tree, I think of our sparkling Canadian intern, Lynn McKay, who gave it to us for Thad's first Christmas. The ornament is a reminder to me that, while situations may seem impossible, we know **THE GOD OF THE IMPOSSIBLE**!

13: FAITHFUL TO ALL GENERATIONS

Little did I realize that our biggest challenge when returning to work after Thad was born would be finding excellent child care. No one could have sufficiently warned me of the intense love that I would feel for my children. I had planned to return to work full-time, but thankfully, Bob and Muriel McDowell allowed me to convert to part-time. Stan and I began to pray for someone who would not only take care of Thad and keep him safe, but who would also love him like her own.

I can't remember how we met Thayla Smith—probably at church. She had three children of her own, but her heart had room for one more. Thayla and Del lived on a mini-farm about six minutes from Camp. As we drove into their driveway that first time, we were greeted by a multitude of dogs and cats. There were chickens all around and a cow stood staring at us, chewing her cud. Their huge house had a lot of unique stone work inside and out which displayed Del's craftsmanship as a mason, and it included a big goldfish pond separating the living room from the den, with water trickling down the rocks.

After agreeing on an hourly rate for child care, we soon came to realize that God had a lot more than just a daycare person in mind for Thad. In no time at all, we were part of the Smiths' extended family. Many days I would linger when coming to fetch Thad, enjoying fellowship with "Auntie Thayla" and learning tips for motherhood. She had a remedy for everything, and it was usually spelled LOVE. "Auntie Thayla" was one of the most creative people I had ever met, and Thad loved being a part of the "Smith Homestead."

I remember one night when both our families camped out in the Smiths' little barn hoping to witness a calf being born. In the middle of the night we got hungry and left to make sandwiches. After a quick bite we returned, only to find that Bessy had given birth to her calf and we had missed it all! And then there were the milking lessons from Thayla, along with making ice cream from the cream skimmed off the top of those big glass gallon jars.

Thanks to Thayla, Thad learned how to pee in the grass, a skill that he proudly displayed during prayer before a barbecue with brand new staff members, Walt and Laree Maendl, and their family. Thankfully, the Maendls were from a farming background too and burst into laughter as Thayla confessed, "I taught Thad that this morning!"

When Thad was three, Thayla decided to start working at Camp as her youngest was ready for first grade. Again we prayed, asking God to lead in the process of finding child care. Upon Thayla's suggestion, I contacted Kathy Brown, Wrangler Rod's wife. They had two boys, Zach and "Tim-Bob," and lived only three minutes from Camp on Frank Waters Road. Thankfully, Kathy had an opening in her daycare and Thad joined the gang—mostly boys. I remember one time when I came to retrieve Thad that laughter was pouring out of the bathroom. There were five little boys gathered around the toilet, all peeing in unison!

In no time at all, Kathy had become "Auntie Kathy." "Uncle Rod" came home every day for lunch. Any table manners Thad learned, especially chewing with one's mouth closed, were thanks to his "Uncle." Often times our family would be invited over to the Browns' home for pancakes after Sunday morning service or for popcorn and apple sections after evening church. Not only did we spend holidays with the family, but Thad also enjoyed being at their home several days a week. Kathy continued to teach Thad amazing skills, including "tatting," which kept his little hands busy manufacturing colorful strings with left-over yarn.

After Cherith Joy was born to us in March, 1984, we were again fortunate that Kathy had an opening in her daycare. As summer season was quickly approaching, I returned to work part-time when Cherith was just a month old. Kathy agreed to take Cherith until summer, but warned me that when the boys were out of school in June, she wanted to be free to take the older ones to the beach. Those first months, Cherith adapted quickly and loved being at Kathy's home along with her big brother. But time was flying by, and as June got closer we prayed for another person who would be a good fit for our wee little daughter. I just couldn't imagine anyone but Kathy! No one could measure up, and I seriously considered quitting work.

It was nearing the end of May when Kathy asked if we had found anyone to take care of Cherith for the summer. I was embarrassed to admit that I couldn't bring myself to even start looking. Kathy let out a sigh of relief and said, "Oh, good! We talked as a family and we couldn't imagine Cherith going anywhere else! If you don't mind her eating a little sand at the beach this summer, we would love to have her as part of the daycare!" Stan and I were relieved and gratified, and Cherith remained with her brother and the Brown family.

We wondered if Kathy would continue the daycare when her youngest started school full-time. The answer came one day while I was dropping the kids off: Kathy excitedly told me that she was expecting another baby! Soon little Katy was born and Cherith and she became fast friends as soon as Katy was old enough to play. Both Thad and Cherith stayed in Kathy's daycare until they were nine years old. The Browns even threw a daycare graduation celebration for Cherith, complete with a little picture book of memories from her time with them. After graduating from daycare, Thad and Cherith palled around with two other children at Camp, Michael and Elizabeth, checking in with us as needed throughout the day and always reporting for lunch at noon.

I once told Rod that if I were God, looking for someone today to be the mother for his Son, I would choose Kathy. Kathy is the most humble, patient, Christ-like woman that Stan and I know. Sometimes I feel that it was wise of me to keep working just so my children could experience Kathy's amazing love and care.

A few months ago, while Thad was relaxing in our big lounge chair he shared something parents long to hear. After relaying that someone had complimented him on his parenting skills with his little daughter, Julie, Thad said, "I realize that you were good parents, and I am just modeling what you did!" Actually, as I have watched both Thad and Cherith parent their children, I praise God for His faithfulness in providing the very best daycare people, Kathy and Thayla, to love our children. A huge part of the good parenting skills they experienced came from these two amazing women of God.

After also soaking in prayer the daycare needs for our grandkids, we have witnessed God supply the very best for our grandsons, Preston and Eli, while Cherith works to contribute to her family's financial resources. Thayla even filled in a few months for Preston when he was very young. Last year we took our grandsons to a birthday party hosted by Eli's daycare person, Meg, who is an incredible mom in the neighborhood! And more recently, Cherith's close friends, Loren and Erin, have continued to provide outstanding care for Eli.

At our wedding in 1971 we selected "Great is Your Faithfulness" as the congregational hymn. The words of that song have rung true throughout our married life: in "summer and winter and springtime and harvest" God hears and answers our prayers and is **FAITHFUL TO ALL GENERATIONS**!

14: THE HARDWIRER

Before the days of routine ultrasounds, I knew without a doubt that the child within me would be active. Thad Johan was doing jumping jacks and climbing the walls of my womb to get out! Two weeks before my due date and after I had already worked a long day, Thad jumped so hard he broke my water and demanded to be born around five p.m. on January 21, 1980.

After being married nine years, we were elated to have a healthy, nine-pound, two-ounce baby boy! Thad broke all the records for what babies are to do in their first months of life. He was way ahead of the pack in learning to roll over, crawl, and walk. To our astonishment, before he was a year old this now light-weight, agile boy, who had surpassed the upper limits of the growth chart during the first month of his life, hoisted himself out of his crib and came crawling into the living room.

Thad was in constant motion, and it took both of us to keep him safe. He couldn't even sit still long enough to watch cartoons. Our pastor declared that Thad was the most energetic child he had ever seen. But Thad was delightful and accompanied us everywhere in the back pack. He was game for anything, including cross country skiing on his tiny skis before he was two.

When the big yellow school bus swallowed Thad up to begin kindergarten, he waltzed his way through the year with his well-developed social skills. From being reared on the campgrounds, Thad didn't know the definition of a stranger, and was tender-hearted and caring to all. But everything changed in first grade, when he found it impossible to stay in his chair. His teacher claimed Thad spent more time under his chair than sitting on it. By the end of first grade he was behind and could not read.

We met with the principal and he gave us the summer to make the decision as to whether Thad should repeat first grade or be sent on without the foundational reading skills. This brought back shameful memories for me, as I didn't begin to read until fifth grade. Stan and I earnestly sought God for guidance. After meeting with a psychologist and Thad's pediatrician, we got a prescription for Ritalin to help Thad settle down before second grade, and we continued to pray.

For some reason, we just didn't feel comfortable starting Thad on the medication. During midsummer I chatted with the Camp's volunteer nurse, Linda Visser, to see if she had any experience with Ritalin. Linda had not worked with this medication, and so our prayers continued as we sought guidance. The summer was passing, and as August began I became nervous: a decision had to be made soon.

One day the phone rang. It was Linda, back home in Wenatchee, Washington, and she said, "Nancy, I don't know you well enough to be doing this but the Lord won't give me any peace until I call you, so here goes…" Linda had recently seen a friend, a school psychologist, at a gathering. Upon being told about our situation he advised, "Instruct your friends to wait and give the Ritalin *after* his teacher has had a chance to get a base line on his behavior without the drug. The only way to know if the Ritalin is effective is if Thad's teacher observes a change in his learning behavior after he has been on the medication."

Peace flooded my spirit. I knew this "WAIT" was God's answer concerning Ritalin. We decided to have Thad begin second grade without the medication. Knowing his situation, the principal placed Thad in Mrs. Lemke's class. She was an experienced teacher who used "cooperative learning" in her class, a method whereby everyone worked together on the same things and helped one another. Not only did this cut down on classroom distractions, but it also brought out Thad's highly developed social skill of caring for others in community.

Mrs. Lemke used many "hands-on" learning techniques along with powerful motivational aids. Thad was paired with a good reader and each was required to move a ruler under a line of text while the other one read. Mysteriously, Thad's hands on the ruler caused his brain to focus on the words. There was a huge chart on the classroom wall to track the number of books each student read at home to their parents. There were incremental awards along the way. But Thad set his eyes on the grand prize. After reading 300 little books, he was thrilled to be a part of the elite group that got to stay overnight at Mrs. Lemke's home.

Within months Thad was reading and was leading the pack with his creative skills in art and science projects. At his first conference session, Mrs. Lemke confirmed our own assessment: Ritalin would not be necessary.

Four years later, when his little sister had Mrs. Lemke as her second grade teacher, Thad attended an "open house" with us. He pulled Mrs. Lemke aside and we heard him exclaim, "I would have never learned to read if it hadn't been for you!" Mrs. Lemke pointed toward the ceiling and declared, "Don't thank me, Thad, thank God. You don't know how many times I sat in your chair before and after school and prayed for God to help you learn how to read."

In his senior year, Thad wrote a story about the most influential person in his life, Mrs. Lemke. His creative writing teacher passed his story on to the Stanwood-Camano School District office and, with Thad's permission, it was published in the district newsletter that went out to every household in the Stanwood/Camano area just before Thanksgiving. On the front page was a picture of Thad sitting at a tiny desk with Mrs. Lemke proudly standing behind him. Thad's story beside the picture ended with, "I thank God for Mrs. Lemke." He was honored to invite and to have Mr. and Mrs. Lemke among the guests at his high school graduation party, and a few years later they also attended his wedding to Abby.

The Creator has hard-wired Thad with DNA to be active, and to be a kinesthetic, hands-on learner. Anyone who follows him on Facebook or looks at our 2014 and 2015 Christmas presents—beautiful calendars with gorgeous photos he has taken of his favorite expeditions—can see that Thad is still climbing the walls—the rock faces of high mountains. He is using his hands as an excellent journeyman commercial electrician, and his social skills come in handy as a foreman leading his crew.

God is **THE HARDWIRER** who creates each of us uniquely. And whenever we ask, HE can direct each and every person to what is most effective for that hardwiring, and gather the people around us to enhance and develop that which He has ordained.

15: THE MULTI-TASKER

When Thad Johan was growing up on the Campground he used to declare, "I am the luckiest kid on earth because when Camp is over, I don't have go home: I live here!" But at eight years old, he longed for a buddy at Camp to share in his adventures. During bedtime prayers he would often ask God for a boy his age to join the staff family.

After serving as Food Services Director I became Bob and Muriel McDowell's assistant for several years. Then Muriel, the Director of Administration, died in 1988. I took over her responsibility of directing the Human Resources Department. My first year-round, salaried vacancies to fill were a maintenance position and an accommodations worker. Bob had graciously sent me to a few workshops right after I had become the department leader, and so I was better prepared for the hiring task ahead.

Right as the summer ended, I received a call from a "Kurt" in California who had seen our summer positions listed with Intercristo. He was wondering if we had any year-round positions available. I told him about the accommodations job and sent him the information packet. After reviewing his application and checking scads of references, I knew beyond the shadow of a doubt that Kurt was our kind of guy.

About the same time, one of our bookkeepers, Jeannette Dozier, asked if she could notify her friends, Peter and Becky Collins, then living at Rawhide Ranch near San Diego, about the maintenance position that had just become available. Jeannette raved about this couple. After we received their applications and thoroughly checked references, I could see why she was so excited about them.

The Camp has a policy to interview the finalists for all year-round, salaried positions in person. The management team was registered for the November Christian Camping International (CCI) Conference at a hotel in Anaheim, California, just a couple of months away. Kurt had applied to several camps and I was afraid we would lose him if we waited; I wanted to move forward but that would have cost money to arrange an in-person interview. With our budget so tight, Bob McDowell held his ground and, even if I had stood on my head, it wouldn't have changed his mind. I thought November would never arrive! I prayed that God would somehow save this young man for Warm Beach. Each day I wondered if Kurt would call to withdraw his application after being scooped up by another camp.

Finally the day arrived. Our management team attended the CCI Conference and I arranged interviews with Kurt and also with Peter and Becky Collins, all of whom connected with us while we were in Los Angeles for the conference. The entire team participated in the interviews conducted in the hotel's restaurant. We had all prayed for God's guidance, as selecting the right fit was extremely important. I still remember when Kurt Hovatter entered the large booth sporting a pony tail! I wondered how this would end up with the dress code at that time outlining collar length hair as the maximum allowed. As for the Collinses, they revealed that they not only had a nine year old son, Michael, but a seven year old daughter, Elizabeth!

All candidates passed the scrutiny of the interview panel with flying colors, and were hired. The Collinses and Kurt all arrived in December, 1988, to begin work in January. Peter and Becky had their kids in tow, but Kurt came without his ponytail.

Later Kurt shared that while he had offers from other camps, the Lord had confirmed to him that he was to wait and come to Warm Beach. All of these Californians moved to Camp, sight unseen, and trusted that we would provide adequate housing. We made good on our promises, except Peter still claims to this day that I lied to him about the Pacific Northwest weather, telling him that Camp hardly ever got snow and if it did snow, it only lasted a day or two. And Kurt insisted on walking around in his Bermuda shorts all that first winter with us, even though the snow lasted for weeks.

Thad, Michael, Cherith, and Elizabeth became fast friends. They were inseparable. While the girls played house and dress up, Michael and Thad built forts in every corner of the woods, in trees, and even one underground. We had many camping trips together as families, including a three-week trip to volunteer at Rancho Betania Camp in Mexico. Back home, the four of us adults would play games late into the night while the kids rode their bikes around the Camp in the moonlight. The boys had a lawn-mowing business and kept the lease lots on the campground looking sharp.

After saving their money for a year, the young "business partners" bought trick "gyro-bikes" with rotating handlebars. Tales have been told about riding those bikes everywhere imaginable throughout Camp, including the shop roof. And then there are the stories of the fearless four playing in the hay mow, picking each other clean of hay until Pat Patterson, then the Head Wrangler, finally caught them in the act!

As a cracker-jack bookkeeper, Becky Collins would have loved to be placed in the Accounting Department, but there were no positions open in her specialty. Instead, she agreed to fill in as the part-time receptionist. Her first day of work, January 16, 1989, was a tragic one at Camp. Becky patched through a call to me from Arlington Hospital asking how to reach the "next-of-kin" for Jeannette Dozier, who had just been in an accident.

Less than an hour before, Jeannette had been standing in my office when her pager went off. Since her lunch hour was just about to begin, Jeannette, a volunteer fire fighter, was thrilled to jump in her big truck and respond to a call. Minutes afterwards, the load in the back of her truck shifted, and within sight of the fire station she went off the road and crashed into a tree. I asked if we should come to the hospital since Jeannette's family was in California and we were like family. The nurse called the doctor to the phone and his words will forever be engraved in my memory: "I am so sorry; Jeannette is dead."

Dr. Frank Thompson had just arrived at Camp to lead the Pastor's Prayer Retreat. He and Bob McDowell gathered the entire staff for a time of prayer and to begin the process of grieving the loss of our young "cowgirl." When Jeannette wasn't at her desk crunching numbers or at the fire station, she had been clad in her western boots and hat, hanging with the horses at the stables or strumming her guitar for the Horse Camp chapel time. Today the covered riding arena at Warm Beach is named in her memory.

Right after Jeannette died, the annual audit was about to start and Sharon Shaw, business manager, quickly requested that Becky move to the accounting office the next day. As unbelievable as it seemed, Jeannette had recruited her own replacement. Today, Becky directs the Business/Human Resources Department.

Twenty-nine years later, Peter is also still on staff, managing the Maintenance Department. Kurt not only changed his last name from Hovatter to Von Pessler, he has filled different roles at camp including accommodations, food services, and recreation. Kurt is a legend. All the staff kids love him, and every young camper knows who Kurt is too: he is the lifeguard at the pool who keeps them safe, but is also the "King of Fun!" His laugh is legendary and can be heard all over Camp. His humble Christ-likeness is obvious to all. To celebrate Kurt's twenty-fifth year of service, the recreation staff had special shirts made to honor him.

One look at Thad and Abby's wedding photos will reveal how special these three staff members and their children have been to us over the years. Michael was Thad's best man in the wedding and Kurt was a groomsman. Becky was one of the special people that Thad selected to pray a blessing over them at the end of the ceremony.

In addition, these three hires have loved and discipled many of the college-age staff through the years with their infectious hospitality and grace-filled lives. Peter and Becky have opened their home and hearts for many lonely summer staff who need a "mom and dad" to cure home-sickness. Kurt has discipled countless young men and holds the record for the most weddings as an attendant—probably well over fifty! When asked about it, he blushes and just says, "It's such an honor and privilege to be asked."

After evening swims, Kurt used to bring our daughter, Cherith, home from the swimming pool on the handlebars of his famous bike with the big balloon tires whenever the other three kids would leave her. We finally figured out Cherith would purposefully dawdle just so she could sail through the air while riding home with Kurt. Now our thirteen-year-old grandson, Preston, lingers at the pool so that he too can talk to "Mommy's friend," Kurt.

God is indeed **THE MULTI-TASKER**! Not only did HE answer a little boy's prayer for a buddy, at the same time HE brought us three amazing staff members who have been gracefully woven into the lives of scores of people at Warm Beach Camp, including Stan and me and our family.

16: ABBA

There was never any doubt growing up that I was "Daddy's girl!" Or rather, I should say, "Daddy's tomgirl." As the second daughter I quickly filled the role of the companion that my Dad had hoped to someday take fishing with him. It wasn't until high school that I realized it was rare for a girl to go fishing with her father almost every weekend, including winters when we would bore a hole in the ice!

Dad was a farm boy at heart. While he was trapped in the city as the head of the Vehicle Maintenance Department at the naval air station there, he migrated to the country as often as possible. It never occurred to me that we were poor and couldn't afford vacations and eating out. Our weekends were simply delightful. Whenever Dad and I weren't trolling in our old boat fishing the lakes around Minneapolis, our family was picnicking with permission near some farmer's pond in Wisconsin.

And then there was the love of camping that Dad instilled in us. As soon as summer vacation began, our family would be off to pitch a tent in some lovely natural setting. While there were established parks, this was before the days of designated campsites, so it wasn't long before Dad had talked his way around the campground and knew everyone else vacationing in the park. We had our "extended camping family" who met from a three-state area every summer in northern Minnesota to swim and waterski. Dad had connected us with them our first year at Cass Lake, and by springtime every year the annual summer reunion would be on our calendar.

Deep in the core of our being, we all long for our parents' approval. After my mom and dad sacrificed to pay half of my way through college, I wondered if they were disappointed in my husband's and my decision to throw away our professional careers to go into Christian camping, which in 1976 was just coming of age. As I was at the top of my graduating class at the University of California at Davis, my folks had always imagined me in a starched-white hospital lab coat, making my education pay off. I will never forget the first time they visited Stan and me after we had landed at Hartland Christian Camp, hidden in the mountains near Badger, California. When my folks entered the camp kitchen, they saw me clad in jeans, topped off with an old work shirt covered by a stained chef's apron. I was behind the grill flipping hotcakes for 200 hungry campers.

Then, in January of 1980 when their first grandchild, Thad Johan, was born, Mom and Dad started coming regularly to Warm Beach Camp (our new home) as part of the "Grandparent Volunteer Program." Funny how parents all of a sudden start visiting more regularly and staying longer after grandchildren arrive! Dad became part of the maintenance staff and was affectionately termed "The Wood-chuck" as he would have a ball cutting up fallen trees with his chain saw on the Camp's 268 acres. Every January he would care for the Camp's sixty horses when the staff would go for our annual retreat at another camp. Mom would tend to the home front and take care of our children and their best friends, Michael and Elizabeth, whose parents were also on staff.

One day, that long-awaited parental affirmation came from my dad in an unexpected phone call. He had just sold his deceased brother's farm in Wisconsin. While they were empty-nesters, Mom and Dad had made many fond memories camping with friends at Uncle Rudolf's farm by Goose Lake, which was located on one corner of the property. Dad was in a tender, reflective mood and needed someone to talk to in an attempt to lighten his grief over the loss of the farm. In the process, he shared how fortunate we were to be a part of the Warm Beach Staff and to raise his grandchildren at Camp. He was amazed at how the staff family loved one another and couldn't think of a better environment in which to have Thad and Cherith grow up.

Dad also marveled at the staff events that we had at Camp, like the Christmas party. He felt that he was a part of this yearly event, for he had played Santa Claus a couple of times when visiting us in December. One time, Thad, in the midst of the gang of staff kids gathered around Santa's feet said, "Hey, those are my Grandpa's shoes!" The wonderful memories continued to flow, and at the end of that precious phone call Dad expressed how proud he was of Stan and me. He loved how we were investing our lives in the camping ministry at Warm Beach. Those words were music to my ears. I floated around for days after hanging up the phone.

In December of 2000 I received a call from my Aunt June, who had never called me before. She was concerned for my mom, who was very depressed. We had prayed for years to know when it was time to move my parents to Washington so we could be involved in their care. Upon retiring they had moved to the vacation town of Balsam Lake, Wisconsin, to spend twelve years entertaining in their lovely home on the lakeshore. With Dad's progressing Parkinson's disease, however, the isolation during the harsh winters had become more than Mom could manage. That confirming phone call was an answer to prayer and I made an emergency four-day trip back to Wisconsin to accompany my folks on a flight to begin the next phase of their lives.

Shortly after his arrival at Warm Beach, it was necessary to place Dad in the nursing home right next to Camp. It became obvious that Mom, Stan, and I could no longer physically juggle the twenty-four-hour care regimen that was necessary. I begged God for months to take Dad home to be with Him in Heaven. Dad was trapped in his body, unable to chop wood or fix things that needed repairing. As his muscles lost control, we proceeded to lose Dad, "one brain cell at a time."

After countless days of wrestling with God in prayer, I realized that He wasn't going to do it my way. I will never forget the day that I fully surrendered to the journey ahead. I had stopped that morning at the nursing home to spend a few minutes with Dad in his room at the far end of the hall. After a quick visit, I kissed him goodbye as I had to lead a meeting over at Camp. He insisted that he would walk me to the front entrance. While he could still walk using his walker, I knew that it would take a long time. So, I suggested he let me push him in the wheelchair. In a voice I recognized from childhood, Dad emphatically said, "NO! *You* get in the wheelchair and I will push *you* to the entrance!" There was no sense in arguing with this strong-willed Swede! Even though I was late to the meeting, somehow, mysteriously, after that long ride down the hall in Dad's wheelchair with other residents and staff pointing at us and laughing, I relaxed and leaned into our new extended community and sensed God's presence.

After five years of experiencing community at the nursing home, hospice was brought in as Dad was on his final trek through the horrendous destruction of Parkinson's disease. That Sunday morning, the hospice nurse estimated that Dad had about two weeks to live. With spiritual intuition, our daughter, Cherith, and her husband, Chad, insisted on coming that same evening to visit Grandpa. The following morning while I was showering I took my fist and slammed it into the wall and screamed at the top of my lungs, "Take him now, God! He has suffered long enough!"

I had promised Mom that I would visit Dad in the morning before going to work so she could sleep in, as we were preparing for the long two-week goodbye by his bedside. As I rounded his bed that last morning I momentarily observed him breathing. Yet, as I sat down by his bed I looked at Dad and his face was deathly still and cheeks hollow. I put my ear to his mouth and there was no breath. Within the hour God had answered my prayer.

Numbness set in during the next days of planning two memorial services and receptions—one in Washington, and the other in Wisconsin. There were also arrangements to be made for shipping Dad's body back to Wisconsin for burial in Balsaam Lake's cemetery next to my sister's grave—a promise that I'd made to my mom before the move. There wasn't time to ponder anything with so many details to put into place.

In order to make things easier, we used the same printed program for both memorial services. Mom and Dad's pastor in Wisconsin warned me that people in the Midwest were not used to offering tributes spontaneously during the service. He advised that I have several people primed to follow my tribute. However, I only remembered this detail halfway through my speech, and I quickly prayed that God would somehow cover my forgetfulness.

After I sat down, when the pastor asked for other tributes, Kelly, a nineteen-year-old neighbor gal with Down syndrome, walked up to the microphone in the little mortuary chapel. She simply said, "I loved Carl because Carl loved me. Last time we visited Carl in Washington, I forgot to kiss him goodbye. I got to kiss him goodbye today before they closed the casket. I loved Carl because Carl loved me!" After she sat down, I think just about every friend and relative got up and shared through tears how much my dad had meant to them.

While I would never pretend to understand how the spiritual realm works, months later while I was pondering my slow, five-year goodbye with Dad, an overwhelming thought crossed my mind: could it be that my Dad loved me so much he waited until I could transfer my strong love for him to my Heavenly Father and feel my Abba's embrace?

I am "Abba's girl" and He loves me unconditionally and affirms me, just because I am His child. I can crawl up in Abba's lap anytime to pray or just to be held. I can love, because Abba first loved me! Now, my breath prayer is so simple: "Abba, embrace me!"

Of all the names for God, **ABBA** is my very favorite.

17: THE KEEPER OF WARM BEACH CAMP

It was 1994 and I was working in the upstairs office complex with Director Bob McDowell. I had learned to tell when Bob was carrying a heavy load by the sound of his footsteps as he passed the copy machine and rounded the corner by the old dumbwaiter before reaching my desk. That morning, by the sound of his shoes on the linoleum floor, he was weighted down with a huge burden. A few moments later, upon reading the letter in his hand, I understood why Bob's face was downcast.

An environmental group was suing the Camp and the Department of Ecology (DOE) in federal court because they claimed the wastewater treatment plant was out of compliance with the state's standards. This was documented by a few test samples that were on record with the DOE. Warm Beach Camp was not the only one that was getting sued by this environmental group. The newspapers in surrounding areas were also reporting other agencies and towns that were receiving similar legal papers. Within a few minutes, the atmosphere at Warm Beach Camp took on a heaviness that would invade everything and cause the Camp to be seen in a negative light throughout the community.

The Camp had already been working closely with the DOE in order to solve the problem and provide better wastewater treatment. To make the situation even more complex, the Washington State DOE had granted the Camp an administrative extension to the wastewater treatment plant's discharge permit after it had expired. The Federal law had been changed to allow private individuals to bring lawsuits if wastewater treatment plants did not meet the state standards. Even though the Camp's plant had been operating within limits during the previous six months, the attorney for the environmental group claimed that "any failure is failure to meet the absolute standards of the federal law."

In God's providence, a Board member, Art Smelser, a civil engineer who had recently retired as the district administrator for the Olympic and southern Puget Sound area of the Washington State Department of Transportation, knew his way around the Olympia government offices and had years of experience with environmental and legal issues. God had strategically placed Art on the board at Camp "for such a time as this." Art began to work closely with Director Bob McDowell and board chair, Frank Cranston.

The staff and board began to pray in earnest. Seeking legal advice on how to proceed, the Camp hired an attorney in Snohomish who had experience in environmental issues. It was at this time that Kelly Wynn from Water and Wastewater Services was hired to continue the testing and oversee the Camp's wastewater treatment plant (WWTP.)

The management of the Camp desperately wanted to arrive at a solution as quickly as possible to be good stewards of the environment. A complete overhaul of the WWTP would require planning time in addition to a major campaign to raise the funds needed. It became obvious to those in leadership that we could lose Warm Beach Camp due to the lawsuit.

A few days after the legal papers were delivered to Bob McDowell, I was praying in the outdoor amphitheater overlooking Puget Sound. I remembered the scripture where Jesus instructed his followers to "pray for your enemies." While I didn't know who any of the environmental group members were, I figured that Jesus would want me to pray for them, whether they were actually enemies or not. I started praying for their executive director and for their members, those who must love Puget Sound enough to be combing the records at the DOE and hiring an attorney to file lawsuits against agencies and cities.

After praying for the environmental group members, I sat quietly overlooking the mudflats of Port Susan Bay, taking in the beautiful panoramic view of Puget Sound. That's when the Lord impressed these words into my spirit as if He were sitting right next to me: "I made the land masses. I made the waters. I am the Keeper of Puget Sound and I am the Keeper of Warm Beach Camp!" It was a holy moment indeed, after which the Lord injected a peace that passed all understanding into this very frightened director of administrative services. I hurried to tell Bob and the staff what the Lord had spoken to me.

Later, Art Smelser shared a similar experience he had while driving to the first meeting in Snohomish with the lawyer the Camp had just retained. As Art was traveling north on Highway 9 from Bellevue he was praying, "Lord, the Camp is yours; it's really not ours. If you chose to minister in some other way, then we will have to abide. We are turning it over to you." As Art crested the hill with the town of Snohomish in view, he felt a huge burden lift when the Lord impressed on his heart, "I am going to take care of it."

After the legal counsel for the environmental group left that first meeting, the Camp's newly hired lawyer said, "Since the Camp has been operating the last six months within the limits of its permit, there are reasonable grounds to protest the law suit." Art felt a ray of hope beginning to rise that the Camp could win the case or delay it long enough to get the needed improvements in place to guarantee that in the future there would be no tests out of compliance.

Meanwhile, intercessors continued to pray for the Camp to be saved. Two months later an administrative law judge in the Olympia area called a meeting of both parties to review the case. Both attorneys were present, along with a representative from the State DOE and Bob and Art from the Camp. After the environmental group's lawyer outlined the case, the Judge asked exactly how the system worked. After Art described the plant's operation in detail, the judge turned to the DOE representative and asked if that was an accurate description. Upon receiving a "yes," the judge asked the environmental group's attorney if he had ever seen the plant in operation. After he said that he had not, the judge then asked the young attorney if he had ever tried a case in federal court. When he admitted that he had not, the judge advised that there be a settlement out of federal court. To this day, with tears in his eyes, Art continues to exclaim, "That only could have been God at work."

The environmental group, the State DOE, and the Camp worked together to arrive at an agreement that would be best for the environment of Puget Sound. The DOE had to issue a new operating permit for the WWTP in a timely manner. Without any admission of liability, the Camp agreed to make a $5,000 contribution to a local agency to replace a degraded fish ladder on a local creek, install water conservation fittings in facilities, move the fencing in the horse pastures to allow for a greater buffer by the streams, and make several improvements to the existing wastewater treatment plant process to help ensure compliance. In 1995, the Camp fulfilled the final promise by completing a modification project to the lagoon that improved the treatment plant until a new one could be built in the future.

Desiring a quiet WWTP that would honor the environment, the Camp began researching different ways to process wastewater. Kelly Wynn recommended a new concept for constructed wetlands after contacting leaders in the field at Humboldt State University in California. Since Art was retired, he agreed to monitor with Kelly the design of the proposed new WWTP that would include constructed wetlands.

Meanwhile, the feasibility study for the Journey of Faith Campaign had begun so that there would be a way to fund the $1.5 million needed to construct the new WWTP. Art helped interview contractors and the board chose one with the most experience and willingness to work with the Camp. Art came aboard as the Camp's engineering consultant to monitor the contractor's work.

The Warm Beach Senior Community—the Camp's next door neighbor—helped raise a portion of the funding for the new WWTP as their operation required two-thirds of the treatment provided. Thanks to many generous donors and a $320,000 grant from the M.J. Murdock Trust, the Camp was able to begin construction of the new plant in 2002. God gave exceptionally dry weather through early December for the completion of the project—another answer to prayer. And, part of the grant from the Trust funded a $25,000 interpretive walkway around the constructed wetlands for environmental education.

In 2005, the M.J. Murdock Trust leadership asked if they could include a site visit to the new WWTP as part of their staff's field trip to see projects that had been funded. One of the trustees, Neal Thorpe, had great interest in the plant. He and his wife, Kay, came a week before the scheduled staff trip to make certain that all details were in place. When Ed McDowell took Neal on the interpretive walkway around the most environmentally sound wastewater treatment plant in the Pacific Northwest, Neal had all kinds of biochemical questions as to what was actually happening in the wetlands. Ed did an amazing job explaining the process until Neal's questions got too complex. I laughed and told Ed he was no match for Dr. Thorpe, who had a PhD in biology and used to be the chairman of the Biology Department at Augsburg College in Minnesota. I knew, because he was the professor who had helped me with my independent study for Biology 101 in 1971!

The next week, a fancy charter bus pulled up with all the Trust's staff, including the program directors and three trustees. My husband, Stan, and Gary Kocher, Warm Beach's annual fund director, drove smaller buses down to the new WWTP so our guests could see what the Trust's investment had accomplished. The group ended with lunch in the staff dining room where they got to use the old restrooms downstairs in Cedar Lodge. Those restrooms needed to be moved upstairs, and that project would be a part of the next grant proposal to the Trust.

As a part of the Embracing the Vision campaign, a multi-million outfall solution for the WWTP was completed in 2008 to give the WWTP the capacity to function as a Class A wastewater system—more than was required. The WWTP has continued to work excellently, winning awards for its operation. Most importantly, the goal had been achieved to earn and receive a new WWTP permit, and to guarantee that the state discharge standards are met—thus protecting the environment in Puget Sound. In addition, the plant has become a destination point for many who are considering an environmentally friendly way to process wastewater. In the spring and fall, many students can be seen using the interpretive walkway around the WWTP.

By representing the Camp in the Warm Beach Community Association for the last twenty years, I have gotten to know some of the environmentalists in the community itself. They are our neighbors, and are good people who love the environment. Director Ed McDowell continued to work with some of them while obtaining a new conditional use permit for the Camp. These same people who expressed environmental concerns in 1994 are now trusted partners with the Camp in pursuing environmental solutions.

God is **THE KEEPER OF WARM BEACH CAMP**. The Lord set apart these beautiful, wooded 268 acres which sit overlooking Port Susan Bay on Puget Sound. He has appointed the Camp to be a good steward of the environment, and He delights when we work in unity with our neighbors.

18: THE GOD WHO ANSWERS PRAYER

Excitement mounted as we packed up our kids and all the gear for our annual camping vacation in the middle of July, 1990. We were leaving early on Friday morning to secure the best camping spots at Deception Pass State Park Campgrounds right next to Cranberry Lake. Since Peter and Becky Collins had to work that day, Stan and I had agreed to take their kids and their tent with us in order to reserve them a campsite right next to ours before the weekend crowd arrived.

With a trailer full of bikes, lawn chairs, and cooking equipment, we pulled up to our favorite stomping grounds only to find a sign across the entrance that read, "Closed due to water quality problems. Campground will reopen tomorrow at 6 a.m." With four very disappointed youngsters seated behind us, we decided to scout out motels in the neighboring town of Oak Harbor. After being turned away from every possible place, we realized that the sailing regatta advertised throughout the town must be the reason why there were no vacancies. At the very last hotel we found one room available for an outrageous price—but it was the bridal suite!

After we explained to the children that we could not afford the only available room left in Oak Harbor, our ten year old son, Thad, asked, "Well, what can we afford?" Stan replied that $40 would be more within our price range. Right from the back seat Thad demanded that we pray about the need. Four little kids bowed their heads as Thad laid his request before the Lord: "God, You know we need a motel room because the campground is closed, and we have $40. Will you please help us find a place so we don't have to go home?"

Oh, what faith! We had already turned around and were heading back over the Deception Pass Bridge towards Camp. Just as we rounded a curve, there on the right-hand side of the road appeared the Lake Campbell Motel. Stan pulled into the driveway and parked the car full of noisy kids as far from the office as possible. When he returned, his big smile told us that it was a positive answer. The owner had agreed to rent us a room with a kitchenette for the night and his rate was $40! And Stan had even told him that we had four kids in our car with the possibility of another set of parents on the way! Soon we were comfortably settled into our large motel room containing a double bed and a couch that made into another bed.

We quickly called Peter and Becky and told them that if they wanted to wait until morning to join us that would be just fine, but they were also welcome to squeeze into the motel room as well. The kids swam and fished all afternoon in Lake Campbell on the other side of the road. Sure enough, before dark Peter and Becky pulled up in their rig, and as nighttime settled in, it became an adventure of epic proportions as the kids used every inch of the floor to arrange their sleeping bags. We ate a very late supper and bedded down for the night. Early the next morning the men and boys were at the Cranberry Lake campground at six a.m. to set up camp on the best site in the park that was big enough for both tents. When the dads returned with their sons to the Lake Campbell Motel, we women folk were waiting with hot cinnamon rolls and eggs.

It was a fantastic week! We hiked, swam, biked, and spun tales around the campfires. The kids spent hours on the beach building elaborate forts out of drift wood. Peter and Becky would arise early every morning to have breakfast ready for us late sleepers. It didn't even seem like work having Becky to chat with as we prepared and cleaned up after the other meals.

Even now, years later, every time we drive by that Lake Campbell Motel, someone always recalls the day that God answered the prayer for a $40 room. God is **THE GOD WHO ANSWERS PRAYER** even if it takes a ten year old boy to remind us to pray about everything.

19: THE GIVER OF ALL GOOD GIFTS

When our children were very young we began to dream of having a boat. I had grown up with a boat, spending many hours on the slalom ski and making giant "rooster tails" around many of the 10,000 lakes in Minnesota. I can still hear my dad say as he would bring me the tow rope after a wipeout, "Whatcha doing down there?!"

Years ago, it would have been a stretch for our family to buy a boat on Camp wages, even with both Stan and me working. But, after a family meeting with Thad (age eight) and Cherith (four years old), we committed ourselves to saving money. A large "boat chart" was constructed to hang on the wall by the washing machine. Decorated by the kids, it had a large thermometer to indicate the progress towards the $3,000 goal.

The kids knew that saving $3,000 would mean eating Camp left-overs and foregoing all costly entertainment. Thankfully, newly-retired Grandma Johnson, my mom, was addicted to garage-sales and thus kept our kids in clothes. Stan's sisters, "Auntie Sugar Bump" and "Aunt Cindy," also sent care packages with adorable dresses for Cherith before the holidays.

As we pinched pennies for many months, the line on the thermometer continued to rise as the money accumulated in the bank. As a family we would regularly pray for the Lord to save just the right boat for us. After a couple of years and with the goal nearly met, Stan and Thad began to study the boat-trader magazines listing used vessels for sale in the Pacific Northwest. Sadly, most were way over our $3,000 goal.

One Tuesday in March, 1990, while perusing the magazine Stan spotted an older 17-foot Beachcraft boat with an eighty-five horse Evinrude motor listed for $3,500; it would be perfect for our young family's use. From experience, Stan knew that if he waited until the weekend, the boat would be sold. After phoning the owner, Stan jumped in the car and headed south of Seattle to Lake Tapps—about two-and-a-half hours away—where the boat was being stored under a shelter attached to a dock. The owner had been out of town, and while there was a long recording full of inquiries on his answering machine, Stan was the first person to call right after he had walked through the door.

Upon inspection, Stan knew this was the boat we had been praying and saving for as a family. The owner told Stan that there was only one catch. Lake Tapps is a man-made lake used for water storage, and it would not be refilled until the end of May. Because of that, it would be impossible to do a test run until the lake had risen. The boat was there, safely stored, but could not be picked up before summer. As a matter of fact, the owner had received an offer before Stan arrived, but when the bidder from Oregon realized he couldn't take the boat with him, he withdrew his offer. Stan took no chances and put money down to secure the boat.

Months later, the seller called to inform us that the lake was high enough to get the vessel to the boat launch. With expectations high, the entire family went to fetch our long-prayed-for boat. The Lord had given us a waiting period not only to save the remaining money, but also to test our faith. Clad in life jackets, our little family of four took a spin around the lake in a boat that raced perfectly through the water and into a future packed with the many adventures that lay ahead.

Our cherished boat came in handy during camping trips with the Collins family. Memories of times on Mayfield Lake near Centralia still fill our minds: we discovered small tributaries, and a rope swing hanging over the water. The "Fearless Four Kids" spent hours flying through the air and landing in the water. In addition, many fishing trips, both in fresh and salt water, became standard for the father/son teams.

We also became grateful for special neighbors, Stan and Alice Poyser, a retired couple who lived only ten minutes from Camp on Lake Goodwin. The Poysers let us use their yard and dock for large ski parties with the summer staff and the church youth group. With their grandkids so far away, the Poysers really enjoyed the laughter and commotion coming from their lake front. Their kindness and hospitality will forever be engraved in our memories.

Then there was that Sunday in July of 1997, the day before Thad was scheduled to go to a Waterski Camp over at Sun Lakes with the Stanwood Youth for Christ (YFC) gang. Stan and I had gone on all the YFC winter ski trips up to Whistler Ski Resort, helping organize the food and overseeing numerous details. But with the jam-packed summer schedule in the Recreation Department, Stan knew that it wasn't a good time to ask for a vacation. Instead, we had been praying for the upcoming week, asking the Lord to provide safety and everything that was needed for the kids to have fun while getting closer to Jesus.

The YFC Director, Shawn Rowles, was standing in the church lobby that Sunday morning after the service. As we passed him I asked how everything was lining up for the week. Shawn, with a look of exasperation, retorted, "Not good! We just lost our driver for the bus we rented." I looked at Shawn and pointing at Stan said, "Why not see if there's some way that he could get off work for a week to drive that bus; he is even licensed for air brakes." Surprisingly, Stan quickly responded that there might be a chance since it was a week with no swimming lessons. As the Camp's only water safety instructor, he could not be gone if there were lessons at the Camp's pool. Stan then added that there was only one problem: if he went to Sun Lakes he would want to bring his boat. At that news, we thought that Shawn was about to suddenly launch into orbit right from the lobby floor, for they had also been praying for one more boat!

A quick call to his supervisor, Peter Collins, secured permission for Stan to take a week of vacation. Stan's staff rallied together to cover for him at Camp while another parent towed our boat over the mountains so Stan could drive the bus full of kids. Since our boat's motor was one of the slower ones, Stan spent the entire week pulling the beginners who were just learning to ski and the kids who wanted to try tubing. He was just the right fit, full of patience and encouragement for the inexperienced students.

A few weeks later, Shawn showed up at the ten a.m. staff break at Camp to thank Stan in front of the entire staff for his last-minute part in the YFC Water Ski Camp. Shawn also expressed gratitude for the staff that filled in for Stan when he was gone. It didn't cost anything, but it was the most meaningful thank-you Stan could have received as Shawn then shared how Jesus had touched teens' lives that week at Waterski Camp.

Thad graduated from high school and moved on to rock climbing. Cherith lost interest in our old boat when she began attending Camano Chapel's "Summer Breeze" high school waterski camp. She fell in love with Bill and Lauri Lee, the owners of a powerful new Ski Natique boat. Cherith also fell madly in love with their son, Chad. Even though young, the two were meant for each other. While Bill has stepped into heaven, his boat sits in the shelter right next to Chad and Cherith's home on their cul-de-sac. Our grandsons are already riding the waves in Lake Stevens, just minutes from their home.

Meanwhile, our boat sits under its shelter by our lake. Every now and then, she gets to take a spin around Lake Goodwin, towing our grandson on the tube. Several years ago, the vessel was called out of retirement to be part of Thad and Abby's extended family vacation on Lake Roosevelt. Abby's parents, Chuck and JoAnne Krause, paid for some needed repairs in order to ensure that the aging craft would make it through the week. The old Beachcraft's days are numbered. But for now, we keep her licensed and insured, just in case there is still one more adventure ahead.

God is **THE GIVER OF ALL GOOD GIFTS**. The boat was God's answer to prayer, gift-wrapped for safekeeping in a land-locked boat shelter on Lake Tapps. Through the years this present has provided memories that will be cherished forever—not just by our family, but by the many teens who have come through the ranks at our church, at Camp, and in YFC.

20: THE KING OF HOOPLA

Shortly after leaving the Food Service Department in 1986 to begin working as Bob and Muriel McDowell's assistant, I was summoned to the front office and assigned the chairmanship of the Social Committee. To be honest, this sounded more like a disease than a task to be joyfully embraced. After realizing that Muriel wasn't kidding, I agreed, but with the stipulation that I would choose my own committee members.

Until that time, the Social Committee had been an all-female cohort that designed beautifully decorated wedding and baby showers. It was high time to spread the joy around to some of the male staff and expand the offerings to include a wider range of laughter-producing events. After wooing Cowboy Rod Brown and several other staff with "partying personalities" to join the committee, we carefully laid out the year. In addition to making some of the wedding and baby showers "co-educational," we added monthly "ten-minute parties" before morning devotions to stir grace into the staff, using laughter as the main ingredient.

On a very limited budget, the committee discovered that, by waiting at least two weeks after seasonal holidays, decorations and candy could be purchased for 75-80% off. The stage was set for our monthly doses of "the first, but hopefully not last, belated" ten-minute parties. We carefully crafted the announcements for a list of holidays, from Valentine's Day, the Ides of March, Saint Patrick's Day, Easter, the 4th of July, and Christmas in the summer through Halloween and Thanksgiving to finish each year. We even created a couple of new holidays.

I remember the ten-minute Easter egg hunt when the staff synchronized their watches to report to the lobby of Cedar Lodge before prayer time to find hidden candy eggs. Then there was the ten-minute Valentine party when we drew names ahead of time. The person receiving the zaniest valentine from a "secret admirer" received the prize. A panel of judges determined Walt Maendl to be the winner thanks to the Valentine cake he received. Walt almost broke his hunting knife when he tried to cut the cake, which turned out to be a metal cake pan turned upside down and beautifully frosted.

Soon it was so much fun to serve on the Social Committee that I feared we would need to put term limits in place! We expanded into planning the "all-staff summer event," and one of those probably became the most talked about event in the history of Camp: the WACKY MYSTERY TRIP held during the 1980s. We prayed for creativity as the Camp was on a tight budget.

Before the big day arrived, the staff was instructed to bring an exact assortment of pocket change, Dramamine if they were prone to dizziness, a wrapped white elephant gift, swimming suit, towel, sun glasses, and a jacket. The gifts were collected as the staff boarded the bus to an undisclosed destination.

What the staff didn't realize was that while they were loading up in the parking lot four well-known staff members were shaving off all their facial hair. Walt Maendl, Rod Brown, Ed McDowell, and Mike Hall were also dressing in clothes that were totally out of character for them. The newly-shaven four took off ahead of the gang to hide themselves in the Everett Mall. In the meantime, as these four characters traveled to the mall, to kill time the bus stopped at the little Lakewood store and the staff used their pocket change to buy ice cream.

When the gang arrived at the mall for the "man hunt," they were given instructions to find the four mystery staff members who had promised to be in plain sight. The searchers had a code word to speak to each staff-member-in-hiding, and with a confirming response from those members, the searcher would be given credit for finding them without revealing their identity.

Ed and Mike were the easiest to find. Ed was dressed like a little old man sporting a derby hat, hobbling along with a cane. Mike was clad in shorts and carrying a tennis racket. Rod was in a classy three-piece suit without his cowboy hat and boots, and stood right in the middle of the mall with his hair greased down. I finally found Rod only because I recognized the friend that he was talking to while using his famous hand movements! But no one, including me, found Walt, not even his own teenagers. A couple of hours before, Walt had shaved off the long beard that he had been growing for years. Clad in a light-green polyester leisure suit with a distinguished-looking pipe in his mouth, he spent the entire time in the Hallmark Store browsing through the cards.

At the designated ending time, we all met in the center of the mall. When Rod and Walt came walking up and identified themselves, our mob went crazy. The police ushered us out of the mall, claiming that it was illegal to raise such a ruckus in a public place. Back on the bus, we headed to a vacant field to play "lodge ball" until it was time to put on roller skates at the Skate Deck in Marysville.

In the middle of the skate, the music stopped and everyone was instructed to sit down. One of the program interns came skating in dressed as Santa (thought it was actually August). He carried the sack of White Elephant gifts to distribute. After the skate we returned to Camp to have a pizza party by the pool. The evening ended with a campfire, s'mores, and a sing-along. It was probably the least expensive all-staff event in the history of Camp. It just goes to prove that it doesn't take a lot of money to create fun memories.

I started using the word "hoopla" around Camp. Once, when challenged by other staff that it wasn't even a word, we went to the Stanwood library to see if "hoopla" could be found in the huge dictionary there. As it turned out, even though the word was not in that official book in the 1980's, we continued to create "hoopla" anyway! At Camp we discovered that like music, "laughter is wound down into the soul." Not only is it good for one's health, it mysteriously opens up other emotions and allows us to cry together as well. The 10 a.m. break every weekday at Camp is still filled with laughter, as are many other parties and events. And as the "Queen of Hoopla," through the years I have helped organize numerous celebrations, including goodbye parties and retirement shindigs. One of my favorite tasks is to be the official "roaster- toaster" of the honored guest. Anonymity is promised to all informants, and if we can't find enough stuff, well, we just make it up! Since my development work requires me to frequently be on the road, today party-planning has been reassigned to other capable and creative staff.

As February 2014 approached, I wondered who would be planning Stan's retirement party. I prayed for Stan to be honored appropriately. Here was a man who had worked quietly behind the scenes at Camp for thirty-six years! While my positions often put me in the limelight, most of the time Stan "played for an audience of one." Along with his volunteer staff, Stan worked endless hours to keep the grass green and the grounds looking beautiful. In the early years he also kept the camp's two pools running as director of the Recreation Department. It was common for Stan to spend an entire night fixing a pool pump or, dressed in a wetsuit, to be submerged underwater patching the pool in time for campers to swim the next morning.

Little did I realize what the Lord already had in store for Stan! At the January board retreat we were surprised that Dan Bolin and his wife, Cay, were with us. Dan, Director of Christian Camping International (CCI), was our keynote speaker. It was like "old home week" as Stan and I had been a part of a team with Dan and Kay in the early days of CCI, helping put on national conventions around the U.S.

During the retreat, Dan likened the account of Jesus feeding the 5,000 to what we do in camping. Comparing the account in all four Gospels, Dan kept highlighting the fact that Jesus had the crowd sit down in the "green grass" to be comfortable, not realizing that Stan had taken care of the Camp's own grass for years! At the Saturday banquet, the board chairman, David Goodnight, presented a plaque and gift to Stan, accompanied by amazing remarks from different board members. They had even calculated how far the 156 hoses would extend that Stan rolled up every Thursday night so the mowing crew could mow on Friday mornings.

Two days before Stan's official retirement party, the Staff Alumni Reunion was scheduled. To make the reunion festive, Nikki Rossiter did an outstanding job decorating Cedar Lodge Chapel with pictures on all the tables and walls. Everything was left in place for Stan's party with Nikki rearranging a few things to highlight Stan's time at Camp. Jessica Wilson sent invitations so the room was packed with staff, volunteers, former staff, and friends. My mom, our children, their spouses, and grandkids were all there to see Papa awarded the plaque a second time and to hear the comments sending Stan off in grand style.

We are made in the image of God, **THE KING OF HOOPLA**, who throws parties when His kids come home from the far country. And HE is the Master of the ceremony, weaving together all the fine details. The Party Planner makes certain that "laughter is the best medicine" as He uses it to knit us together as a community of grace.

21: THE ORCHESTRATOR

It was rare for year-round salaried positions to come open at Camp. During the spring of 1995, during the final stages of the Camp's search for a new executive director, we were also hunting for the best candidates for a dining room manager and a guest services associate. Appointed that year as HR Director, I was coordinating the hiring and was eager to find the perfect fits.

After directing a day camp for his church in California, a young man, Brent Allee, was longing to pursue a career in Christian camping. Like so many, he was interested in programming and soon discovered that very few camps have a year-round program director position. With a college degree in business, specializing in human resources, Brent was willing to get his foot in the door with any available job, and after interviewing him in person, I was very impressed.

Sometimes called "Prince Ali" (after the character in the movie, *Aladdin*, and the fact that he is a "prince of a guy"), Brent would be excellent at either position. What was I to do? I paced around my office that morning in April, knowing that in a matter of minutes I needed to offer one of the positions to him. I desperately prayed for God's direction. Just then the phone rang. It was Franklin Ridgeway, a former guest service host, calling from Ecuador where he and his wife were serving as missionaries. His wife, Gina, had been very sick and they were burned out. Franklin wondered if there were any openings at Camp as they needed to return home to the States. Instantly, I knew that God was orchestrating details behind the scenes and had saved a place for the Ridgeways at Warm Beach Camp.

In a matter of moments I called Brent and he accepted the position of dining room manager. Franklin, needing no training, returned to step into the vacant role in guest services. While Brent had zero background in food services, he was a quick study with exceptional organizational skills. His HR training had prepared him to test out many motivational techniques on his young high school staff, including our son, Thad, and best buddy, Michael. Brent got the teens involved in designing labor-saving ideas. It worked: one night Thad got home highly energized because the team had knocked off several minutes during clean-up using their latest idea that they called, "Scrap-a-rama."

Later Brent would share that he was thrilled to be given the dining room position as he wanted to influence young people, and the venue of food service was an excellent way to connect with young staff. It was common for Brent to host the teens after hours, providing popcorn with movies at his little home, which is now the "Kringle Cottage" during December. We will be forever grateful for his influence on Thad. Brent saw the leadership potential in Thad and encouraged him to be the dining room supervisor in the summer of 1998. Thad claims that some of the organizational and training techniques Brent taught helped thrust him into success in his career as a commercial electrician.

But the Lord was orchestrating far more than any of us realized at the time Franklin and Brent joined the staff. One week after Brent joined the team, the food service director quit. Since another member of the management team had also moved away several months before, Bob McDowell had just put the Food Services Department back under my umbrella since I had previous experience. On May 1, right before the busy summer season was to begin, I found myself with two jobs, the HR Director and the Food Service Director, in addition to having to finish the executive search process.

Since failing to provide food for hungry campers wasn't an option, I stepped into the role as if I were jumping onto a fast moving treadmill at the gym. There were menus to plan, summer staff to hire, and employee schedules to post. I began getting up in the wee hours of the morning to get the office work done while doing the family's laundry. We still had two kids at home, one in high school and the youngest just beginning junior high. Fortunately, Brent was a quick learner and by the end of the summer could begin picking up the hiring process and the overall scheduling for the Food Service Department.

The executive search process was completed by the end of May, 1995, when Bob's son, Ed, was chosen. There were three retirement parties to plan for Bob McDowell, all requiring extensive food service coordination. After being honored at Annual Conference, Family Camp and a staff family celebration, he was more than ready to retire! His "passing the baton" to Ed was legendary, and they have taught workshops together for CCCA Conferences on the topic, "Making Transitions Smooth." Bob was highly supportive of Ed, but purposely removed himself from the Campgrounds for many years unless specifically called upon. This allowed long-time staff members to easily transfer our loyalty to the next director.

Ed inherited me along with the treadmill that I was running on at a breakneck speed. We quickly put plans in place for Brent to assume the job of food service director by March, 1996 with the understanding that I, as a registered dietitian, would still plan the menus. Brent would do everything else, including hiring the food service staff. God had orchestrated things well: this exceptional young man was placed in food service so that within less than a year, he could take the reins of a department with over forty staff.

I didn't make it until March. After nine months of juggling both jobs and my home responsibilities, I came crashing off the unrelenting belt. I had become boundary-less, and I was physically, emotionally, and spiritually exhausted. Looking back on it now, it is both sad and ironically humorous that I had previously given a workshop at a CCI conference entitled, "How Not To Burn Out in Christian Camping!" One day, when a dear colleague phoned and simply wanted a "Yes" or "No" answer to a request for 300 sack lunches, I began sobbing as the phone receiver fell out of my hand. I hadn't cried for months— there hadn't been time. I couldn't even make my hand work to hold the phone.

Ed's assistant, Joanie Yonker, heard the gut-wrenching sobs coming from my corner office and came rushing into the room. She got behind me, putting her arms around me, gently drawing my body together. I couldn't tell who it was but could hear her praying. After a while I was able to quit crying and become orient-ed to my surroundings once more. I now realize how fortunate it was that Joanie knew what to do. Before that grand "hug" it seemed as if my body was about to fly into pieces—a sure sign of my serious mental state.

Ed and Board Chair Frank recommended that I get counseling while I took an "administrative leave." While I would never want to go through extreme burn-out again, I wouldn't trade the experience for anything. Through some excellent counseling, I learned a lot about myself and the importance of self-care, and that such care was my responsibility. After reading several assigned books on "bound-aries," I was held accountable by my counselor for putting those boundaries in place in my life. One of the decisions we made at this time was to move off the campgrounds and into our first home on 81st Street, so as not to be always avail-able to everyone twenty-four hours a day every day of the week.

Thankfully, Brent was ready to step into the challenge of the food service director role a few months before the planned transition. He later would lead that department through the massive tasks of *The Lights of Christmas*—opening the concession stands, three restaurants, and the six-course dinner theater. His favor-ite line when asked if he could do something: "Piece of cake!"

Franklin went on to be the first director of the Camp's Environmental Educa-tion Program. He was instrumental in getting the learning stations in place around the Camp's newly-constructed wetlands that were the educational component of our new, environmentally sound waste water treatment plant. Franklin also collabo-rated with Kelly Wynn on some of the tasks needed to ensure the proper function-ing of the new plant.

God is **THE ORCHESTRATOR** of every detail, even when we don't know what we are fully asking! He is behind the scenes, with a long-range view, strategi-cally moving people into place to assure that HIS kingdom plans advance.

22: THE ANOINTER

During my interview in January of 1978, Bob McDowell made it clear that as Food Service Director I would need to focus on quality and safety. What he didn't share was that his seventeen-year-old son, Eddie, a young man sporting a huge afro, had recently participated in a dining room food-fight! Upon arriving at Camp a few months later, I spoiled the fun for the young staff with new safety standards: no more hurling "pink fluff" through the air nor riding in the old dumbwaiter.

With such "fun" now a thing of the past, Eddie quickly transferred to become the head of the print shop, now the site of the new walk-in cooler. Thankfully, he was still willing to come back to train new dishwashers and sweet-talk the Camp's old Hobart machine into working a little longer.

In the beginning of 1979, Stan and I began helping with the youth group at the church across the street from the Camp. Eddie was a natural born leader among the other teens. During his senior year, Stanwood High School asked him to serve as a "peer counselor," giving him a heavy load of troubled students to mentor. Still, he found time to remain mischievous. During those years, my office was right next to Ed's print shop desk. He loved to scare the living daylights out of me by crawling on his belly to shoot rubber bands from under the office partitions.

It didn't surprise us at Camp when Ed married his high-school sweetheart, Bev, after attending Central College in Kansas for a year. During his second year at Central College, he was the resident director of the boys' dorm. At twenty years of age, Ed returned to work at Camp while commuting to Seattle Pacific University in order to finish his B.A. degree in Christian Education.

I have often told people that Ed took the greatest strengths of both his parents and rolled them into one enchilada. His young age didn't matter; Ed was sought out by many for counsel. One day while still in college, he asked me to pray for God's guidance for him, in that he had been asked to expand his Promotion/Marketing position to include directing Guest Services. Ed wanted my honest opinion as to whether I thought he was qualified for the job and how I would feel about having him for my supervisor in this new role.

After praying, I wrote a long note to Ed, promising to pray for wisdom and affirming the fact that though he was young, like David in the Old Testament he could do the job with God's help. God had uniquely gifted Ed and I let him know he was up to the task. Furthermore, I told him he was highly respected, and I would certainly have no trouble answering to him. Ed did accept the expanded position and even though he was only twenty-two, in the next several years we witnessed his phenomenal leadership of the Guest Services team, which included me as Food Services Director.

Fast forward to 1994. After twenty-four years as Camp director, Bob Mc-Dowell was getting ready to retire. The Camp's board had appointed a nine-member search committee to begin the task of seeking his replacement. As HR director, I had been selected to represent the staff on the search committee led by board chairman Frank Cranston. One day as I was sitting in my office praying about the next director, I asked God for wisdom and to lead the committee to the person of His choosing. Just then the phone rang. It was Ed McDowell! I hadn't talked to him in ages and we enjoyed catching up.

Ed shared with me the main reason behind his call. While he had been cleaning his file cabinet at the Denver Free Methodist Church where he was senior pastor, the note had resurfaced that I had written to him years ago. As he read it out loud, I was stunned that the Lord was refreshing our memories at that precise moment in time. Here are snippets from that letter I wrote to Ed in the early 80's:

> ... *"The key to the whole matter is exactly what you shared in Sunday School last week. When we are truly 'broken' before the Lord, then He can fill us with the Holy Spirit. We then have the power to accomplish whatever task He sets before us... Yes, my initial reaction was, 'He's too young and inexperienced.' But God immediately and firmly stopped that line of thinking. I gently heard Him remind me that David was only a youth when he killed Goliath. He didn't have the military training his competitors did for the job of giant-killing. He also used an unconventional method, something that surely must have been predicted by human wisdom to fail. But David did have faith, obedience and a heart ready to hear God's command...Ed, for the next five years you will be too 'young' in the world's standards for whatever task the Lord calls you to do...you are ahead of your age. ... The best piece of advice that I can give you without telling you what to do is to 'let your life be its own defense.' Your mom drove that lesson home to me during some very difficult times...over time, without a word it will become very evident to everyone else that you are in tune—God uses your life as its own defense. ...if He wants you to take the camp's proposed expanded position, then He will see you through regardless of people's possible concerns of being too young and/or another McDowell...."*

While I didn't tell a soul about this experience, after hanging up the phone I knew beyond the shadow of a doubt that I had just talked to the next director of Warm Beach Camp!

In February 1994, I attended a workshop on "Hiring the Right Staff" given by Don Goehner at the Sectional CCI Conference at Cannon Beach, Oregon. It was geared for executive searches as that was Don's specialty. The timing was perfect and afterwards Don and I had lunch together. Upon hearing that Warm Beach was about to start a search, Don pleaded with me to advise our board chairman to hire a consultant, especially since I hoped the director's son would be applying. Don had never met Ed, but he had seen too many cases where a son following his father in leadership hadn't turned out well. If Ed McDowell did apply and ended up with the job, a professional search process would help pave the way for success.

Since the Camp had already used Don Goehner as consultant for management training and a $230,000 fund-raising campaign, Frank Cranston secured Don to consult during the search process. Frank was also on the SPU Board, and with the permission of the college, in order to keep costs down we fashioned our executive search after the one they had used, tweaking the written questions to fit a camp. After advertising in several national Christian magazines, we received fifty-six applications.

I was the secretary of the Search Committee and met with Frank once a week to get instructions as to how to proceed with different applicants as we screened for the ones who met the qualifications outlined in the job description. From there the committee selected the top candidates for reference checks by Goehner's firm and for an initial phone interview with Don.

Toward the end of 1994, Don and I teamed together to present a workshop at the St. Louis CCI National Convention on "Hiring the Right Staff." I would address the issues involved with hiring hourly and summer staff, while Don would handle the hiring of management staff. While sitting at a restaurant planning the last details of our presentation, Don said, "I interviewed Ed McDowell last night on the phone." After a pause he went on to declare, "I was literally blown out of the water!" After sharing how insightful Ed was for his age, Don continued, "When I hung up the phone I told my wife, 'I have just talked to the next director of Warm Beach Camp!'" There were now two of us who had a secret to keep, so as not to destroy the necessary and formal process which had been put in place.

After a thorough, rigorous reference-checking process by two Goehner Group specialists, the committee selected the top two candidates for the final interview process. Both candidates and their spouses were brought to the Pacific Northwest for an in-person interview. After careful consideration and prayer, the Search Committee chose Ed McDowell to follow his father. The huge "Executive Search" notebook still sits on the shelf in my office as a historical record of the process. Ed would later share that the selection experience with the written questions and interviews was more rigorous than earning his Master's Degree in Counseling from Kansas State University!

Ed, at age thirty-four, arrived at Warm Beach Camp with Bev and their four children in the summer of 1995 to lead the Camp's ministry into the future. God had gifted him specifically for this phase of the Camp's life. Ed is not perfect, as no one is; he has had to learn by experience, making mistakes along the way. And when those mistakes occur, as a servant leader he leads by example and is quick to ask forgiveness.

Early in Ed's time as director, a master plan was set in place, including two huge $6.5 million campaigns that were completed in order to renovate facilities, build new ones, and update Camp utilities so as to guarantee the future. The board also allowed Ed to oversee the huge risk of bringing *The Lights of Christmas* into reality. Under Ed's leadership the Lord has also opened up streams of ministry to the marginalized, and a spirit of adoption has fallen over the Camp. People are invited to "come home to the Father, and grace is extended to be adopted into the family of God." On a personal basis, I count it one of the greatest blessings of my life to have Ed as my supervisor.

Twenty-two years later, there is no doubt that the Lord selected Ed, full of vision, to be the next Director of Warm Beach Camp. What the Lord said to Samuel holds true today: "The Lord does not look at the things man looks at. Man looks at the outward appearance, but the Lord looks at the heart." The youngest of Jesse's sons, David, was tending sheep when the Lord told Samuel, "Arise and anoint him, he is the one."

The Lord is **THE ANOINTER**. And just like King David, Ed has received the anointing of the Lord to lead by the Spirit the ministry of Warm Beach Camp for this chapter of its history. Like David, Ed (who now has no hair left), is still hurling rocks at giants and successfully meeting the considerable challenges of his time.

23: THE GOD OF BRILLIANT LIGHTS

December is traditionally not a busy time for camps. For years some of our staff prayed for a way that the Camp might be used for ministry during December, when many people are most open to the message of the Gospel. Ideas were often discussed, but none of them fit Warm Beach.

While floating aboard a charter boat, *The Mystic Sea,* through the channel at Deception Pass in December, 1996, none of those aboard realized that the traditions at Warm Beach Camp were about to be radically altered when a Board member, Roger Hancuff, started drawing on his paper napkin. Roger had recently returned from Nashville, Tennessee after purchasing a business in the country music capital of America. He and his new staff had attended *Christmas in the Park* at Opryland's theme park. After sketching out the different venues of that event, somewhere between the main course and dessert of that 1986 Board Christmas dinner, Roger, in a Spirit-filled moment, realized, "That's what we could do at Warm Beach Camp with all volunteers!"

A week later, Pat and Jeannie Patterson, Laurie Fertello, and I were summoned to Director Ed McDowell's office. Roger and his wife, Cheryl, had felt the Lord leading them to sponsor a research team to Nashville to check out the possibility of Warm Beach Camp doing a country-spun, volunteer-driven version of the holiday light show that they had seen. Right after Christmas, the "Nashville Four" boarded a plane to that city in order to "spy out the land."

Armed with yellow tablets and a huge video camera, we felt like Joshua and Caleb entering a land overflowing with beauty, performing talent, and stunning lights. The Hancuffs graciously provided their suite and extra hotel rooms near Opryland and paid all our expenses, including two nights in the park. While the park was not operated by a Christian organization, the Gospel message was evident in the traditional music, the dramas, and the gorgeous larger than life-size, white, fifty-six-piece nativity illuminated by colored spotlights. I still remember the first time we gathered at the nativity and I saw Pat Patterson standing in awe, wiping tears from his eyes.

That first night I lay in bed in the hotel room, unable to sleep. Who in the world did we think we were to attempt an event like this at Warm Beach Camp? We were used to setting the stage for camps and conferences. We had no experience in designing light shows. But as we walked around the park that evening, the other three visionaries kept pointing and saying, "Oh, look! So-and-so could make that, weld that, or manufacture that!"

Surely, the board was counting on someone to be rational! Had we lost all common sense? In an attempt to get my team members' feet back on the ground, I had occasionally interjected a comment such as, "Do you have any idea how many volunteers this would take?" or, "Do we have any idea how much it would cost just to get the electricity into Camp for an event as huge as this?" I felt like one of those negative spies in Joshua and Caleb's scouting party. To be honest, I had begun to wonder how in the world I'd gotten myself into this mess.

After that first mind-boggling trek around Nashville's *Christmas in the Park,* as I tried to drift off to sleep, I asked the Lord for a "fleece," a sign that HE was really in this. If we came back recommending such a large scale event, we would be risking a lot of resources that weren't presently in the coffers. I had heard that it was not good to ask God for a fleece. But this was a huge proposition, and if God wanted a band of plain, ordinary folks with no experience in designing light shows to do this, then I figured HE wouldn't mind giving us a divine "wink." I had also heard that when we ask God for a fleece, we need to be prepared to go with His confirmation, regardless if it defies all human understanding.

The next night, as we were standing in line to enter the event, a stranger approached us and inquired how many were in our party. Upon hearing our answer, he shoved four free passes worth seventeen dollars each into Pat's hand. On a tight budget, we were thrilled at this unexpected blessing. After we thanked him, the stranger disappeared into the crowd.

Our yellow tablets were filling up with notes as we interviewed staff members in the park, getting the scoop on what it took to develop this event, what had worked best, and what had failed. The video camera was filled with footage of the petting farm and the "Talking Christmas Tree," along with all the professional entertainment on the different performing stages throughout the venue.

As we entered one of the gift shops, Laurie spotted a display of huge Christmas tree balls, about two feet in diameter. Originally priced at sixty-nine dollars each, they were now on sale. Laurie pointed at them and said, "We have to have these! Where else can we get them?" It didn't concern Laurie that we had not yet gotten Board approval even to do the event. Neither did it matter that we only had a compact rental car, and no way to get the balls home to Washington. Trying to reason with her was impossible: she had her creative mind made up, already envisioning how we would use them.

Laurie started wheeling and dealing with the shop attendant. Could she cut us an excellent deal so that we could have these balls, which came in three sizes, for the Christmas event that we would be hosting next year an hour north of Seattle? At the same time, another lady was also expressing interest in some of the ornaments. Finally the clerk laid out a deal that Laurie couldn't resist. If we promised to take the entire inventory, we could have the big ones for two dollars each, the medium-sized ones for one dollar each, and the smallest for fifty cents each. What she didn't tell us was that there were more cases in the storeroom!

After the other bargain hunter purchased the balls she wanted, the shop keeper tallied up the remaining cases. The total cost came to exactly what we had saved coming in the entrance that night when an "angel of a stranger" handed us free passes. I had just received my "holy wink" from the Almighty, and was swept into the craziness with the other three. We were about to experience a wave of God's activity in our lives that was intoxicatingly exciting, risky, overwhelming, and almost fierce enough to drown us if it weren't for His grace.

Pat Patterson made multiple trips that evening back to Roger's suite in the little car stuffed with boxes of Christmas balls. After vacation, Roger returned to find his cozy Nashville suite full of balls, including in the bath tub. We figured since Roger got us into this, he could figure out how to get these treasures back to Stanwood. Fortunately, he was gracious enough to have his assistant ship the balls to Camp.

Using every waking hour as we traveled through airports back to Seattle, the "Nashville Four" put together a sketch of the proposed Christmas event along with a business plan. After review by the Marketing and Finance Committees of the board, a special meeting was called in January of 1997 for us to present our plan, which, to the best of our calculations, would lose money for the first few years. I was pretty sure our proposal would not fly.

Getting a fifteen-member board to approve something so risky and radical takes a miracle! And of course the board asked tough questions, including, "How is this in line with the Camp's mission?" and "How will this affect the staff who usually take their vacations in the month of December?" But after much discussion the board voted unanimously to approve *The Lights of Christmas* (LOC) to be up and running by the end of November, 1997—just ten months away.

A few days after that amazing Board decision, the staff gathered for the annual staff retreat at The Firs Chalet on Mount Baker. When the planned keynote speaker cancelled days before, Roger and Rachel Williams from Mount Hermon Conference Center in California agreed to come. Roger walked us through the story of The Prodigal Son, showing how the village customs in Jewish culture had to change in order to make a way for the son to come home to the father. The Lord had strategically planned for us to hear Roger's messages as the backdrop for the first LOC and the radical shifts that were on the horizon for the Camp.

Under the leadership of the first LOC Director, Jeannie Patterson, the Camp became like a start-up corporation. While doing our regular duties, we also made plans to deck the halls, trees, and buildings by Thanksgiving time. Laurie Fertello became the artistic designer for everything on the outside, and after summer camps were over, she began working almost round-the-clock at The Pines, a building at the entrance of the camp. With enough creativity to keep her busy for years to come, Laurie spun visions of a star-studded path into our event: mountain ranges, three-ships a-sailing, giant lighted poinsettias, and even a reflecting pond where none existed.

The first light-hanging crew, mostly volunteers, was led by board member Bud Timm. They put on the OSHA-required harnesses and got into giant rented lifts to wrap the trees in colored lights. Vern Ritter signed on as the electrical engineer to design the electrical package. Former Director Bob McDowell got the word out for volunteer electricians to assist Vern.

Jeannie ordered 500,000 lights and the essential pieces for the larger than life size nativity scene which would be placed at the center of the event with the *Hallelujah Chorus* playing overhead. She also recruited volunteers to lead in decorating each facility, and lined up entertainment for the six performing stages, including the dinner theater. Most of the entertainers were volunteers, or were paid an honorarium that barely covered their transportation costs. As the human resources director, I helped organize the volunteers needed to staff the event during twelve nights in December that first year.

Part of the plan to cover the $250,000 start-up cost was to secure sponsorships. Ed and I canvassed the local businesses. But we struggled: the LOC was an audacious idea, probably too unbelievable for anyone to attach their name to it. At the next board meeting I was sweating bullets, as we would have to report to the board our lack of success in finding even one corporate sponsor. What a surprise when a board member declared, "Let's let God sponsor Christmas at Warm Beach Camp!" After some discussion, Cowboy Rod Brown was instructed to take off his hat and pass it around for board members to put in personal commitments to help fund that first LOC. Yes, this was to be a God-event!

I will never forget the Saturday before we would open to the public the following Thursday, when the "Nashville Four" toured the event with Ed. It was the first time that all the lights were on, and every lobby and sleeping room throughout Camp was creatively decorated beyond words. The astounding beauty, the wonder of it all, had happened seemingly overnight as volunteers brought decorations out of their garages and reassembled them at Camp. They had stretched their tiny decorating budgets beyond belief. When we stopped to peek into the "Joyland Auditorium" we saw those huge colored Christmas balls attached to giant ribbons, hanging from the ceiling and divinely winking at me one final time!

Around the first of November, before that first LOC, Jeannie shared that she was pregnant. Their long-awaited, prayed-for baby would arrive in seven months. Not only was the Camp birthing an event to lavishly celebrate the birth of Jesus, but the miracle of new life was happening inside Jeannie's womb at the same time. Kaleb Patterson made his appearance the following June. We wouldn't have been surprised if he came into the world humming *Deck the Halls!* Our fourteen-year-old daughter, Cherith, delighted in pushing baby Kaleb around the second LOC in his stroller. And as he grew, at a very young age Kaleb began volunteering in the Toy Shop and Petting Farm. In 2016, at eighteen-and-a-half years of age, Kaleb, a full-fledged paid staff member, served for the third year as one of the leaders for the parking crew during the 20th LOC, helping to direct as many as 2,500 vehicles to parking spaces over nineteen nights.

After successfully getting the LOC through the first creative seven years, Jeannie handed the reins to Keith Yarter, who for the next six years fine-tuned the organization of the event. For the last seven years, Loren Isaac, full of the grace of God, has directed the production, seeing the event cause Stanwood to be rated in 2015 as "one of the top best American towns for Christmas" by *Coastal Living Magazine* and the "best place to see Christmas lights in Washington State" by *Travel and Leisure Magazine.*

Today the LOC has over 1 million lights and hosts 70,000+ guests during the month of December. It has become a platform for people to express their God-given creativity as they reflect His image. In 2016 over 750 volunteers helped to make the event a reality with hospitality that woos people to come home to the Father. It's an extension of the grace God provides by becoming flesh in the person of Jesus, born that first Christmas.

The other day I heard a song on the radio by Aaron Shust called, *"God of Brilliant Lights."* My spirit soared within me as I realized the first three verses and chorus perfectly summed up the reason Warm Beach Camp does *"The Lights:"*

> *Sing it out, shout it loud*
> *Cover all the earth*
> *Let the sound of the saints*
> *Everywhere be heard*
> *Praise the God who has come*
> *To cure every broken heart.*
>
> *He is Lord over all*
> *His reign will never end*
> *Through the fire and the flood*
> *He draws his children in*
> *He's the light of the world*
> *Brighter than the brightest star.*

Chorus:
> *The God of brilliant lights*
> *is shining down over us*
> *Breaking through the darkness*
> *Covering all the earth*
> *Ooh, his love is like an ocean*
> *Oooh, forever overflowing*
> *The God of brilliant lights is shining over us.*
>
> *Sinners come to the cross*
> *And lay your troubles down*
> *At the feet of the one whose mercy will abound*
> *He's not afraid of our filth*
> *He will never turn away*
> *The God of brilliant lights is shining over us*
> *He's shining over us.*

Album: Morning Rises / original release date: July 16, 2013

I was asking the wrong question while scouting out Nashville's *Christmas in the Park*. It's not, "Who are we to think we can do this?" but rather, "Who is God, and does HE want this done at Warm Beach Camp?"

God is **THE GOD OF BRILLIANT LIGHTS**! In Scripture, light often portrays and reflects the glory of God. Only the Sovereign God of the Universe knows why HE picked Warm Beach Camp (to host *The Lights of Christmas*), a sweet spot on the "interface" of the Pacific Northwest, where not only 350 non-profits and many Christian denominations gather, but where heaven overlaps earth and His grace abounds.

24: THE RAINBOW PAINTER

Even though it was springtime, Christmas was in the air at Warm Beach Camp, and had been ever since the board had voted unanimously in January of 1997 to begin a home-spun, volunteer-staffed event fashioned after Opryland's *Christmas in the Park* event in Nashville, Tennessee. The plans for Warm Beach Camp's *The Lights of Christmas* program were in full motion. The Camp's culture had taken on a fast-paced, corporate-like, start-up energy. The full-colored brochure was printed and ready for distribution throughout the Puget Sound region. Christmas music could be heard coming from offices as plans were made to "deck the halls" of every meeting and sleeping room at Camp. Since this event was to have a wildly high percentage of volunteer help, the first *The Lights of Christmas* director, Jeannie Patterson, reported to me, the human resource director.

One of the first volunteer efforts to be organized was the electrical team needed to prepare for energizing the 500,000 lights advertised in the brochure. Former Camp director, Bob McDowell, had agreed to round up the volunteer electricians to wire it all together. I will never forget the meeting in June that Bob and I had with the power company's electrical engineer, a lady from the local Public Utility District office. I opened up one of our beautiful glossy brochures, hot off the press, and asked this professional what we would need to do in order to turn on the switch for our light show by Thanksgiving time.

Trying not to be deterred by her stunned look, we listened intently to her response. "First of all, you will need your own electrical engineer, and secondly, you will need to tell us where every one of those 500,000 bulbs will go and what size they will be!" I tried to remain calm and not give her any indication that her requirements would be next to impossible to fulfill. We already had a lot invested in ordering the nativity set and a half million lights in addition to the printing of brochures. There was no turning back, so we started praying earnestly for a volunteer electrical engineer.

Bob McDowell had worked with Vern Ritter, a retired electrical engineer, who had helped with several projects at our sister camp in Mexico, Rancho Betania. He gave Vern a call to see if he'd be up to this gig. Vern sounded interested but informed Bob that there was only one thing holding him back: he was recovering from brain surgery. Vern told Bob that if the doctor gave him clearance in two weeks, he and his wife, Sammie, would be parking their RV at Camp so that he could serve as the electrical engineer for designing *The Lights of Christmas*.

Those two weeks seemed like an eternity. One afternoon I was hiking on the dike by the mudflats below Camp, which overlooks Port Susan Bay on Puget Sound. It was one of those misty, rainy days with the sun peeking in and out. I was by myself and started calling out to God in the loudest voice I had, shouting as if He had a hearing problem! I reminded God (as if, with His infinite memory, He needed reminding!) that HE had gotten us into this and that we needed an electrical engineer who would volunteer, since we had NO money! And we needed one SOON.

I went on to ask God to heal this Vern Ritter, who was recovering at his home near the northern border of Eastern Washington, because we needed him. At that moment I looked eastward and saw the most huge, vibrant rainbow I'd ever seen arching over the A-frame peak of the Camp's main administrative building, Cedar Lodge. I knew in that moment that somehow God would provide the electrical engineer who was required to launch *The Lights of Christmas*!

Just a few days later, Vern received clearance from his surgeon and he and Sammie were on the way with their RV in tow! Vern stayed until the switch was turned on for the Saturday night of Thanksgiving Working Weekend. There was never such a stunning sight as those 500,000 lights brightly announcing the beginning of the first season of this annual December event which twenty years later displays more than one million lights and welcomes over 70,000 guests each year.

To ensure that the electrical package would be finished, Vern gave up spending the holiday with his family in November. He, along with several other volunteers, became part of our Thanksgiving family. After the big turkey dinner, we went around the table taking turns telling what we were thankful for. When it was Vern's turn, he shared, "I am thankful that I lost my arm in a hunting accident while I was in high school. It forced me to change my plans and go to college for a degree in engineering. Because of this, I have gotten to participate in so many exciting projects like *The Lights of Christmas*!" Our thirteen-year-old daughter, Cherith, was sitting next to him and said, "I didn't know you only had one arm!" Vern promptly lifted up his jacket to show her his stump with his sleeve pinned up around it. Missing an arm didn't deter Vern. He could work circles around most people and pull wires better with one arm than most could with two!

The rainbow over Cedar Lodge is not the only one God has painted during the history of *The Lights of Christmas*. Fast forward to 2008, a year that the staff will never forget! The early attendance was stunning and by all predictions, this twelfth year would break all records. Then, just before the busiest stretch of *The Lights* when children would be on school vacation, the weather turned cold and snow was predicted. Now to Midwesterners, snow is no big deal. But in Western Washington, when there is even a hint of snow in the forecast, people hunker down and stay home.

Right before the staff was to meet for the 2 p.m. prayer time, I parked in back of Cedar Lodge. The sky was really dark and it looked like a bad storm was brewing. I was trusting God to spare the event from stormy weather and to hold it off until December was over. As I got out of the car I noticed a huge, brilliant rainbow touching down in the horse pasture below. The rainbow was so stunning that I literally pulled Director Ed McDowell outside from his office so someone else could be a witness to this second rainbow in the history of *The Lights*. I was positive that it was God's way of assuring us He would hold off the bad weather.

Anyone who lived through the winter of 2008 knows that it was one of the worst seasons of ice, snow, and wind that the Pacific Northwest had seen in years.

Several nights we had to close the event because we had no electrical power. Other nights we remained open only to have 500 or fewer people brave the icy roads. One night we closed the event because we didn't want staff, volunteers, or guests to risk traveling to the Camp. By the end of 2008, *The Lights* had lost about a quarter of a million dollars of budgeted revenue for that year.

God had painted the first rainbow I saw at a strategic time to remind us that He has promised to never let us drown while we are in the stream of His activity. But after the winter of 2008, I was left pondering the second brilliant rainbow I had seen in the pasture below the Camp. A few days after *The Lights* were over, a check arrived from a charitable remainder trust that had been set up many years before by a dear couple. Earlier in the year Ed and I had a chance to be with the surviving widow and her family just days before she died. When we opened the envelope, we were stunned and delighted to see that the check covered a large part of the money lost during the snowy season, and the meaning of that second rainbow became clear in an instant.

God is indeed **THE RAINBOW PAINTER**, and HE is very strategic about where and when He places these reminders of HIS promise to not let us drown! I have learned He delights in delivering on His promise in His own way!

25: PRAZABLE

In the midst of the crazy November before the first *The Lights of Christmas,* Thad, at the ripe old age of seventeen, announced that he was going to buy the car for which he had saved every dime since beginning to work three years before. Because I was a controlling mother hen, this just about sent me into orbit. I had visions of him packing his car full of teens and heading off through the icy mountain passes to snowboard.

With less than divinely-inspired motivation, I tried slowing him down by suggesting that we pray about this huge decision. After all, he would need a road-worthy car in September to travel to job sites around Puget Sound for his electrician's apprenticeship. In order to get his hovering mother off his back, Thad retorted, "Fine, let's pray!" He then proceeded to *place his order* with the Lord: "God, I want a car, either a burgundy Honda or Toyota with a standard transmission and four doors. As you know I haul a lot of kids to Youth for Christ. And, Lord, I have $3,000 to buy it. In Jesus Name, Amen!"

Oh my! I then began to worry that my son's faith would be disappointed when God didn't deliver to his precise specifications. At that time, things were so fast-paced at Camp that I didn't even have time to share with Stan the very specific request that our son had just prayed. But events were moving forward, guided by a divine hand. A few days later, Stan flew in the door and shouted, "Thad, come quick! I think I have found a car that would be perfect for you!" To be honest, I was ticked at Stan. He was encouraging this car-buying whim while I wanted Thad to wait until after graduation to buy a car at the end of summer when he would have saved more money. Besides, we had much more control over his driving escapades when he had to ask permission to use our old station wagon.

As Stan and Thad were about to pull out of our driveway, I jumped into the back seat so that I could see this "perfect" car waiting for inspection about seven minutes from our house. As we got closer I saw a burgundy-colored, four-door Toyota Corolla. Just as we parked behind it, I saw a metal symbol of the Christian fish on one side of the license plate, and a dove on the other side. All at once my eyes focused on the Washington license plate which read, "PRAZ HM" imprinted over the familiar picture of Mount Rainier. The sign in the little car's window said, "FOR SALE, Excellent Condition, 115,000 miles, Standard Transmission, $4200." There was no doubt, even in the mind of one over-protective mom, that this was Thad's car!

The woman who was selling the car was moving to Arizona the next day. After she had tried to sell the car for a long time, a friend advised her to put it in his yard along Lakewood Road so that commuters would see it on the way to the freeway, and that is where Stan spotted it. After the test drive, he pronounced that it ran "like a top" and told Thad to buy it. After Thad relayed his story of prayer and that his life savings totaled $3,000, the Christian lady agreed to come down to his offer. Because she was moving the next morning, we quickly drove home to fetch our money market check book to close the sale. Thad would pay us back the next day after he withdrew his savings from the bank.

But upon returning to the car, we found that another person had offered the seller her full price. It was a challenging moment for Thad. I was tempted to tell him we would loan him the rest of the money when he boldly stood his ground. He had asked the Lord for a car for $3,000, and deep inside, Thad told us later, he knew this was a test of his faith. Because this fine woman stood by her word, she helped one young man's faith in God grow leaps and bounds that day.

We affectionately called this car the "PRAZMOBILE." After the odometer turned over 350,000+ miles, up until fairly recently the car had acquired a place of honor in Thad and Abby's driveway as a reminder that God hears and answers prayer. While the lining on the ceiling was falling in and the body showed a lot of wear and tear, the PRAZMOBILE was used in case of emergencies when Thad's work car needed repair. That little car not only got Thad through his five-year electrical apprenticeship and early years of his career, it took Thad and Abby to Kentucky for Abby's master's degree program at Asbury Seminary.

For two years those "PRAZ HM" Washington license plates hung on Thad's bedroom wall. When he left home I inherited the plates. One sits perched next to our wood-burning stove where I can see it from my prayer chair early in the morning. It serves as a template for prayer, a reminder to "PRAZ HM."

The other plate sat for some time on the wood-burning stove itself and turned really dark from the blazing heat. Today I keep it behind its companion as a good reminder to PRAZ HM even when things look dark. Praising God not only brings Him sheer delight, it brings HIS presence and accompanying light into the darkness. I have often used both of these plates while teaching about prayer.

In 2008 I had a chance to put into practice what I teach. It was the morning after an accident in which a delivery truck had driven into the hood of my car, totaling the car and injuring my dear assistant, Theresa, and me. After x-raying every part of my body, the ER doctor determined that nothing was broken and released me. The accident left me with ribs that were badly bruised, an ankle three times its normal size from slamming on the brakes so hard, and aches all over my body. I was on so much pain medication that I barely remembered that we had left our teammate, Gary Kocher, to run the "Kids 2 Camp" fundraising breakfast all alone that morning. My blurry vision came into focus and I saw the PRAZ HM plate on display by the stove.

And praise Him I did! In the wee hours of that morning, I started calling God every name in the book—the GOOD BOOK that is: "PROTECTOR, PROVIDER, LOVE, LIGHT, RESTORER, GOOD SHERHERD, HEALER, RECONCILER, WONDERFUL COUNSELOR, COMMANDER OF THE ANGEL ARMIES, and on and on. After shouting every name I could think of to describe the Almighty, I felt a peace settle over me and I started praying min-ute-by-minute for the program that I had helped arrange for the breakfast as it was happening at Camp. Who knows, maybe in the end I was concentrating on the most-needed function for the event, the foundational prayer!

It is now twenty years later and I still marvel at how the God of the Universe divinely dropped that PRAZ HM license plate into my lap right before the first *The Lights of Christmas* and the journey into my new position as development director, all needing intensified prayer. At that time I would never have dreamt of requesting a desire of my heart, a little Lexus SUV with an automatic transmission—something that was definitely a "want" and not a "need." Somehow I think that God has an extra soft spot in his heart when young people earnestly pray, and Thad's car and its license plate were an answer that rewarded his faith.

God is indeed **PRAZABLE!** We are to enter His presence with thanksgiving and praise. As Eugene Peterson paraphrases *The Message* in Psalms 100:4: *"Enter with the password: 'Thank You!' Make yourselves at home talking praise. Thank him. Worship Him."*

26: THE SUPERSIZER

At the same time as the first *The Lights of Christmas* was about to be launched, the first major $6.5 million campaign, "The Journey of Faith," had just successfully passed the feasibility study phase at Camp. Under the direction of our campaign consultant, Don Goehner, as human resources director I had helped put together a national search for an experienced development director who would help the Camp take this giant leap. Even though the Camp didn't really have any major donors at the time, this campaign was desperately needed to begin new programs and to renovate and build facilities, including a new wastewater treatment plant.

The search for a development director had been narrowed down to two finalists and I had arranged for these two men, along with their spouses, to come at separate times for a day-long interview process with Camp Director Ed McDowell and some board members. Shortly after the interviews were completed, one morning as I was praying I asked God to give Ed and the board guidance as to which of these outstanding candidates to hire. I specifically requested that God would reveal which man would sense and develop a passion for Warm Beach Camp most quickly. Then a strange thing happened: in my spirit I heard the Lord say, "You have the passion; that's something you could do!"

When I got up from the chair the most amazing feeling followed. It was as if God took liquid peace and poured it into my body from head to toe! I floated through the rest of the week with a feeling that if they offered me the job (for which I had not applied), it would be wonderful. But if not, that would be great too because I loved handling the human resources functions for the Camp.

At the tail end of the first *The Lights of Christmas,* Director Ed McDowell came into my office and closed the door. My first thought was to wonder if I was in trouble. After quickly scanning my memory for any issues, I relaxed and heard him say, "You will never believe this. A few days ago, after the first candidate withdrew his name from the search, now the second one just withdrew. They both gave the same reason: they had NO peace about taking the job if it was offered to them." Ed went on to explain that he had never really felt comfortable bringing in someone from the outside for this position. Therefore, he had asked the Lord to stop the process if He didn't want it to proceed. God had obviously stopped it. Then Ed simply said, "Nancy, you are good at coordinating projects; would you consider coordinating the Journey of Faith Campaign?"

It only took me a second to respond, "YES!" I had no idea at that moment how much this one "YES" would radically affect my life. There was no way to comprehend the magnitude of change that I was about to be swept into by embarking on this "Journey of Faith." Within two months that liquid peace I had experienced during my prayer time turned to sheer terror! I was literally sick to my stomach for months.

I had been raised in a Midwestern blue collar family; entering the world of major donors was like taking a distant journey into a different culture while still remaining on the continent. We had a Sponsorship Committee on paper which never materialized. So, after signing a $35,000 contract with a major hotel in the Seattle area, I found myself needing to round up one hundred sponsors at $350/table. I literally cut my teeth in development work asking for $350 gifts. This was a huge stretch for me. In the beginning, I would recite, "I can do all things through Christ who strengthens me" before picking up the phone to make those calls.

Several times I tried to give this new job of development director back to Ed. Whatever potential Don Goehner and Ed saw in me, I certainly couldn't see in myself. I literally would lie face down on the floor early in the mornings and cry out to God for help. I had always succeeded at everything I had attempted since high school. My behavioral narcotic of choice was performance. But as Abba's child I felt as if I had been kidnapped by God and placed in a role so impossible that if HE didn't come through I would be toast! And not only would I fail, but the Camp would suffer because it so desperately needed the projects that first campaign would fund. My world was crashing down as failure loomed overhead.

I begin to pray a version of Eugene Peterson's paraphrase of Matthew 11:29-30 from *The Message,* adding my own words: *"Abba, take me in your arms, pull me close, I want to feel your heart beat. I want to walk with you, I want to work with you, I want to watch how you do it. Teach me your unforced rhythms of grace."* This became my frequent prayer for the next few years, and in greater peace I watched as God carried the "Journey of Faith" to a wonderful conclusion.

After watching God complete the campaign, I realized that, like *The Lights of Christmas,* He could do whatever He wanted at Warm Beach Camp. The question wasn't, "Who are we to think that we could do this?" but instead, "Who is God, and does He want it done?!" Yes, we had to work very hard and we had an excellent consultant holding our feet to the fire as we finished the $6.5 million campaign with God constantly present and directing us. But as amazing as completing the campaign was, it was not the total answer to my prayer for God to pull me close to Him. If I had known what I was really asking God at the time I would have been too afraid to pray!

In 2007 I received an email from board member David Goodnight asking if I would mentor Denise Patch, the brand new executive director of a new non-profit, Sister Connection. This newly-formed 501c3 was established to help widows and their children in Burundi, a small heart-shaped country in the middle of Africa. Most of these widows had lost their husbands as a result of the horrific genocide that had raged in this region. The need was great. Still, I had very little interest or time to get involved. But because David was the Camp's board chairman, I said yes.

After many "email cups of coffee" and phone calls with Denise (who at that time lived in Indianapolis), I at last got to meet her when the Camp gave the founding board of Sister Connection a complimentary retreat at Warm Beach in May, 2007. The distinguished board members flew in from all over the country along with Bishop Elli and his wife, Joy, from Africa. My assignment was to give this group a short talk on how to put together a prayer team for their newly-formed organization.

The Sister Connection Board was planning a women's retreat for the widows at the end of August. When Ed caught wind of this he inquired, "What will the children be doing when their moms are in retreat? Why don't you let us come to Burundi to run a camp for the kids?"

Through a wild set of circumstances, five months later I was thrilled to be part of a team boarding a plane to Burundi. After having enough vaccinations to last a lifetime, I was prepared to teach a workshop on "Using the Word of God in Prayer" at this most amazing women's retreat. Four of Warm Beach's younger staff went along to help begin the first youth camp for 300 teens, some of the most traumatized youth in the world. Many had seen their fathers killed in front of them during the war. Our goal was to help the national staff launch their own camping program for future years.

Before the retreat was to begin, the nationals had planned a beautiful ceremony to recognize Sister Connection as a formal organization in Burundi. The Governor of Gitega, the local province, was to speak. The president had sent his drummers, who beat huge drums while dancing in unison over and around the drums. It was a magnificent performance with the drummers' red and green attire flying through the air. The governor was late, but the drummers kept beating the drums until he arrived about forty minutes behind our schedule. They were performing so close to us that we could feel the ground shaking. I was minding my own business, trying not to think about the heat, when in my spirit the Lord impressed on me these words: "Do you feel my heartbeat now? My heart beats for the widows and orphans of Burundi!"

In our living room is a huge sign that sits at eye level where I can see it from my prayer chair. It reads in bold letters: "PRAY BIG." I have come to believe that when we pray for the small assignments—the things that are a part of our lives (like who the Lord's choice is for a position or for HIS nearness when we are afraid)—when God answers...well, HE is **THE SUPERSIZER!** He takes our finite requests and he answers with His infiniteness! Like any father, He simply can't resist when His children cry out to Him in dependence. God SUPERSIZES His answers!

27: PERFECT A.T. (ABBA'S TIMING)

Early in my career I longed for an accountability group. Many male Christian leaders had assembled these groups and I was asking God for a small team of women with whom to share the challenges of ministry. As a young mother I felt lonely and different. In the 1980's it was rare for a Christian mom to have a career, especially one that had a husband working at the same location. At church socials, I was more comfortable chatting with the guys about the latest cafeteria plan for employee benefits than discovering what the other women were feeding their kids.

For a fleeting moment I considered putting an ad in the local newspaper: "WANTED, SMALL GROUP OF PROFESSIONAL CHRISTIAN FEMALES LOOKING FOR ACCOUNTABILITY AND FELLOWSHIP, contact Nancy." After having changed careers five times at Camp, I had resigned myself to the fact that God had answered my prayer for an accountability group with a "No." As a new development director, my world was spinning and I didn't have time for another meeting anyway.

A week before the Free Methodist Family Camp in 1999, our director, Ed McDowell, decided that we would tithe the family camp offering to New Horizons, a ministry for street kids in Seattle. The Camp's goal for contributions was so high that, in my mind, this latest brain wave was completely ridiculous and I made certain that Ed knew my feelings. After listening to my concerns, Ed gave instructions for the offering flier to state that half of the offering would go to missions and half to Camp *after* a 10% tithe was taken out for New Horizons. There was nothing else I could do but submit to the authority God had placed over me. To be honest, I was like a strong-willed child who had been told to sit down. While appearing on the outside to be sitting down, on the inside I was still standing up and shouting, "This is crazy!"

Upon tallying the offering, the Business Office cut a check totaling around $2,000 for New Horizons. Ed asked me to deliver the check to the director of New Horizons, Rita Nussli. I had met Rita at an Essentials of Development training workshop a couple of months before and knew that she was a force to be reckoned with after her experiences dealing with street kids. Surprisingly, when I called to arrange a meeting, Rita invited me to lunch. When I handed Rita the check, the look on her face revealed that it had far more significance than what $2,000 could purchase. Later, I learned that not only was the $2,000 exactly what they needed to make payroll, but it also represented to Rita that her own denomination, the Free Methodists, recognized the street ministry.

Half way through our lunch in Seattle, I asked Rita this question: "How do you stay accountable in development work?" She leaned in and said, "Funny you should ask! I was just talking about this with my good friend, Nancy Murphy, who directs Northwest Family Life, a ministry for prevention and intervention in domestic violence." Rita then invited me to ride with the two of them the following week to the Murdock Trust's Women in Ministry Conference in Vancouver so we could explore further.

That six-hour round trip from Seattle to Vancouver and back seemed like thirty minutes as we shared our hearts together in an environment of grace. None of us wanted it to end. When we finally pried ourselves apart, one of the women said, "Why should we wait four more months to have fellowship and prayer down in Vancouver? Let's meet together each month, just the three of us." From then on we have continued to meet almost monthly for several hours, sharing our journeys together and soaking each other with prayer.

In Abba's perfect timing he brought these two powerful Christian leaders into my life to not only support me in prayer, but to speak the truth in love. They both had far more experience fund raising than I did as they had been raising their organizations' entire budgets for years. I remember one time I was whining about the fact that it was insane for Camp to begin the $6.5 million Journey of Faith Campaign with no real major donors. Rita's response was, "It might as well be $17 million; if God doesn't come through, you will be toast anyway!"

Until I met these two women, I had very little understanding about kids who had gone through trauma. In their work, Nancy and Rita lived on a steady diet of investing love into traumatized youth. Little did we realize that in the coming years the Lord would be opening up multiple streams of ministry at Camp to many marginalized children who had experienced the kind of brokenness that Rita and Nancy confronted on a daily basis.

Throughout the years our little triad has prayed for each other and our families. These two women have embraced me when I just needed someone to lift me up and remind me that God can do anything. We have been there, standing in the gap for each other, and sometimes, that has gone way beyond prayer.

About six years ago Rita asked if we would consider adding two younger women to our threesome. These women, Heather Tuininga, then Director of the Luke 12:48 Foundation, and Linda Ranz, then Vice President, Marketing and Development Director for Medical Teams International, were putting together a small inter-generational group and wanted to add some older Christian professional women to it. After seeking God for wisdom, we agreed that the Lord was leading in this direction even though it seemed a huge stretch to incorporate younger women into an established group that had been meeting for eleven years.

Although scheduling became a greater challenge, the expanded group not only increased our prayer coverage but the younger ones mentored us in ways that are helping me to relate more effectively with younger leaders. I am old enough to be their mother yet God has uniquely bonded us all with his sheer pure grace.

Technological advances in the last few years have tied the five of us into a texting group where we can, at a second's notice, send out prayer requests and words of encouragement to each other. When necessary, we have all gone to the wall for each other, standing in the gap and covered with the blood of Jesus against the forces of evil.

Four years ago we had the joy of standing by as Heather went into labor to deliver their long-awaited, much prayed for baby. Heather sent updates via a group text and it was like we were in the labor room with her. The excitement could be felt through our smart phones! We were some of the first to receive a texted picture of tiny "Miss Kate," who was healthy and beautiful. A few months later we gathered around Heather and Eric as their pastor dedicated this marvelous miracle child to the Lord. The ceremony was followed by a most amazing sermon on prayer!

In 2014 Linda left her position at Medical Teams International to return to the corporate world. For ten years she served on the board of the Seattle Union Gospel Mission (UGM). While in that role, several years later she was also appointed as a trustee of the Stewardship Foundation. In God's master plan, He used Linda to initiate the expansion of Warm Beach's "Kids 2 Camp" program to include UGM kids.

Heather has now started her own company, 10/10 Strategies, working as a consultant with families who want to make a bigger impact with and get more joy from their philanthropy. Rita has joined an organization called Soul Formation. In addition to a lot of speaking and teaching at the Spiritual Academy, Rita helps Christian leaders connect with God through spiritual direction. Nancy Murphy is still directing Northwest Family Life but is also concentrating on domestic violence training world-wide by the use of the web.

Since Rita moved to Sumas near the Canadian border several years ago, our little group mostly stays connected via texting. That a plain, ordinary camp development director landed in this influential group of women is still astounding to me and definitely one of God's supersized, priceless answers to prayer that HE orchestrated through a $2,000 tithe.

I have a clock on my office wall that has stopped. For years, as the battery was dying, it ran really slowly, hardly moving. Since falling off the wall, the clock also has a big crack across the glass front. I plastered a little yellow sticky note right at eye level that reads, "A.T." It is a constant reminder that Abba's timing is perfect, even if it looks like nothing is happening.

Dutch Sheets, in his book, *Intercessory Prayer* (Bethany House, 1996), claims, "We humans are into microwaving and God is into marinating." I must confess that at times I remind God, "You are infinite and have all the time in the world, but remember that I am finite and would like to see an answer in my lifetime!"

I have another little sign at the front of my desk that reminds me, "Don't quit five minutes before the miracle!" It sits right next to a 1979 note from Danny Cook which is taped to my wall: "There are enough hours in each day for us to fulfill God's particular and perfect will for our lives. We never need more time than we have to fulfill the whole will of God."

We can count on Abba to come through in HIS TIMING for HIS Kingdom purposes. There is A.M., P.M., and A.T. Of the three, **A.T. is PERFECT,** because everything about God is perfect!

28: THE ROOM PREPARER

One phone call in late December, 2000 changed everything. Within a day I was on a flight to Wisconsin to move my parents in with us so that we could help them during the final chapter of their lives. After initially surviving the craziness of the Nelson household, however, it became evident to my mother that she and Dad needed their own place. Cherith had given up her bedroom to Grandpa and moved into the rec room downstairs. She and her teenage friends loved this get-away, complete with private bathroom and T.V. all to themselves. But my dad needed to go into the nursing home at Warm Beach Senior Community as his Parkinson's disease had taken a serious turn for the worse. Even with Stan and me helping my mother, Dad was getting too hard for us to manage. The three of us were wearing out quickly as we tried to keep up with his twenty-four-hour needs.

Mom and Dad's names were at the top of the list for the Manor Estates, the Warm Beach Senior Community's manufactured home park right next to the Camp. We were praying for a home to come available soon. It was toward the end of December when we retrieved a letter from the mailbox announcing that #41 had just been put on the market. After only a year, the couple who lived in #41 had decided to move. Fortunately, Mom and Dad had put their names on the list twelve years earlier in case they needed to move closer to me, their only living daughter. After a quick tour, Mom decided to purchase this large three-bedroom home. While we didn't think it wise, Mom insisted that Dad live with her in #41 for a while before he was placed in nursing care. She wanted Dad to know that she would be just across the street.

In the middle of January, 2001, Peter Collins accompanied Stan on a flight to the Midwest to move all of Mom and Dad's belongings to Washington. Coming to grips with the finality of their time in Wisconsin, Mom had packed most of their belongings before they left on the emergency trek to Stanwood right before Christmas. True to her organized nature, Mom had attached color-coded sticky notes to each box and piece of furniture indicating which to take, which to leave at the thrift store, and what to give to relatives. My Aunt June had promised to be at Mom and Dad's home on Balsam Lake when Stan and Peter arrived with the moving van they had rented locally.

The entire Camp community was praying for the guys as they left on this winter-time mission of mercy, and everything went off so smoothly that they arrived back in Washington two days before they were expected. Stan and Peter had packed the truck in record time and, with Mom and Dad's Chevy in tow, left late in the afternoon of the same day their plane landed at the Minneapolis airport! Between the two of them, they drove extra miles each day, stopping only for a few winks of shut-eye along the way. Fortunately, they didn't encounter any ice or snow until they got to Washington and crossed over Snoqualmie Pass.

Meanwhile, Mom and I were at the Everett courthouse with the previous owners of #41 finalizing the sale and receiving the title to their manufactured home. Late that afternoon, Mom and I pulled into the driveway with all the needed paperwork completed. Much to our surprise, a few minutes later Stan and Peter arrived with the moving van full of all my parents' treasured belongings. In no time at all, with the help of several staff, Mom and Dad were nestled in their new home perched on a corner lot near the entrance of the Manor Estates with a view of everything happening in the park.

After a few weeks Mom realized that she could no longer manage Dad by herself. That dreaded day when Dad would need to be admitted for full-time nursing care had come. Their new doctor leveled with me in front of Mom, stating rather matter-of-factly that if we didn't place Dad in nursing care soon, I would lose Mom before Dad. Fulfilling my promise to Mom, I broke the news to Dad. Out of love for my mom, Dad agreed without a struggle. Because the nursing home was right across the street, Mom walked over almost every day to visit and to help feed Dad his meals. None of us realized that this would become a five-year routine.

Mom and I had the joy of going on a cruise to Alaska in May, 2010, a dream that she and Dad had put off too long during their retirement. A couple days after the delightful cruise was over, however, Mom had her first stroke. If it had occurred a few days earlier, Mom would have gotten an "air-lift" off the ship! After speech therapy Mom became her independent self once more, but she moved a bit more slowly, both mentally and physically.

Then in April, 2011, Mom suffered a compressed fracture of her vertebrae while the rest of our family was in Santa Cruz for Stan's mother's memorial service. Fortunately, Cherith's mother-in-law, Lauri Lee, took Mom to the doctor and stayed overnight with her in #41. It became very apparent that Mom needed nursing care immediately, so Lauri arranged for Mom to be admitted to the Warm Beach nursing facility while we were still in California.

After two months of care, mom's back had healed enough that she could graduate to the senior community's "assisted living" care unit, Cedar Court. Her doctor said that Mom's independent living days were over for good. There was only one problem: all the places in the Cedar Court Assisted Living Unit were filled. There was no way to know when one would come available. Since we didn't have a bedroom on the main floor of our lake home, we scouted the area for other interim options. Finding none, after much prayer we decided to move into #41 with Mom until an opening came available in Cedar Court.

I paced outside the social worker's office for several days. Having lined up help for most days of the week, I hoped that we could fill the remaining slots so that Mom would have the twenty-four-hour assistance needed. In addition, there were some "accommodations" that would have to be in place before we brought Mom home. Finally, I got up enough courage to arrange with the social worker to start the discharge process at the nursing facility. Actually, it took a nudge from the Lord as HE impressed upon my spirit this question: "Don't you trust me to provide all that is needed?"

After meeting with the social worker, I had just sat down in the chair next to Mom's bed when the lady in charge of Cedar Court came flying into the room. She was so excited that she was almost ready to bounce off the walls. She exclaimed, "You will never believe this, but a room in Cedar Court just became available!" She went on to tell us that just minutes before a family had taken their mom home to live with them and, while it was not normal for a room to be shown until all the former resident's belongings were removed, the family had given us permission to look at the room.

As we went down the hall to Cedar Court, which was attached to the nursing wing, there was a slight peppiness in Mom's steps: she was on her way to a private room with more freedom. Upon viewing the room, we both knew that this was the perfect place for the next phase of her life. All meals would be provided along with housekeeping and a call button for assistance.

Mom picked out the furniture that would fit into the small room and we held a massive moving sale with the remainder of her belongings. She agreed to letting all the profits go to "Kids2Camp" scholarships. Her mobile home sold before an advertising flier could be printed, as a gentleman residing in the apartments across the street had his eye on the beautiful site for a new manufactured home to grace this prime spot in the park.

Cedar Court was an amazing place for Mom. During this time, Chad and Cherith's little Eli was just a baby and we brought him to visit often. For nine months, Eli was the "Cedar Court baby." He delighted in visiting each table during mealtimes. A baby brings smiles to all, especially the women who remember their own children and grandkids. Chad and Cherith's Preston also loved visiting Great Grandma (G.G.) at Cedar Court. Mom would often accompany us to the little pool in the basement of the Senior Community to watch Preston swim. We were also able to eat with Mom in the fine dining room where she had her meals.

But then Mom began to have a series of small strokes. After five trips to the ER, it was no longer safe for her to stay in Cedar Court. We had hoped that she could step into Heaven straight from Cedar Court someday. But after the fifth trip to the ER, she was transferred back to the nursing unit. We had already been looking around for another place as it was becoming evident that Cedar Court was not going to be Mom's last home on earth, and Mom did not enjoy life in the nursing unit. We began to pray again.

Chad's great grandma, Sylvia, had been in an adult family care facility called Abundant Living Care Home (ALCH), which was just twenty-five minutes from Camp. We had heard wonderful things about Abundant Living and Sylvia's daughter, Dianne, suggested I visit right away as there was an opening at the care home. After touring the home and talking with the owner, Michelle, I had to agree that it was the most loving, caring atmosphere one could find for a loved one. I returned the next day with Mom so she could get a peek, and she graciously agreed to move to ALCH. It was a mad rush to get her furniture moved from Cedar Court so we could bust her out of the nursing home the next day.

Mom enjoyed being with Sylvia for a couple of years. Sylvia and Mom had become friends before Chad and Cherith got married. I remember being at Sylvia's house with both families tying bows onto all the programs and favors for the wedding in 2004. Chad's dad, Bill, was observing the process and made a comment that has become a sacred memory: "I think we are tying more than bows together; we are tying two families together!"

Days before Sylvia died in the care home, Chad's mom, Lauri, posted a precious picture on Facebook of my mom sitting next to Sylvia's bed talking with her. They had become tight friends, together until Sylvia, at age ninety-nine, died three years ago at ALCH.

After almost six years, my mom just stepped into Heaven while a resident at ALCH. At ninety-four her bones were brittle and she suffered another serious compressed fracture of the vertebrae. For the last year she was confined to a wheelchair due to her inability to walk without falling. The loving staff did everything possible in order to keep Mom there while managing her pain with the assistance of Hospice. Michelle, Linda, Crystal, Jessica, Tara, and Rebecca, long-time staff members, were like daughters to Mom, and their love and care was beyond anything we could have ever provided ourselves.

For example, after Mom had been at the home for just a couple of months, we were invited to attend Linda and Rick's wedding, and hanging on Mom's dresser mirror until her passing was a precious photo of the bride behind a row of her five residents. Recently Linda and Tara moved on to attend school, and several additional staff have been added, including Maria and Sonny, continuing to see that all of Mom's needs were met up until the very end.

Before Mom became so frail, the staff at ALCH made certain she got to church and went on field trips. They took her shopping (letting her drive the motorized cart at Costco), and took her out for meals. A while ago, with tears in her eyes, Crystal exclaimed that Mom was like a family member, and described how hard it is to lose people the staff had grown to love so much. For five years Crystal painted beautiful designs on Mom's long finger nails. And as for her feet, Mom had never had her toe nails polished until Crystal came along. There have been many fun posts of Mom's nails on our Facebook page!

After Mom's second compressed fracture, Michelle comforted Mom by heating up a blanket in the dryer and placing it all around her while stroking her face. No wonder my Mom exclaimed, "This is home: they really love on me here!" On July 2, 2017, the family gathered to say their goodbyes to "G.G." (Great Grandmother). Mom had a window of several hours where she knew us, was talking, smiling, and able to receive the last hugs from her great grandchildren. After that afternoon, her body shut down and she no longer ate or drank. Just five days later, on July 7, Mom stepped into eternity directly from her beautiful bedroom at the Abundant Living Care Home just minutes after her great granddaughter, baby Clara, and I left the room. Leave it to the Lord to choose 7/7/17, a date chuck full of 7's, to be the day Mom felt His final embrace and is now face-to-face with Jesus in Heaven.

God is **THE ROOM PREPARER.** HIS house has many rooms and HE not only prepared places for my mom and dad throughout this journey after their emergency flight to Washington, but HE prepared a place for my mother in eternity where my dad, sister, and unborn nephew have recently welcomed her home.

29: THE TERRITORY ENLARGER

Excitement mounted as the old camp bus pulled up in front of The Firs Chalet at Mount Baker that January in 2001. Loaded to the gills with staff, baggage, snacks, and games, we were more than ready for the annual retreat. Fresh white snow beckoned the adventurous. The plow had just provided a spot for the bus to park, leaving a huge pile of white stuff that almost covered the entrance to our favorite retreat location.

Besides the fierce card games and ongoing yearly Farming Game and Scrabble tournaments, the staff was ready to let down, experience community, and spend time in worship. It was our turn to be fed the Word, to be campers ourselves. We were always thrilled when The Firs staff traded staff retreats with Warm Beach Camp. This particular venue provided a unique atmosphere to blend us together because everything was contained in a four-story building with a spiral staircase on one side.

That year Director Ed McDowell would be the keynote speaker and his messages revolved around Bruce Wilkinson's book, hot off the press. As we gathered around the circular gas fireplace in the meeting room of the main floor, Ed passed out a tiny little book, *The Prayer of Jabez* (Multnomah Books, 2000), to each staff member.

We spent all four sessions on one verse, I Chronicles 4:10, that records Jabez's prayer:

> *"Oh, that You would bless me indeed,*
> *And enlarge my territory,*
> *That Your hand would be with me,*
> *And that You would keep me from evil."*

Following Wilkinson's lead, Ed encouraged the staff to begin corporately praying this prayer for Warm Beach Camp. If one only read the first couple pages of the book, there might seem to be a suspicion of "prosperity theology" being advocated. But Ed beckoned us to keep reading, asking God to bless us indeed to be used in greater Kingdom work. None of us realized how this simple, direct request was about to change the trajectory of the Camp forever!

Wilkinson, in the very first chapter, puts it this way: "Instead of standing near the river's edge, asking for a cup of water to get you through each day, you'll do something unthinkable – you will take the little prayer with the giant prize and jump into the river! At that moment, you will begin to let the loving currents of God's grace and power carry you along. God's great plan for you will surround you and sweep you forward into the profoundly important and satisfying life He has waiting!"

Jabez's request for blessing is radical, as "he left it entirely up to God to decide what the blessings would be and where, when and how Jabez would receive them." This is not today's popular prosperity gospel, but rather focuses on "wanting for ourselves nothing more, nothing less than what God wants for us." Wilkinson goes on to say that it's as if "we are throwing ourselves entirely into the river of HIS will and power and purposes for us…to become wholly submerged in what God is trying to do in us, through us, and around us for HIS glory."

The staff began to get excited about God blessing the Camp and enlarging its "territory." Many had ideas of what this could look like in the future. Several hoped that the Camp could find a way to minister to the homeless. Many had dreams of reaching at-risk populations. While this was adventurous, as a fairly new development director, it was also terrifying to me. Since the marginalized can't pay, I could sense the need for increased contributions.

The staff began to boldly ask God to "bless us indeed and enlarge the Camp's territory." We were soon to experience the fact that God always intervenes when, as a corporate body, we put His agenda before ours! But it didn't take us long to understand the importance of "the touch of His Greatness"—HIS hand on us. Wilkinson puts it this way: "As God's chosen, blessed sons and daughters, we are expected to attempt something large enough that failure is guaranteed…unless God steps in."

It wasn't long after the retreat before Ed McDowell got a call from a board member, Roger Hancuff, who had just returned from morning worship at Overlake Christian Church in Kirkland. During announcements in the service he heard that the committee that organized the delivery of Christmas gifts for Angel Tree kids (children who have a parent[s]incarcerated), was trying to find a way to get these children to a Christian camp in the summer. Ed was given the phone number for Elbert Silbaugh, the man who directs the Christmas outreach to these Angel Tree kids— some of the highest risk children in American society.

In God's perfect timing, Ed was introduced to Elbert soon after he had called the national office of Prison Fellowship to obtain permission to round up some Angel Tree kids for a summer camp experience. When the national director of Prison Fellowship heard that the Lord had laid this desire on a group of believers in the Pacific Northwest, he was on a plane in two days to meet with Ed and Elbert. Prison Fellowship had just received a grant from a private foundation to help fund a pilot program to send Angel Tree kids to camp. They had not planned to target the Pacific Northwest, but sensing the Spirit's leading, they quickly added the Puget Sound area to the pilot program.

On the following Sunday, just one week after Roger's phone call, Ed inquired if I could attend a meeting that evening forty-five minutes away in Lynnwood, to discuss the possibility of Angel Tree kids coming to Camp that summer. Not knowing what to expect, I found myself crowded into a tiny living room with a handful of plain, ordinary people who seemed to have dreams out of proportion to their means.

The evening ended in a prayer time and a commitment from Ed that Warm Beach Camp would accept 100 Angel Tree kids at Camp in just a few months. I felt a sickening knot forming in my stomach. While the grant would pay a large portion of the cost, there were still added expenses, not to mention the nosebleed we were about to experience on yet another steep learning curve. I started wondering if my plea to the search committee in 1995 for a camp director with vision might have been a bit over the top!

Still in a fog of concern, while we were walking out of that little house just north of Seattle one of the committee members handed me a small card and said, "We have been praying this." Having plunked myself back into Ed's car, I focused on the card. It contained "The Prayer of Jabez"! Somehow, God had connected their prayers with our staff's prayers in the Heavenlies. He had taken us all seriously. We had jumped into the river of God's activity and would soon experience what dependency felt like. As Wilkinson outlines in his book, "You do not become great, you become dependent on the strong hand of God."

Through the diligent work of that little committee that had gathered in the living room in Lynnwood, about forty Angel Tree children were brought to Camp that first year. The Lord knew we were not yet equipped to handle more. In the coming years the staff, under the direction of Youth Camp Director Laurie Fertello, would grow in their knowledge and ability to handle forgotten, traumatized kids who have unique issues due to an incarcerated parent.

More and more we prayed for God's hand to be with us. As Wilkinson explains, "'The hand of the Lord' is a Biblical term for God's power and presence in the lives of His people." This is witnessed over and over again in Acts as "the phenomenal success of the early church is attributed to one thing: 'The hand of the Lord was with them'… A more specific New Testament description for God's hand is 'the filling of the Holy Spirit.'" We would soon testify with the prophet of old in Zechariah 4:7: "…it's not by power, it's not by might, but it is by the Spirit…"

That first plunge into the "river of God's activity" with the Angel Tree kids was just the beginning. In the spring of 2002, following the aftermath of the events of 9/11, when it appeared our summer youth camps would be practically empty Ed walked into the registration office and declared, "We can't minister to empty beds! Don't turn anyone away based on their ability to pay. Ask them what they can pay, and we will trust God to find the money to fund the rest." Needless to say, as a fairly new development director, when I heard this I about fainted. The current was picking up in the river of God's activity, and the flood gates were about to burst open.

God had a "holy surprise up His sovereign sleeve," as Mark Batterson says in *Draw the Circle*. As program planning grew in the next several years, a couple put down money to begin the partnership program to bring the poorest-of-the-poor children to Camp in the summer of 2005. At the last minute, the Lord arranged for Grace Community Church in Auburn to be our pilot partnership. The following summer, the Camp was slammed with requests from other groups ministering to the poor.

In 2006 I received a call from Doug Jonson on his first day of work at New Song Church in the Hilltop area of Tacoma, the most gang-involved part of the city. Doug, who had worked at Camp during high school, said, "My mom says that you guys have money to send the poorest-of-the-poor kids to Camp. Is that true?" When he heard "Yes," he went on to say, "Well, I can bring 200 this summer!" Doug combined forces with Youth for Christ (YFC) in Tacoma and, starting with around fifty kids that first year, grew their camping program so large that after four summers at Warm Beach they spun off to attend a larger camp in Oregon.

The river has continued to expand, with tributaries going to over twenty partnerships in the Pacific Northwest, including the latest ones: in 2014, Union Gospel Mission brought children from the women's shelter in Seattle; in 2016, Jubilee Reach brought immigrant children, and Raven Rock Therapeutic Riding Ranch brought traumatized youth to camp as well. Each opportunity reached further into the world of the marginalized, requiring God's hand to be more and more over the Camp. God funds what HE wants done! While the development staff has worked diligently seeking funds, we have seen HIS provisions in ways that cannot be explained. In 2016, a total of $221,000 was given by generous donors to help over 1,800 children with full or partial camperships to make certain that no child was left behind.

The ripple effects are astounding. The staff helps Elbert, Director of Eagle Outreach Ministries, and his crew stuff their annual camp mailing for the Angel Tree kids. Last year, before our prayer time at our 10 a.m. break, two helpers shared their stories. Former Angel Tree campers themselves, they are now working with Eagle Outreach, making a way to bring other kids to camp whose parents are incarcerated. One of them, Stephen Couldry, also attended Father/Son Camp with Elbert where he committed his life to Jesus. They later returned to Warm Beach Camp to volunteer as buddies in the Special Friends program. Stephen is currently attending a Christian college to become a pastor. Elbert exclaimed, "Because of Warm Beach Camp's faith in partnering with Eagle Outreach, through the years God has given more than 800 campers an opportunity to be immersed in a Christian camp experience."

Several years ago, at our annual Partner-in-Ministry dinner, Doug Jonson, now on staff with Tacoma YFC, presented a seven year look-back. He showed a picture of kids from that first camp at Warm Beach, many right out of juvenile hall. After describing the typical trajectory of a kid from Hilltop, many who are fatherless and/or involved in gangs, prostitution, and drugs, Doug showed a current picture of those same kids. They are now young adults who reserve the week of summer camp to return to be cabin counselors. Some have gone on to college; one is currently working at the YFC Tacoma Office. It's the ripple effect which comes from jumping into the river and experiencing the wild ride fueled by God's grace and power.

Early on in my journey as the new Development Director I came upon a disturbing and challenging passage that has forever been seared into my heart. In *The Message,* Amos 5:22-24 records the prophet speaking to the family of Israel:

> *"I'm sick of your fund-raising schemes,*
> *Your public relations and image making*
> *I've had all I can take of your noisy ego-music.*
> *When was the last time you sang to me?*
> *Do you know what I want?*
> *I want justice—oceans of it.*
> *I want fairness—rivers of it.*
> *That's what I want. That's all I want."*

God is **THE TERRITORY ENLARGER** and royally places HIS hand of blessing on those who plunge into the rivers of ministry HE initiates, according to HIS agenda, not ours!

30: THE REALTOR

Plans were underway for our first major campaign's banquets in Central Washington. During the first months of 2001, I was on the other side of the Cascades quite often nailing down arrangements at hotels in Wenatchee and Yakima. While sharing "windshield time" with Director Ed McDowell, I mentioned that Stan and I would love to do more entertaining of volunteers and donors in our home, but that it was just not correctly configured for it.

Our split-level house on 81st Street bordering the Camp had been perfect for our kids when they were teens. The large rec room downstairs was the place for many parties and Bible studies. But the small dining room and separate kitchen did not allow for entertaining big groups. After my dreaming out loud that day in the car, Ed's response came in the form of a question: "Why don't you sell your house and buy one with more open entertaining space?" I laughed out loud. My world was spinning as I navigated the whirlpool of banquet details. The thought of putting our house on the market and looking for another house was terrifying. Dismally, I imagined ending up in an apartment while searching for the perfect place.

A few weeks later I received a call from Brian Smelser. After an awkward pause he asked, "Have you ever thought of selling your house?" I smiled and knew he must have been talking to Ed! Brian went on to explain that he and Kim had leased a house on Camano Island with an "option-to-buy." Their lease was up on May 1—just a couple of months away. They had decided they wanted to live closer to Camp, where Kim was working in our Registration Department. Brian knew every inch of our house, including Thad's uniquely decorated bedroom, as he came weekly to disciple our son.

The first words out of my mouth let Brian know that we did desire more open entertainment space for large groups with my new job in Camp development. But I went on to explain that with the banquets on the east side of the mountains in the near future, there just wasn't time to go house hunting, especially with their May 1 deadline looming. That didn't sound too spiritual, so I ended the conversation by promising Brian that I'd talk to Stan and we'd pray about it. After supper that evening, Stan and I had one of the shortest prayer sessions ever, giving the whole matter over to God.

To be honest, I had been surprised when we had moved into our own home about six years previously. After living in Camp housing for seventeen years, I figured we'd never own a home. I would often look around and exclaim, "God, you own all of this. I don't have to own it to enjoy it!" We regularly took in the beautiful sunsets over Port Susan Bay. Beauty was everywhere as we walked on the dike, watching the tide creep in over the mudflats.

Three days after Brian's call, I met Dodie Weiland in the staff dining room. She had just come from the bakeshop where her daughter, Diane, was working.

Excitedly Dodie said, "Nancy, you know a lot of people. We just put our house on the market and are selling it ourselves; do you know anyone looking for a house?" I laughed and told her that someone wanted to buy our house. Dodie pointed her finger right at me and declared, "Then you can buy our house!"

Again I laughed, certain it was way more than we could ever afford. We knew their house well as the Weilands had graciously hosted the Camp staff there for 4th of July parties. Their three-story home sat right on Lake Howard with a big deck overlooking the lake. The middle floor of the house was designed for entertaining large groups, as the kitchen, dining room, and living room were one giant, open space. Furthermore, the kitchen had a huge center island, readymade for potlucks.

Dodie urged me to come look at the house. Because it would be such a financial stretch, I assured her that while it was a perfect house for what we wanted to do, I didn't want to waste their time as we could never afford it. Two more times she demanded that we look at the house the very next day, Saturday. So as not to offend her, I promised Dodie that I'd talk to Stan and we would pray about it. After she left the room, I quickly dismissed the idea as utterly impossible.

Later that Friday, while Stan and I were having dinner at Arlene Scott's lovely home overlooking the Sound, Dodie's wild proposal resurfaced. In front of the other guests, Rod and Maggie Allen, I told Stan about my conversation with Dodie earlier in the day. Arlene immediately inquired what the house was like. After describing the perfect location (just seven minutes from Camp) as well as the open entertainment floor and the huge deck overlooking the lake, I added that it had a two bedroom apartment downstairs. Quickly Arlene asked, "Does the apartment have a separate entrance?" When I said "Yes," Arlene began exclaiming her enthusiasm. It was as if we had jumped on a magic carpet that was hurling us into the future.

Arlene explained that no one lives somewhere forever—we just think we will. She coached us to look at the house as a business investment, renting out the two bedroom apartment to help pay the taxes. Then when we were done entertaining for the Camp, we should take the equity in the house and downsize to a small place where we would have a bedroom on the main floor and no stairs. She neatly tied a bow around the package by adding, "Go see that house tomorrow!" To hold us accountable she threw in, "I want to hear all about it at Sunday School!"

Needless to say, Stan and I hit our knees when we returned home, as the whole thing was intoxicating but scary. We were on a careful plan to be mortgage free in our home on 81st Street by the time we retired. While I was used to jumping into risky streams of God's activity at Camp, our own personal finances were a different matter. Having been raised in a frugal, conservative home, this was WAY out of my comfort zone. We did go to see the home on Lake Howard the next day and realized that what Arlene had outlined could actually work. Still, while we would have a nice down payment from the equity from our first home, I was certain that no bank would loan us the balance that we would need, given our Camp wages.

The Weilands accepted the offer we made a few days after touring the house. It was just in the nick of time for them to make an offer on a smaller one-level home in Stanwood that was under construction. The builder would have had to secure a realtor if he hadn't had a firm offer by the end of the week, as the house was scheduled to be ready the second week of May. Because of their timing, the Weilands were able to save money on their offer. Furthermore, the Smelsers were still very interested in our home, and made us an offer that we accepted. It was truly a "win" for everyone!

I was speechless when our loan was approved. When the loan officer inquired about setting a time for signing, I named the only two days that would fit into my crazy work schedule that spring. He laughed and said the likelihood of us actually signing papers on one of those days was pretty slim, as closing loans was sometimes dicey and unpredictable. He was unaware that the Lord was weaving this deal together behind the scenes, because as it turned out, all three parties signed on one of the days I requested. All three houses closed within twenty-four hours. No one went through a realtor. Two of us used the same lender. And all three of us used the same title company.

The builder finished the Weiland's house a week earlier than scheduled. On May 1, just a couple months from Brian's original phone call, our Sunday School class helped us move into our new home on Lake Howard. Our furniture and pictures matched the décor perfectly. In addition, the Weilands had included all the curtains with the deal along with two counter-high stools and their paddle boat. All we had to purchase was a rug set for the bathroom on the entertainment floor. After mounting pictures on the walls, only one week after the move we had our first group of volunteers, the Sowers, for a potluck.

That first year we hosted over fifty events, the largest being the staff's annual 4th of July Party. Our home has become known as the "party house" and we have had a steady stream of guests—too many to count—during the last sixteen years. As for our downstairs apartment, while never advertising we have had a total of five renters over the years. God has multi-tasked throughout, providing the extra money we needed and doing amazing things in the renters' lives at the same time. When the apartment has been free, many people in ministry have used it to rest, relax, fast, and pray, including Chad and Cherith's pastor, Daniel Espy, senior pastor at The Bridge Church in Snohomish.

In his book, *Playing for an Audience of One,* our pastor, Josh Brooks, adopted a quote by Abraham Kuyper: *"There is not one square inch of earth's real estate over which Christ, who is Sovereign overall, does not cry, 'Mine!'"* We will probably never fully own this wonderful grace-filled spot on Lake Howard. God not only owns it along with everything else, HE acted as **THE REALTOR**, tying three deals together, staging and showing the houses without anyone realizing what He was strategizing. He engineered every detail down to the signing day and the May 1 grand shuffle. And God continues to use this three-story house by the still waters of Lake Howard to fulfill His Kingdom purposes.

31: TRUSTABLE

It was the first *The Lights of Christmas* after 9/11. As the American public was still reeling from the horrific acts of terrorism that December of 2001, people's hearts were tender and craving the eternal. When tragedy strikes, even newscasters dare to claim that their prayers are with the families of the victims. The big A-frame Cedar Lodge Administration Building at Warm Beach Camp displayed a large banner across the front: "IN GOD WE TRUST."

The Camp's first major $6.5 million campaign, The Journey of Faith, was almost finished, with only $300,000 to go. Somehow, that last little bit seemed more impossible than the millions already raised. Under the direction of our consultant, Don Goehner, and a supportive Board, we had made it to this point. As I was coming up the sidewalk of Cedar Lodge my eyes were glued on the words, "IN GOD WE TRUST." I prayed out loud, "God you are TRUSTABLE, you got us into this, and it's up to you to finish the campaign. We have done everything we know to do; it is in your hands, and it's in YOU that we trust!"

Several months later, right before Valentine's Day, I received a call from "J.B.," a woman who was a donor and who had just lost her husband. On my last visit with them at their home, her husband, even though he was in the final stages of cancer, had wanted an update on everything happening at Camp, especially the construction of the new waste water treatment plant that was part of the JOF Campaign. The widow was now calling to see if we would be interested in some huge glass vases that had been given with flowers for the memorial service. She thought they would look wonderful with colorful balls in them for next year's *The Lights of Christmas*. After telling her I would have someone contact her from *The Lights of Christmas* Department, I continued working on the project in front of me.

As I was walking across the office to place a folder into the interoffice mail bin, the Lord nudged me and advised, "She wants to see you; go pick up those vases." I quickly cancelled the message that I had just sent to *The Lights of Christmas* assistant and called the widow back to arrange for the pickup of the vases, and added, "If you have time, I'd love to take you out for a cup of coffee."

While we sipped our favorite hot drinks, that first visit on Valentine's Day in Starbucks began an amazing friendship with this Camp supporter. Whenever I was in her area, I would whisk her away for lunch and we would bring each other up to date on our lives. Somehow, mysteriously, the Lord was working out HIS plan as our relationship grew deeper and deeper. We marveled at the many similarities in our lives. While she was old enough to be my mom, this pioneer knew what it was like to work among males as a full-time professor rearing a family at the same time, before it was commonplace for moms to have professional careers. We both had been blessed with incredible husbands who were not threatened by our accomplishments and cheered us on. God had arranged a soul-friend, someone who had gone through similar things a generation ahead of me!

To top it off, I was losing my dad at the same time. My friend had experienced losing her mother to dementia and was so helpful as I processed my feelings. I felt very special when she saved a place for me right next to her at her granddaughter's wedding reception. We delighted with each other as I became a first-time grandparent and she became a first-time great-grandparent. J.B. didn't just want to know what was happening at Camp; she wanted to really know me!

I enjoyed being with J.B. so much that I took every opportunity to connect with her. One day while getting in my car after a lunch, she said, "I would like to donate a home with acreage to the Camp." I couldn't believe what she had just said and honestly wondered if my ears needed cleaning! Still in shock, not knowing how to respond, I simply said, "Let's talk about it at our next visit."

Being new in the Development field, I needed wise counsel from someone with more knowledge than I to map out how to make this offered gift a reality. After I made a phone call to Don Goehner, J.B. had a statement notarized indicating her intent to gift the house to the Camp. Working closely with her attorney, she transferred ownership of the house to Warm Beach. Upon the sale of the house, God came through with the $300,000 needed to complete the $6.5 Million funding for the JOF Campaign.

My friend and I still take every opportunity to meet whenever we can. Our lives are intertwined in amazing ways—too many to spell out. She has attended Rotary meetings as my guest in Stanwood when she is in the area. We follow each other's kids and grandkids, praying along the way. I know all about her thirteen year old neighbor, a precious gal with Down syndrome who is a special friend that J.B. has loved since birth. Recently, before Mom died, J.B. visited my mom with me in Mom's family care home nearby. She continued to travel this journey beside me as my second parent slipped away "one brain cell at a time."

Several years ago J.B. began to sell a collection of guitars that her husband had owned, with the intent that the proceeds go to the Special Friends Program at Camp for people with disabilities. At the end of 2014 she helped to finish another $427,000 mini-campaign when one of these guitars sold. This gift helped build the second accessible overnight cabin just in time for the 2015 summer season. The gift is in honor of her neighbor gal, Anjulie Grace, who will soon be old enough to be a Special Friends camper. And I just betcha that she will someday stay in one of those cabins overnight, experiencing the rhythms of grace!

God is indeed **TRUSTABLE**. Not only did HE finish the Journey of Faith Campaign HIS way with J.B. and her husband's incredible investment in Kingdom work at Warm Beach Camp, but in the process HE gave me the most incredible friend to invest in my life along the journey.

32: THE RESCUER

A heavy feeling hung in the atmosphere that January of 2002 as the young staff, suited in their OSHA-approved harnesses, were taking down the lights. The effects of 9/11 were just about to crescendo, reaching a crisis point at Camp. It was four months after 9/11, but fear still permeated society. While many families had attended *The Lights of Christmas,* experiencing a welcome relief from anxiety, the American public was hunkering down in the security of their homes.

Groups that had reserved facilities at Camp began to cancel after 9/11 or arrived with numbers way below their minimum guarantees. Our Guest Services Department started to waive the guarantees just to have a few campers to serve. It wasn't just at Warm Beach: these effects were being experienced throughout the entire travel and recreational industry. There was a sense of helplessness at Camp as the bills piled up from *The Lights of Christmas,* including the huge food and electricity invoices that always arrived in January.

To make matters worse, we had forged ahead on some of the projects that were in the Journey of Faith campaign based on pledges received. We were inexperienced in campaigns and didn't realize that, in addition to the unstable nature of the economy following 9/11, larger commitments made during the "quiet phase" are often fulfilled toward the end of a five-year campaign cycle. But there were contractors to pay for work already completed.

All of this spelled a financial disaster brewing for the Camp, one that none us could have predicted before 9/11. But as we neared the end of January, those in the Business Office were well aware of the situation—not enough cash on hand to cover all the bills. Of course, we kept praying and hoping that the American public's icy level of fear would thaw, allowing the scheduled February groups to arrive with their promised minimums. But it soon became a stark reality that there was no way out of this. The lines of credit used for the normal yearly cash flow cycle were exhausted, an abnormal condition for January, which typically provided an influx of cash from *The Lights of Christmas.* We were out of cash, with months to go before the busy summer season.

Our young director, Ed McDowell, didn't know what to do. This man full of vision was about to begin a crash course in "Finance 101 for Nonprofits." Thankfully, we had the right man in place on the board's Finance Committee, Daryl Miller, a successful businessman with an MBA. Daryl had the needed experience to not only help the Camp navigate the crisis, but to educate the board and management team in the following years.

With no immediate solution in sight, Ed did the only thing he knew to do: turn to the Lord in prayer for guidance. He followed the pattern laid out by Jehoshaphat, King of Judah, in II Chronicles Chapter 20, when he got word that there were armies coming from every direction to attack Judah and Israel.

King Jehoshaphat cried out to the Lord for help and called for a nationwide time of fasting and prayer. Ed started with the board and staff. Next he notified the Camp's prayer warriors throughout the Pacific Northwest, including the east side of the Cascades. We hosted several prayer meetings at the Camp, in Olympia, and one in Wenatchee.

At the same time Ed alerted the entire constituency that supported Warm Beach Camp through donating finances and/or volunteer time. In February, with the help of Gary Kocher, the Annual Fund director, Ed sent out the now-famous "Jehoshaphat letter," describing in detail the financial situation and truthfully revealing the sobering situation: by March 5, $200,000 was needed in order to pay all the overdue bills and make the payroll that would be handed out on March 6. It was the kind of crisis letter an organization can only send out once in its history. Ed urged the Camp's supporters to pray and give.

The staff was well aware that we might not be paid in March. Many had let the Business Office know that they would be willing to wait until the Camp's finances improved. There were some on staff who had no financial reserve and this would mean their families would go without the necessities of life for an indeterminate amount of time.

While I had read about fasting, I had honestly never done it. Ed encouraged the staff to give up at least one meal a day and use the time to plead before the Lord for the Camp to be saved from financial ruin. What a time it was for me to be a fairly new development director at Camp! In addition to the financial crisis looming, the economy had tanked, affecting many donors' ability to give. All my life I had been a late-night owl, watching "Nightline" before falling into bed after midnight. But facing this crisis, I couldn't sleep anyway, so I began giving up breakfast in the mornings and getting up around 3 or 4 a.m. to pray.

Somewhere during the wee hours of February, 2002, the Lord changed my "circadian rhythms." Much to Joanie Yonker's delight, I became a morning person and have continued to wake up early, eagerly anticipating time alone with the Lord to pray. When Joanie, an "early bird," was my assistant during the late 80's, we used to claim that there were only a couple of hours we were both fully functioning together, since I didn't completely wake up until around 10 a.m., even though I was at work a couple hours before that time!

During February, at one of the staff's daily 10 a.m. staff prayer times, the young *The Lights of Christmas* assistant, Cami Cook (now Blue), made a prophetic statement: "This will be a story that we tell to future generations—how the Lord rescued the Camp." While the Camp was birthed in prayer and has always had a mantle of prayer over it, this was definitely the most concerted prayer effort Stan and I have ever experienced in our thirty-nine years of being at Warm Beach.

Mid-way through February, Ed also instructed the Development Department to plan two huge celebrations in May to acknowledge what the Lord was going to do. He wanted one at Camp in the main auditorium, and the other close to the Bellevue/Redmond area (the "Eastside" area of Seattle). In addition to not knowing exactly what we would be celebrating, we had no budget available, and it looked like a crazy, impossible assignment. We began to intercede and ask the Lord for direction and help in planning these two "Celebrate!" events.

One day, I was scheduled for a thank-you visit at a Starbucks with a Camp donor, Henriet Schapelhouman, whom I had never met. She and her husband, Fred, attended Timberlake Fellowship in Redmond where she was on staff as an assistant pastor. Among various duties, Henriet's specialties were small group ministry and event planning. Henriet had a cadre of creative people who were used to putting on elaborate events at Timberlake. While sipping coffee and sharing deeply at a Starbuck's table, we began a friendship that has had Kingdom significance in many ways.

Henriet jumped right in when she heard of the Camp's need for a place on the Eastside to host the "Celebrate!" event. She volunteered her decorating team and outlined how we could set up round tables in the Timberlake church's huge lobby and use their kitchen. She rounded up helpers for the kitchen and enlisted the youth group to act as wait staff. Henriet assured us that it wouldn't cost anything except for decorations and paper supplies. We had already decided that we would fashion the event after the "dessert potluck" that Rita Nussli had been doing with all volunteers to help raise the operating budget for New Horizons' ministry.

We gave Donna Storm, the head of Timberlake's decorating army, a tiny budget for supplies. They either laid hands on that money to multiply it or added some of their own to supplement the pathetic amount. I could hardly believe my eyes when we arrived that evening in May to place the printed "Celebrate!" programs on the chairs and test out the AV equipment. These miracle workers had turned the church lobby into a festive array of colors, using centerpieces made from two-foot glass candlesticks with ivy and bright red, orange, and yellow silk flowers cascading down from their tops. Tiny bags of colored Mike & Ike candies with matching ribbon were at each place. Red, orange, and yellow confetti was scattered over the white table cloths, shouting that a grand party was ready for 180 guests.

Delicious desserts started arriving in the kitchen, so many that we ran out of counter space. Some had to be set on the floor to await being cut and placed on the silver serving trays by the volunteers Henriet had summoned. The aroma of freshly-brewed coffee filled the air to accompany the platters of unbelievably beautiful desserts. All the stops had been pulled out for this legendary, first "Celebrate!" event.

And was there ever something to celebrate! By 5 p.m. on March 5, just hours before payroll checks were to be distributed, every penny of the needed $200,000 had come in to the Business Office in response to the director's five-page letter—which broke all the rules in fund raising! Usually, a good, concise, direct mail piece will bring in around $20,000 at the most. Thanks to amazing Camp donors, all the outstanding bills were paid and there was enough money left to pay the staff.

A week after the Redmond celebration, the same decorations were unloaded at the Camp's main auditorium and the event was repeated for 250 people with the staff providing the desserts and service in order to meet the health regulations that govern the Camp. For several years we continued to have these "Celebrate!" events. These have now been transformed into a yearly "Partner-in-Ministry" thank-you event that serves as a "report to the stockholders" who invest resources in the Camp.

The crisis experience was a wake-up call for the Camp. While the Lord provided for the needs of the ministry through His people in the short term, the board started setting in place what was needed to change the trajectory of our financial picture for the long haul. Under the board's guidance and the leadership of the Finance Committee, and through the work of a special task force of Daryl Miller, Preston Feight, and Bob King, the Camp has been brought to a new level of stewardship and effectiveness, with a greater safety margin in the budget in case of unforeseen events such as the aftermath of 9/11.

Still, the staff will always remember the Lord's specific words that He gave to Jehoshaphat and also to our small group: "Stand quietly and see the incredible rescue operation God will perform for you" (II Chronicles 20:17, *The Living Bible*). It is indeed a treasured story that we continue to tell to future generations.

God is **THE RESCUER**, and HE responds to the cries of HIS people when they fast and pray. The words from Eugene Peterson's paraphrase of Psalm 91:14-16 in The Message ring true for Warm Beach Camp: *"'If you hold on to me for dear life,' says God, 'I'll get you out of any trouble. I'll give you the best of care if you only get to know and trust me. Call me and I'll answer, be at your side in bad times; I'll rescue you, then throw you a party...'"*

33: THE RESTORER

As the first year anniversary of the tragic events of 9/11 was approaching, Thad and Stan were finishing up their long-awaited back-country trip around Ross Lake near the Canadian border. The weather was fantastic for sleeping under the stars, and the lake was smooth-as-glass for waterskiing. Meanwhile, back on the home front, I was helping Cherith get ready to leave for college. Just past midnight that Saturday morning, Cherith finished her visit with some high school friends and returned to her car only to find that a huge rock had been hurled through the back window of her cute little '93 blue Ford Probe.

Stan usually took care of car maintenance issues. But he wouldn't be back until Sunday evening and Cherith would be leaving us with an empty nest the following Monday morning. Cherith needed her car to commute to junior college from the home where she would be boarding. That left it up to me to be resourceful. After calling a window repair company, I found out that a new window for a Ford Probe back hatch would cost over $800 before installation. While it was a sporty car with fancy tire rims that perfectly fit Cherith's personality, it had traveled a lot of miles and wasn't worth that kind of money to repair.

I took off down the road by the lake for my early morning walk. It wasn't long before the usual pack of neighborhood dogs were trailing behind me. I often prayed out loud while walking. There was no one in sight and the animals were used to listening to my prayers. Given my tone that morning, I didn't doubt that the dogs could not fail to understand the seriousness of this situation. I cried out to God and told him that I needed HIS help. I simply didn't know what to do. Cherith needed her car Monday morning and Stan was gone. God already knew that I was a spoiled wife who never handled any maintenance issues outside the house—or in the house, for that matter. Suddenly, an idea popped into my mind. Why not call some wrecking yards to get a used window and hire someone for the installation?

Because there were a limited number of Ford Probes in circulation, I figured it would take a lot of calls to locate a back window. Phone book in hand, I made a big chart to record the calls and responses from the companies within a forty mile radius. This would no doubt be a long process, so I settled in next to the phone with a strong cup of coffee.

After explaining the need, on my very first call I waited as the clerk checked his inventory. I was shocked to hear him report that he had a back hatch window for a '93 Ford Probe. After he quoted me a $50 price I said, "Sold," and asked when they could have it popped out and ready for me to fetch. My learning curve on the wrecking yard world was just beginning!

The clerk told me that they would not remove the window, and he advised that I didn't try popping it out either. Their past experience revealed that these windows break easily. Instead, he recommended that I come and remove the whole hatch door and swap it out for the old one. I laughed and told him that my husband was on a trip and I had no mechanical ability whatsoever. He suggested that if I came right at closing time I could hire one of the guys from the yard who could perform the operation for me. But then there was the issue that the color would probably not match and, because of past experience, I informed the clerk that the repainting would cost more than a brand new window.

Almost out of patience, the man on the other end of the phone blurted out, "What color is your Probe?" I responded, "Blue." He replied, "Well, so is this one!" He then instructed me how to check the exact dye-lot on the little metal plate attached to the car's door frame. When I returned to the phone I said, "T-90 Royal Blue." And then I heard him say with a tone of disbelief, "Wow, so is this one!" I arranged to be at the yard by 4:30 p.m., right before closing, asking that one of the guys be standing by ready to do the swap.

Entering that wrecking yard was like stepping onto another planet. There were little vehicles zipping around that looked like "all-terrain vehicles" used on the moon. A guy missing a few teeth pulled up to take me to the back of the yard in order to inspect the Ford Probe hatch that he was about to take off and install on Cherith's car. I was beginning to wonder what kind of fool I was to be alone with a total stranger hidden in the midst of wrecked vehicles, when he pulled up in front of an ugly, grey-looking Probe. I quickly informed him that there must be a mistake. This was certainly not the promised T-90 Royal Blue color. He said not to worry, that the weather had discolored the paint, and with a special compound rubbed in, the original color would be restored.

Realizing that my naivete was showing, I figured the workman was pulling my leg. But a quick call on my cell phone to Cherith's future father-in-law, Bill Lee, verified that what the man was saying was indeed true: the color would most likely come back. So, without any other options in sight, I went ahead and hired this strange-looking mechanic on the spot. After paying the yard $50 for the part and an additional $100 for the labor, I drove off in a little blue Ford Probe sporting an ugly grey back hatch.

When Stan returned late Sunday night, I handed him a newly purchased can of rubbing compound to work into the ugly grey paint. Using the process as "therapy" because he was sending his only daughter off to college, Stan spent most of the night rubbing the compound into the back hatch. When we got up in the morning, there in the driveway stood Cherith's Probe with a beautiful, sparkling royal blue back hatch surrounding its window. As a matter of fact, the hatch was shinier than the rest of the car! I could hardly believe my eyes!

Sometime later I was pondering this T-90 Royal Blue incident during my early morning prayer time. It was just too divinely arranged to be a coincidence. That's when the Lord impressed on me that some people are like this too. Life has been rough and the storms they have weathered have taken away their original shine. But when the Heavenly Father rubs HIS grace into them, their lives shine brighter than the original because they reflect the glory of God! And then the

Spirit went on to inform me that God most often uses human hands to rub His grace into others.

Countless campers, volunteers, and staff have been restored at Camp as others gather around to gently apply the grace of God. Sometimes, truth spoken in love is needed, but it is done with grace. I can vouch for this because, while I am still in process, the Lord has done this in my life through the ministry at Camp.

The Father is **THE RESTORER,** and HE delights in using HIS people to rub HIS sheer pure grace into His children.

34: THE MENTOR

After Ed McDowell had been director for several years, he gathered the Camp management team together and said, "I've taken you as far as I can. You have sixty days to find yourself a mentor to get to the next level." Of course he was hoping that we could find someone who would do it at no cost, but if necessary, Ed was willing to put Camp resources behind his assignment.

In 2002, "mentor" was not yet a buzz word in leadership circles. To be honest, I wasn't even sure what a "mentor" was, nor, for that matter, what the "next level" was that I needed to attain. I began to pray, asking the Lord to guide me in this search. After all, the Almighty was all-knowing and would surely, if asked, reveal what I needed.

As a fairly new development director, to me the corporate world was like a foreign culture and entering it scared me. But it was now my job, and so, feeling no immediate spiritual nudges at that point, I decided to seek out a corporate mentor to help me understand this amazing world where people with major giving capacity seemed to reside. The trouble was, I wasn't sure how to find a corporate mentor.

A few days later I was having lunch with one of the Camp's supporters, Dee Jonson, who had hosted a table at the Journey of Faith campaign banquet. She lived just a couple miles from us, and both of us were new empty nesters as our "babies" had just graduated from high school. While devouring our favorite entrees at Red Robin, I told Dee that I needed a corporate mentor, the female version of her husband, Lou, who was a consultant in the coffee industry. Without missing a beat, Dee exclaimed, "Corporate-smorporate, you don't need one of those! You are far too serious. You work way too much the way it is. What you need, Nancy, is a 'mentor in fun!' I will be your 'mentor in fun!'"

Dee soon began to fulfill her new role, creating different kinds of outings that brought joy and relief from the pressures of raising resources for Camp. The Lord had placed this tiny 5'1" ball of fire into my life to help me let down my hair and laugh. One day, Dee phoned and asked, "Whatcha doing Saturday night? I have tickets for a Michael W. Smith concert." I had never experienced strobe lights mixed with such amazing music. Dee also taught me how to shop for my grown kids, showing me that it was okay to buy impractical things to stuff into their Christmas stockings. Without realizing it, she gave me an education regarding what it was like to be a corporate wife, for she was often left alone while her husband flew around the world to do business in coffee-producing countries.

Because I don't cry easily, Dee has cried for me when we missed our kids and faced the fact that motherhood, as we had once known it, was over. Dee certainly has specialized in laughter and helped me to not take things so seriously. When Cherith was pregnant with Preston, Dee threw a first-class baby shower by her family's swimming pool. First I and then she joyfully stepped into the realm of grandparenting, where she became a wonderful companion. We have enjoyed outings with Dee and Lou, including a dinner at our home purchased in the Camp's annual fund-raising auction.

Meanwhile, since I didn't think that "a mentor in fun" was exactly what Ed had in mind, I kept looking for a corporate mentor too. The only corporate woman I knew was Joan Wallace, who with her husband, Bob, owns Wallace Properties in Bellevue. A few years earlier Joan had served on the Camp board and I thought she might remember who I was. At least she would know Warm Beach Camp. I finally got enough nerve to contact Joan and ask her if she would consider becoming my corporate mentor. Surprisingly, Joan said she would be honored to serve in such a role. I was ready to bounce off the walls in that Joan had recently been voted "Bellevue Citizen of the Year" by the Chamber of Commerce and was well-known by everyone on the Eastside.

After sharing the news of my precious "find" with Rita Nussli, she commented, "If I had known you were looking for a mentor I would have suggested Ruth Youngsman, a newly retired businesswoman." She and her husband, Jim, had just sold Skagit Gardens in Mount Vernon. Having served with Ruth on the Youth Dynamics' board, Rita assured me Ruth would make an excellent mentor. Having already reported to Ed that Joan had agreed to be my corporate mentor, I filed Rita's suggestion away in my mind.

A few days later Joan called to tell me that she had just returned from a doctor's appointment. She had fallen ill and the doctor was recommending that she take time off and decrease her work load. Joan apologized and promised that if she regained her health, she would still love to be my mentor. I promised to pray for her and proceeded to beg God to heal Joan. Not only did her family and the business need her, but I needed her to be my corporate mentor!

With the sixty-day deadline looming, I picked up the phone and left a message for Ruth Youngsman. When Ruth returned from an overseas trip, we arranged a lunch meeting. In preparation, Ruth suggested that we pray asking the Lord to reveal what a mentor relationship would look like. Halfway into lunch Ruth shared what she felt our relationship could become. In amazement, I read her my written list which was identical to what she had just carefully outlined. It was a holy moment, and feeling so comfortable in this woman's presence, I took off my mask for a second and shared some deep feelings that were troubling me. I told her that I just couldn't shake these feelings, even though they made no rational sense.

Before the end of the meal, Ruth told me that she had training in a special kind of prayer, helping people listen to the Spirit to uncover the lies that we believe about ourselves. She asked if she could pray with me. How could I say, "No?" I had just backed myself in a corner and once again been hijacked by God. I would have never allowed myself to get into this if I'd known what was coming. I thought I needed a corporate mentor, but God knew that what I needed first was a "spiritual director" to help me uncover some of the damaging lies I had believed about myself since childhood.

Thus began many sessions with Ruth as we prayed for Jesus to reveal the lies connected to strong, detrimental emotions that were exhibiting in the present but were really connected to my past. Through the next couple of years I began to experience freedom like never before in my life. Through Ruth's loving friendship, the Holy Spirit began to transform many areas of my life, setting me free to become who God was calling me to be. I couldn't wait to sit in that big chair at their farm house in Mount Vernon and share a cup of tea while experiencing the wind of the Spirit. We also continued to meet when Ruth and Jim moved full-time to their lovely home on the waterfront by Deception Pass. Appropriately named "Eagle's Rest," it made me feel I had stepped into an oasis of grace upon entering their front door.

Midway through my adventure with Ruth, Joan Wallace called me. Her health had improved and she was ready to be my corporate mentor. To be honest, I was scared to death during that first lunch with this classy little lady who knew her way around the corporate world. When Joan inquired what I expected from her as my corporate mentor, I had to confess that I didn't really know. She was prepared to open doors for me; she had connections throughout the region. I finally shared that what I needed most was a true friendship with someone who worked in the corporate world. I needed to feel comfortable just "being" with her, a person who was from a culture so foreign to me.

Thus began the most amazing friendship with Joan. I wanted to know her dreams, about her family, and how she got to where she was: a respected civic leader, a board member at Overlake Hospital, and one of the few females invited to speak at the Seattle Rotary Club. Joan shared stories from her childhood, like when her father took her to the roof one night and encouraged her to reach for the stars. Joan treated me like a queen, taking me to restaurants around the area where the owners would come out and greet her on a first-name basis. Stan and I also enjoyed having Joan and Bob to our lake home one Sunday afternoon for our famous rib dinner.

Joan was also very generous to me. At one point, I shared the tale of my experience arriving at the five-star Keystone Resort in Colorado with a suitcase full of seminar handouts that was duct-taped shut after popping open at the airport. Joan laughed until I thought she would cry. The next time we met, she excitedly presented me with a brand new set of suitcases. Her encouraging remark was, "You are going to need these. You are going places!" Throughout the coming years I would often report to Joan where my suitcase had just been.

A few years into our friendship, it brought me great joy as I watched Joan step into one of her dreams of being involved internationally. After joining Medical Teams International's board, Joan went to Uganda for two weeks and witnessed what was happening to children whose parents had died of AIDS. After that experience she became a spokesperson for the orphans who could not speak for themselves. There were light-hearted moments too. One time, Joan laughingly shared how amazed she was when a group of former Seafair queens kidnapped her for lunch to tell her that she had been chosen to be the next queen to oversee Seattle's famous Seafair that coming August. I couldn't think of anyone more deserving to reign over such an event.

In 2006 I was asked to give a workshop on "Mentoring for a Lifetime" at the Camp's women's retreat. After reading a few books on mentoring, I began my presentation by outlining some principles and quoted a few formal definitions from the experts. Then I shared my definition: "mentoring is what happens when the Holy Spirit connects with two human spirits and the transfer of grace happens both ways." From my experiences I had found mentoring to be more like a dance, not a drill, bringing joy to both parties in the relationship.

I captured the women's attention as I told how God had so graciously answered my prayer, supplying me with three mentors—the best in the world—to come alongside and inject the grace I needed to grow in areas that would help me begin to "reach for the stars." Part way through that workshop my eyes found Joan, smiling in the audience. At the end she came to the front and, putting her arm around me, shared with the women how meaningful the mentorship relationship had been for her as well.

The Spirit of the Lord is really **THE MENTOR**, the best mentor a child of the King can have! He knows us better than we know ourselves. He oftentimes works though others who are willing to speak the truth in love. While mentoring is a lifetime process, sometimes it's as simple as just being a friend, creating an environment of grace where we feel loved, just as we are.

35: THE STRATEGIC "J.J."

It all started with cinnamon rolls. In 2000 the Camp began an annual auction to raise money. Since the auction's inception, one of the hottest items has been the Camp's yummy cinnamon rolls. People will bid outrageous amounts to get their hands on them. In 2001 this highly coveted auction item included a couple dozen delivered every month, and the Overton family secured the winning bid.

One month I delivered the treats to the Overtons' lovely home near Snohomish, Washington, about forty-five minutes from Camp. While the family had been to the Homeschool Outdoor Education Camp at Warm Beach, I had not officially met them. After arranging a specific time for the delivery, I inquired if I could take a few minutes to get to know them. Upon arrival, I was ushered into their living room and the entire family, including five children ages three through sixteen, sat staring at me.

After being introduced to the entire clan, I learned that they had moved up from Silicon Valley in California to be closer to their aging parents who lived in Vancouver, B.C., across the Canadian border. John owed a software company and had staff in other parts of the United States, with clients as far away as France. The Overtons hoped someday to live closer to Camp so their kids could be more involved.

During that first encounter, I found out what kind of home they would be looking for and filed the information away in my memory. They needed a large house with enough bedrooms for their children and a large space for home schooling. John would need office space for the business. Then Carolyn, the mom, tacked on that they would like land for some horses along with a view of the water.

In 2001, the family started volunteering to work at *The Lights of Christmas* (LOC). Carolyn would often be with the younger children at the petting farm or toyshop. John wore a security vest and "walked the beat" a half a dozen nights each December. They were intimately acquainted with the event and what it took to get an entire family placed into the correct slots for multiple nights.

By 2001, coordinating the 500+ volunteers for nineteen to twenty-one nights each December had grown into an overwhelming task still managed with a huge notebook and a pencil. All confirmations were done by hand and snail-mailed, with the individual descriptions for each job included. The Overtons' bulging packet required extra postage: since the family liked variety, rotating the entire clan through different positions during the event, there were many additional sheets of paper covering each person for each day and activity.

Theresa Smiley, my amazing assistant, transformed into the LOC Volunteer Coordinator every October. The phone was attached to her ear through December and she went through many pencils and erasers before the intense pressure ended in January. Toward the end of the run in 2002, Theresa threw up her hands and declared, "By the next LOC, this volunteer confirmation process must be computerized!" The volunteer scheduling task was on the verge of becoming humanly impossible. I knew she was right, but even if we had the money to purchase a computer program, we were certain that there wouldn't be any software developed that could do this unique and monstrous task. So we began to pray for a computer programmer.

From my memory bank, John Overton's name surfaced. Theresa looked up when he would be volunteering next. That night, after he left the staff dining room, like a couple of undercover spies we followed him on the sidewalk heading to Deer Mountain Lodge. When the moment was right, Theresa and I surrounded him on both sides, leaning into him so that he couldn't get away if he tried to flee.

Before losing my nerve I blurted out, "John, you are a computer whiz kid, right?!" His hesitant "Yes" didn't give me much confidence that he would give a favorable response to our request but I proceeded to do "the ask" anyway. "We need a program written that will do everything to computerize the LOC volunteer process except greet the volunteers when they arrive." And then to make sure he realized this would be a donation, I quickly added, "And we have NO money; we would need you do this as a volunteer."

His response took forever, and I feared my request was out of line and too audacious to fulfill. John's face looked like he might be fighting back tears. Finally he found his voice and said, "I have been asking the Lord what I could do to help the Camp with my computer skills." At that moment we all realized that the Lord was way ahead of us! After John's "Yes!" he added, "Besides, it would get me out of walking around all night in the cold wearing this security vest!" Theresa and I were floating on air as we hurried back to Cedar Lodge to dance around the office, screaming with joy.

During the following months, John met with everyone in the Camp who would interface with the software he was about to engineer. After careful study, he devised a program that would allow the volunteer coordinator to assign volunteers to roles and at the same time print out their confirmations with the accompanying job descriptions on the same page, ready for mailing. The confirmation even had a calendar, displaying the days of the LOC they would be working. With the push of a button, a list of volunteer positions which were still needed could be printed to be left on the tables in the volunteer dining room. John had the program running in time to book the volunteers that fall, And during that LOC, the "security-guard turned-computer-whiz-kid" sat in the Development Office every night to make certain that the program was running correctly. God had lined up the very best!

For several years afterward, John kept asking how we wanted the LOC software improved, and we all continued to work on it. Today, everything is done on-line, including filling out the volunteer request forms with one's desired choices, and receiving the confirmations as well. There is still the tedious process of placement, but now two staff members can do the task at the same time. During 2016, over 750 people were inputted into the system to report for volunteer duty at the LOC.

In 2004 while I was having "windshield time" with Ed McDowell, he shared that they were going to put their home overlooking Puget Sound and the Camp's horse stables on the market. I told him not to bother—that I already had a buyer. Quickly I called the Overtons to let them know I found their house, right next to Camp! And, it had everything they were looking for, except the land for the horses. But there was no need to fret: they could enjoy the Camp's horses without having to pay the feed or vet bills.

After purchasing Ed's home, the Overtons have become part of the Camp's extended staff family. Carolyn helps organize our kitchen for the annual 4th of July party so that we can accommodate up to 130 at our home on the lake. Her craft skills have come in handy in designing and sewing costumes for the horse vaulting team. The Overton children have all worked at Camp, wrangling horses, working in food services, hanging lights, and acting and stage managing for the LOC Dinner Theater play. Their oldest daughter, Lydia, met her husband, Curtis, when he headed up the light hangers. Their youngest, Luke, is now seventeen years old and can be found working at the stables when he's not flying through the air vaulting on the back of a cantering horse.

Every August when the "Kids 2 Camp" auction rolls around, John heads up the auction tent, supervising the volunteer team and spreading computer-generated bid sheets next to the items, including cinnamon rolls. John is still using his computer skills to help tweak the auction software so as to try the latest techniques. The Overtons' company puts up part of the matching money each year to make certain that no children are left behind because of their inability to pay for Camp.

God is **THE STRATEGIC "J.J.,"** Jehovah-Jireh (the Provider), and HE is way ahead of us, strategizing details that we have yet to realize are needed. And when necessary, He can even move an entire family into position to get HIS Kingdom work accomplished by enticing them with cinnamon rolls!

36: GRACE FULL

It was toward the end of 2002 and the Journey of Faith campaign had been wrapped up successfully with the $6.5 million goal achieved and the projects underway. After a slight pause, we would begin another huge campaign. I continued to make visits to donors, thanking them and keeping them connected to the exciting ministry happening at Camp.

One day while finishing a delightful visit with Miriam Goodnight in her beautiful mother-in-law apartment attached to her son and daughter-in-law's home, I asked if there was anything I could pray about for her. She quickly shared that she would like me to ask God for a reading partner. My puzzled look caused her to explain that, even though she was in her late seventies, she loved reading deep books about spiritual things. Most of her friends no longer enjoyed reading, and she longed for someone to review books with her. Upon leaving this new-found friend, I promised to pray for God to grant her request.

After visiting Miriam I attended the M.J. Murdock Trust's Leadership Advance. One of the speakers, Dr. Walter Wright, suggested that every Christian leader should read Henri Nouwen's little book, *In Jesus' Name*, at least once a year. Matter of fact, the Trust sent us home with a copy. The next time I visited Miriam, I told her about reading this short book and how much I needed Henri's warning to Christian leaders based on the three temptations of Jesus during his time in the wilderness. Miriam quickly went to her book shelf and pulled down another book and said, "If you loved that one, you will really love reading Nouwen's *Return of the Prodigal.*" Indeed, Miriam was right. In just a short time I had become a "Henri-fan!"

Every few months I would return to Miriam's little home where she would be waiting with another book. She introduced me to Brennan Manning's writings, starting with *The Ragamuffin Gospel*. Without me realizing it, Miriam had me on a crash course for "Grace 101." It soon became obvious that I had become the answer to her prayer! Also, without either of us aware of it at the time, the Lord was setting the stage for me to receive family members into my arms while being able to say, "Yes, I forgive you because God has forgiven me."

During that same time I had a most interesting "thank-you" visit with another senior donor, Dorothy Rosenberger. The year before, Dorothy had initiated her own little fund-raising campaign to get a piano for the Camp. She had recruited others to make it possible for a brand new upright to grace one of the Camp's meeting rooms. I had tried at that time to arrange a "thank-you" visit with Dorothy, who was a force to be reckoned with, but she had replied, "Let's wait until it's a good time." Time passed, until out of the blue one day Dorothy called to inform me, "Next week would be great time for that lunch: my husband will be out of town."

I arrived at Mitzell's on 128th in Everett and reserved a table. After an hour of waiting I ordered my favorite salad and figured that Dorothy had forgotten. The waitress was just delivering my entrée when Dorothy roared up to the table apologizing. She had gone up and down Everett Mall Way looking for the restaurant until she at last remembered it was on 128th. As Dorothy sat down she thrust a book by Joyce Meyer at me; it was entitled *Knowing God Intimately* (Faithwords, 2003).

To be perfectly honest, I had never heard of this author, and if I had gone into a bookstore, I would not have been prone to buy a book with the author's picture masking the cover as this one was. But Dorothy insisted that I read it, saying, "You really need this, Nancy. Skip the first four chapters; those are basic stuff and you already know it. Start with Chapter Five!" Wow! While I hardly knew Dorothy, I felt as if the Lord had just given me a homework assignment.

By the time our late lunch finished, I got on I-5 only to find myself stuck in rush-hour traffic and sitting on the freeway. Intrigued by the unusual event that had just happened, out of curiosity I opened the book with its blue and white cover to Chapter Five, entitled, "Not by Might, Nor by Power, but by My Spirit." Unbeknownst to anyone, I had been struggling to make things happen in my job and dreading the thought of another campaign. The first campaign, while miraculously completed, had taken the wind right out of my sails. The 9/11 tragedy had happened right in the middle of the campaign, and the thought of another big campaign made me want to run away to Never Never Land with Peter Pan and inhale some fairy dust.

Somewhere on I-5, I realized that the Lord had sent this senior citizen to remind me that I couldn't make anything happen through my own strength. Matthew 11 and "the unforced rhythms of grace" kept resurfacing in my mind. Upon returning home I devoured the book that I would never have purchased myself.

In Chapter Seven, Meyer goes on to explain about grace: *"Grace is a wonderful thing. It is the power by which men are saved through their faith in Jesus Christ as Paul tells us in Ephesians 2:8. …The Holy Spirit ministers grace to us from God the Father. Grace is actually the (Holy Spirit's) power flowing out from the throne of God toward men to save them and enable them to live holy lives and accomplish the will of God…I had always heard that grace is God's unmerited favor, which it is; however, it is much more than that. When I learned that grace is the power of the Holy Spirit available to me to do with ease what I could not do by striving, I got excited about grace. I began to cry out to God for grace, grace, and more grace"* (page 102).

And that is exactly what I did. I began to earnestly cry out to God for HIS grace. I went on a search for passages on grace in the Bible and my memory was refreshed with verses like, "My grace is sufficient for you, for my power is made perfect in weakness" (II Cor 12:9). I began resting in our big living room prayer chair in the early mornings, asking God to soak me in His grace. This was before I had even heard anything about the "soaking movement" that was going around charismatic circles.

But that wasn't my only take-away from Chapter Seven. Meyer goes on to share: *"In Zechariah 4 we read of a group of people who were trying to rebuild the temple and who came up against much opposition. Satan always opposes the work of God. In verses 5 and 7 KJV the angel of the Lord told the prophet that the assigned task would be accomplished, 'Not by might, not by power, but by my spirit, saith the LORD of hosts.' The people were promised that the grace of God would turn their mountains into molehills and that they would finish the temple, crying out, 'Grace, grace unto it.' We usually try to push our mountains out of the way with our own strength when we should be calling on the Spirit of Grace to make it easy"* (page 102-103).

Wow! That little passage challenged me to pray my way through Zechariah, the next-to-last book of the Old Testament. Even the introduction to this book of the Bible by Eugene Peterson in *The Message* shot encouragement into me. Peterson claims that Zechariah's "poetically charged messages are at work still, like time capsules in the lives of God's people, continuing to release insight and hope and clarity for the people whom God is using to work out his purposes in a world that has no language for God and the purposes of God."

Here was a prophet encouraging his people in the huge task of rebuilding the temple. I could somehow identify with Zechariah as the Camp, now almost fifty years old, needed major repairs and renovations to be preserved for future generations. I began praying my way through Zechariah, using the language found in the paraphrases of *The Message* and applying it to Warm Beach Camp (WBC): Thank-you, Lord, that you "care deeply" for WBC (1:14); Thank you that you are "going into action" for WBC (1:15); Thank you, Lord, that You will "see to it that" WBC is rebuilt (1:16); Thank you that You already have "the rebuilding operation staked out" (1:16); Thank you that you will "be right here" for WBC (2:5); Thank you, Lord, that you are "a radiant presence within" WBC (2:5).

On and on I prayed through Zechariah, choosing key phrases out of *The Message* for WBC. My favorite passage is in Chapter 4, for it is God's message to WBC: "You can't force these things. They only come about through my Spirit ... So, big mountain, who do you think you are?" Thank you, God, that you "will proceed to set the Cornerstone in place accompanied by cheers: Yes! Yes! Yes! Do it!" Thank you God that WBC has started the rebuilding and YOU, Lord, "will complete it...Does anyone despise this day of small beginnings?"

I continued to be infused with excitement by praying Zechariah 6:15: Thank-you, Lord that people are coming "from faraway places to pitch in and rebuild" WBC. This is confirmation that the "God-of-the-Angel-Armies," in fact is in this. Lord, help us at WBC "to put our minds to a life of responsive obedience" to your voice, God ... on and on, with every chapter containing gems to turn into prayers, like Zechariah 10:5: Lord, help us to "be a workforce to be proud of, working as one ... courageous and vigorous" because you, Lord, are with us.

And by far, one of my favorite passages is Zechariah 12:10: "Lord, pour out a spirit of grace" over WBC, and then later, as in Zechariah 13:1: Lord, open a fountain for all who come onto the grounds of WBC so that they experience your grace to have their sins washed away. Lord, the timing is yours—Abba's timing— when "every evening will be a fresh morning" as in Zechariah 14:6-7. What a day that will be, with "fresh-flowing rivers" out of WBC, flowing year-round, summer and winter! And God will be king over all of WBC, "One God and only one. What a day that will be!"

And, in the same manner as Zechariah 14 concludes, I too prayed: thank-you, Lord, that all the horses' harness bells will be inscribed "Holy to God." Thank you, Lord, that, "in fact, all the pots and pans" in the kitchen of WBC "will be holy" to you, God-of-the-Angel-Armies. I love the fact that Zechariah ends up in the kitchen, for that's where I started at Warm Beach Camp, and it is still my first love in camping! When I need a "pick-me-up," which is nearly once a month, I turn to Zechariah, and pray my way through again, releasing some of the amazing "time capsules" of prayer found there.

God is **GRACE FULL!** And HE used two of His precious messengers, seasoned saints, to bring it to my attention! Miriam called me several days before she died in 2013 and I spent a couple of hours with her two days before she stepped into eternity. Dorothy was in the nursing home right next to Camp, commanding the troops until she too slipped into Heaven this past August. Whenever I think of her today, I am instantly reminded of the day she gave me a book that steered me to Zechariah 4:6, and caused me to cry out for grace and more grace!

37: THE EMBRACER

It was 9:30 p.m. on a December night in 2003 during the second week of *The Lights of Christmas.* I was preparing to exit, heading home to pack for a Christian Camping International conference, when my cell phone rang. A close friend needed someone to sit with his young children while he took his wife to the emergency room. Instead of turning to the right as usual, I immediately turned left as I got onto Marine Drive. After sleeping on our friends' couch for few hours as a babysitter, I returned home and put off the packing until the next morning when we were due to fly out of Sea-Tac Airport.

It was near dawn when Stan crawled around in the attic to find our suitcases. Two extra ones would be needed to carry the handouts for the seminar sessions I would be presenting. I was co-teaching a seminar on "Grantsmanship" with Bart Hadder from the M.J. Murdock Trust. While December is a busy time at Camp, Director Ed McDowell thought it was important that I go, even though the trip was not in the Camp's budget.

We made it to the airport in time to catch our flight, but not without a lot of stress. Later that night, Stan and I pulled up to the lovely Keystone Conference Center in Colorado in our rental car. I was exhausted and had no energy left to cope. In trying to keep our costs to a minimum, we had reserved a room at The Inn, a part of the Keystone complex located a mile from the conference center, where we could prepare our own breakfasts.

We arrived very late in the evening, and I could hardly comprehend the registrar's words as she informed me that they had just given away their last room at The Inn. There was no room for us in The Inn on that dark, snowy night! But before I had the chance to say anything, the registrar quickly told me that they would upgrade us to the hotel in the main conference center. I knew what that would cost and was about to melt down when she graciously declared, "Since this was our mistake, there will be no additional charge." Still, I was concerned that we have a refrigerator, and the only rooms with refrigerators were at The Inn, which would now be a mile away from our room. The registrar assured me that they would have a refrigerator delivered to our room in the hotel.

When we pulled up to the grand Keystone Hotel, everyone from the bellman to the desk clerk treated us like royalty. The bellman insisted on hanging our three plastic bags of groceries from the luggage cart hooks. Everyone in the beautifully decorated lobby could see our yogurt, milk, cereal and juice swaying from side to side as he pushed the cart onto the elevator. In addition to our luggage, we also had two beat-up suitcases full of seminar handouts. One had come open at the airport so the airline had duct-taped it shut. We looked like country bumpkins arriving at the palace!

Five minutes after they ushered us into a gorgeous five-star suite, the hotel staff arrived with a little refrigerator which perfectly held our food. We were in the lap of luxury, complete with two televisions, a kitchenette area, a huge living room, and a spiral staircase ascending to the master bedroom with a king-sized bed. Soft music played in the background and the covers were pulled down, with warm chocolate-chip cookies in a wrapper on the pillow! The next morning, we opened our curtains, which covered the windows across one entire side of the room on both floors, to behold a spectacular view of the mountains. We were just two minutes from the room where I would be presenting my seminar sessions.

I had been at the end of my rope with no energy left. My resources had been totally depleted by the effort to get to the conference. But in that instant, the Lord had gathered me in His arms, and used His people—whether they knew Him or not—to center me and calm me down. I felt His presence, I smelled His breath. He was very near. He had not tested me further than I could go. He embraced me there in Keystone, Colorado. I was Abba's child, and He was taking care of me in royal style.

For years, ever since becoming the development director at Warm Beach Camp in 1998, I had prayed Matthew 11 from *The Message,* crying, "God, take me in your arms, pull me close, let me feel your heart beat, let me smell your breath. I want to work with You and watch how You do it. Teach me Your unforced rhythms of grace." And so it was that after my Keystone Embrace experience, I started journaling:

> "Lord, thanks for the Keystone experience. It will be a key. It will be a rock that I come back to that will remind me of your love, your care and your faithfulness…Lord we have risked the Camp to follow what we thought you were asking us to do…God of the Universe, we are here, ordinary; do the extraordinary though us. We are ready…Lord, do a Keystone experience for our entire Camp. Through all Your people, saved and non-saved alike, do a Keystone… wrap Your arms around WBC, show us the way. Oh Lord, we are always out there, ahead of resources; resource your ministry. Show us the way; Your ways are higher than ours. We have limited views, we go for the low-cost options, the mile-away option when You have the extravagant solution…God, we limit you; I limit you. Forgive me." Then I began praying that "the Lord would let me be a part of a Keystone Embrace in someone else's life."

I ended with,

> "Now do a Keystone on WBC. We are pushed to the limit—our finances, our physical energies, our carpets, our grass; everything is pushed to the limit. Oh God, do a Keystone on WBC, using Christians and non-Christians—your people. God, circle the Camp; all your resources belong to You whether they are in the hands of nonbelievers or believers. Circle this place with Your glory. God, we want to be a light in the darkness. We want people to see Your incredible

power. We want YOU to shine in the darkness. It's Your firm foundation and love that we are building on. Dispense that grace and love through us to all people—Angel Tree kids, foster kids. Flow Your power through us. Lord, it's in You we trust: do a Keystone save on Warm Beach Camp."

When I returned to work the next morning, I started telling Maggie Allen, Ed's assistant, about the Keystone Embrace concept and read a few paragraphs from my journal. Maggie asked if I knew what a keystone was. I replied, "No, we were just at the Keystone Conference Center in Colorado for the CCI convention." Maggie quickly looked up the definition of "keystone" in the dictionary: "The central, topmost stone or piece of an arch, which holds the others in place." We both stood there spellbound. Maggie declared, "Nancy, I think this has something to do with the next campaign."

After visiting several donors that afternoon, I returned to the Camp. Maggie proudly presented me with a drawing and description of a keystone arch which she had found on the internet. Early the next morning, I pulled out the diagram of a keystone arch that Maggie had given me. I began to concentrate on it and began to journal:

Lord, sometimes You allow others to do a keystone, but You are the Keystone. The others are just the stones that take the pressure and transfer it—just the right number of stones. But it's You, God, the Keystone, who holds it all together. Help us to know how to gather all the stones, how to hook them together, the right number to have, which of Your people You want for this embrace. You are the central locking stone. You bear the pressure; this pressure pushes on the stones next to You on both sides. The pressure is relayed from stone to stone. God we need to know who the stones are for WBC. Line up the stones, form a "Keystone save" around WBC. Form an arch of stones; rebuild the walls. Lord, we need the stones; call them forth…

I went on to ask God to identify the two bottom blocks, the "springers," for the keystone arch. As I sat there I realized that the WBC Board was the springer at the bottom of one side of the arch, and the prayer team would be the springer on the other side. Once the prayer team was in place, we could begin praying over the next campaign as it was being organized.

Searching the scriptures, I found Psalm 118:22: "The stone the builders rejected has become the capstone." In the NIV translation "capstone" had a footnote indicating that it could also be the keystone of an arch with a connection to Zechariah 4:7. The word is also interchangeable with one describing a large stone used to anchor and align the corner of a wall, or "cornerstone." The cornerstone for all Christians is Jesus Christ, who is central at Camp. The key phrase that our Camp staff knows by heart is, "Keeping the path clear to the cross." For example, Stan "the nativity man" and his crew place the Camp's larger than life-size nativity scene at the center of the grounds every Thanksgiving weekend before *The Lights of Christmas* begins. All the other parts of the LOC are anchored by and radiate from that center.

When it came time to name the new campaign, there was no doubt in my mind that it would have something to do with this "Keystone embrace." With the support of the Board and the foundational intercession of the prayer team, in 2005 the Camp launched its second major campaign, Embracing the Vision. In addition to the outfall for the new waste water treatment plant, the campaign provided for major upgrades to the Camp's heavily used facilities, including a remodel of Cedar Lodge, the main administration building which in addition to many offices houses the dining room, kitchen, camp store, and a large meeting room.

The campaign brochure carried this scripture on its cover: "God is building … now he is using you, fitting you in … with Jesus Christ as the cornerstone that holds all the parts together…" (Ephesians 2:20-22, *The Message*).

God is **THE EMBRACER**. He is the one who calls forth HIS living stones to embrace Warm Beach Camp. The campaign had many surprises, including more streams of ministry to the marginalized. And there was an unexpected donation from a donor who wanted to put in a new sprinkler system for the Cedar Lodge lawn to keep the grass green—something that Stan as grounds manager had dreamed of for years.

38: THE LORD OF THE DANCE

Dancing wasn't on the "no-no" list at my home church, but the youth group always had an alternate activity planned as a substitute for the dances at the high school. I did go to the senior prom with a fellow who served with me as a co-editor of the Roosevelt High School newspaper, *The Standard*. But because neither of us knew how to dance, dressed in our formal attire, we watched our fellow students dance the night away.

Years later, part-way into my career journey in camp development, I began to add on to Eugene Peterson's paraphrase of Matthew 11, praying: *"Lord, take me in your arms, draw me close, let me feel your heart beat. I want to work with you, I want to watch how you do it. I want to dance with you to your unforced rhythms of grace."* What an unusual thing to pray, especially for someone who didn't know how to dance!

Oh, I had faked it at Thad and Abby's wedding when it came time for the mother of the groom to dance with her son. It was one of the most awkward moments of my life as there wasn't time for dance lessons. Thankfully, when Chad and Cherith's wedding reception arrived some years later, it was Stan's turn to dance with the bride. A few numbers following, I was able to blend in with the crowd when dancing with Stan to show my support of the event.

Where our daughter and grandson got the "dancing gene" is a mystery indeed! Cherith managed to get invited to every dance during high school, including Chad's senior prom when she was a freshman. Her closet contained a beautiful array of formals to commemorate each fancy occasion. Several years later Cherith and her husband were married and she gave birth to their son, Preston. When he was three, as the ring bearer dressed in a tiny tux, he stole the show at their friends' wedding reception. After the DJ announced the dance for the bride and groom, when the music started Preston took to the dance floor alone, entertaining the crowd in his shiny black shoes. He continued to dance the entire evening with anyone willing to partner with him.

During 2005 I foolishly made a promise to dance. We were midway through the long nine-month period waiting to receive word from the M.J. Murdock Trust regarding a $490,000 grant request to help fund the renovation and expansion of Cedar Lodge. This was larger than the $320,000 Murdock grant we had received for the waste water treatment plant. As a matter of fact, when Gary Kocher and I had written the grant proposal, I knew it was a stretch, but we needed that much money. Our first program officer at Murdock, Terry Stokesbary, had advised us concerning the size of a grant a camp like Warm Beach could expect, and our $490,000 was out of the range. Our current program officer, Bart Hadder, had essentially agreed. Feeling pretty safe, then, I told the development staff that I would dance on my desk if the Trust awarded our Camp the full amount of our grant request.

A few months before we were to receive word on the trustees' decision, I shared with Carl Dusek, a Camp supporter in his 90's, the dancing promise I had made to the team. Carl had come alongside us through the years, and had made it possible for hundreds of kids to come to Camp. We used to talk a lot about his investment in eternity. While Carl, a World War II prisoner of war, didn't have any children of his own, he provided a way for children to meet the Savior at Camp. For years, every month Carl would hand Gary Kocher a huge check for the Kids 2 Camp Program. A few days later, I would hand-deliver the receipt.

We engineered all kinds of different ways to package that delivery. Many times he would have dessert and coffee waiting for me in his manufactured home in the senior community, the one with bars covering the windows. After his experience in the POW camps, Carl did not like crowds and his sense of safety had forever been damaged. We expanded into having lunch at local restaurants, picnics at Camano State Park on sunny days, and tiptoeing through the tulip fields in LaConner.

Gary and I would throw Carl's birthday party at the lake every year, as Carl had no family nearby. And most of all, I just listened to Carl tell stories of the sacrifices that soldiers made for our freedom and shared memories from his younger days, including how he loved to dance. Carl had won trophies at dancing contests. Even during his golden years, after his wife died he took to cruising around the world. One of the things he loved about cruising was the dance floor. Carl never had trouble finding partners. He would dance with anyone needing a partner as the cruise ships graced the ocean seas.

Upon hearing my promise to my team, Carl posed a question: "Do you even know how to dance?" I burst out laughing and shared my dance-less tales with him. Instead of practicing our dance steps for the senior prom, my date, who was also the captain of the swimming team, and I had swum across a lake late at night in the moonlight. Thankfully, my swimming skills were much better than my dancing!

Carl saw his chance and blurted out with glee, "Then I will teach you to dance!" I had backed myself into a corner! Was I serious about this? Did I have enough faith to believe that God would answer our prayers and give us the entire $490,000? It was like the tale of the man who showed up wearing his waders at the Midwestern meeting where they had gathered to pray for rain during a serious drought. Would I be ready? After all, the campaign's prayer team were praying and trusting God for the full amount of the grant. The day the Murdock trustees were to meet was even on the prayer calendar so that the team could pray in one accord.

Thus began my dancing lessons in Carl's kitchen. I warned him that my desk top was small; as a matter of fact, when Jack Henry ("Duke" from the Accommodations Department) heard my promise, having cleaned my office for years he declared, "You are going to have to clean your desk off!" So, Carl and I practiced a simple three-step dance routine that would fit on the top of a desk.

In his last call before the trustees would meet to vote, Bart Hadder posed the question, "What will the Camp do if the Trust does not award the entire

$490,000 requested?" Since we had already been warned that this was an amount higher than would likely be awarded for a camp our size, I was ready for this question. I knew the right answer: the Cedar Lodge renovation was our top priority and we would just have to find a way to make it happen by rearranging other priorities or seeking funding from another source yet to be uncovered.

I can remember where I was on the I-405 freeway when my cell phone rang. It was Bart, and he couldn't wait to share the news! The trustees had voted to award the Camp the full $490,000 requested! It took me a moment to blurt out, "Oh, my, that means I will have to dance on my desk!" After a brief explanation to Bart about my promise, he said, "You mean you wouldn't have danced if it had been less than $490,000?" I declared, "No, I thought I was pretty safe!" He replied, "Well, if I was a betting man, I would have bet you were pretty safe too!"

In order to stall for more time, I told the development team that we would need all the required pledges in hand for the total project before I would dance on my desk. The deadline was December 31, 2009. Thanks to many faithful supporters responding to our plea, on the very last day we reached the total project goal of $2.52 million. In January the letter came from the Murdock Trust verifying that the $490,000 would be given to the Camp as soon as we needed the funds.

We moved the "dance floor" to the top of the table in Director Ed McDowell's office so that the development team could witness the occasion. On my office wall today is a large photo of me, with the award letter in hand, dancing on the table top with the development staff gathered around. Along with the board and Major Donor Committee, the staff had all worked very hard to make this victory dance a reality. And trust me: it didn't look anything like what Carl had tried so hard to teach me!

I still run into people who tell me they saw a picture on Bart Hadder's wall before he retired from the M.J. Murdock Trust. It showed a lady who looked a lot like me dancing on her desk. Word soon permeated the extended Camp community at the time, and one Camp board member's husband still doesn't know if he wants his wife hanging around a woman who dances on tables!

God is **THE LORD OF THE DANCE**. And HE is delighted to take HIS children in HIS arms and dance to the "unforced rhythms of grace" which are set in motion by HIS heartbeat. His dance floor spans the universe and HE's ready to partner at any time, no matter how inexperienced we are!

39: THE COMMISSIONER

It was the spring of 2004 when I received a call from our daughter, Cherith. She inquired, "Mom, I know it's short notice, but do you want to go to a women's retreat with our church at The Firs Camp in Bellingham this coming weekend?" Cherith went on to tell me that she hoped to recruit her mother-in-law, Lauri, and sister-in-law, Abby, and a friend to go with us.

I smiled as Cherith went on to tell me all about Women's Retreat and how much fun it would be in addition to the teaching from God's Word. They were having a special speaker from the headquarters of the parent denomination of the New Life Four Square Church where she and Chad worshipped in Everett. Cherith had no idea that I had helped plan women's retreats for years at Warm Beach Camp. Neither did she know that the coming weekend was packed full of previous commitments with Camp supporters, including a dinner at our lake home.

But deep in my spirit the Lord confirmed the importance of attending this retreat. I prayed that donors would understand. After a series of calls, all commitments were rescheduled and even our Camp supporters were thrilled that I would be able to have this special time with my daughter. When I called Cherith back she excitedly reported that everyone else in our soon-to-be-cabin group had said, "Yes."

We felt like teenagers as we dragged our suitcases up the stairs of the dormitory at The Firs. Cherith was pregnant with Preston so she needed extra rest to be able to return to work on Monday. But we managed to slip in lots of laughter and late night conversations while drifting off to sleep. The teaching times were excellent as the keynote speaker, a mature woman of God, brought the scriptures alive for us with a particularly prophetic tone.

Like most women, we enjoyed the meals immensely because someone else was responsible for the cooking and clean-up. Our job was simply to show up on time! We walked around the grounds and did a craft during the free time. To be honest, this was only my second time actually being a camper at a women's retreat. Another time I had stayed overnight with some women from our church, but somehow, there was still the feeling of being responsible within me. This was refreshingly different!

Nothing prepared me for the last general session. At the end of her presentation, the speaker asked all the participants twenty-five years and younger to stand up. Then she instructed all women over twenty-five years of age to gather around the younger ones and lay our hands on them. Conveniently, I was between Cherith and Abby, so it was easy to lay a hand on each of them. The speaker then led us in a commissioning prayer for the younger generation. It was very unexpected, but overwhelmingly powerful. The Spirit blows where HE wills, and there was no doubt that the Spirit was directing the speaker's words for all to ponder as we commissioned this younger generation for great work in the Kingdom of God.

As I kept one hand on Abby and the other on Cherith, the speaker advised us not to put any expectations on these younger women to use the same methods that had worked in our generation. She also prophesied that some of these younger women would go on for further training in order to reach many for Jesus in traditional full-time ministry. Without missing a beat, she also shared that we were commissioning the rest of this younger generation to reach their neighbors and love people right where God would plant them in their neighborhoods and everyday working worlds.

It was a powerful moment. Abby and Thad were just getting ready to leave for Kentucky so Abby could begin her Masters of Divinity program at Asbury Seminary. Cherith was in the banking industry and had a knack for making instant friends. She has always had a kind spirit and can see through people's baggage, connecting with them at the heart level. Here I was, positioned in between the two most important young women in my life, and the Lord was allowing me to be a channel through which HIS Spirit was commissioning them into further Kingdom work!

Abby did receive her master's degree at seminary and served as the children's pastor at the Warm Beach Free Methodist Church for several years. Then Abby served with Sister Connection, assisting Denise Patch with administrative work. While Abby is now pastoring her own little family, she also serves part time at the Hillcrest Community Chapel in Mount Vernon. On occasion, she sometimes fills the pulpit at The Church of God on the Tulalip Reservation when their pastor needs a break. We rearrange our schedules at a minute's notice to hear Pastor Abby preach! Abby is loved by all, including all the children who flock around her. Watching her reminds me of what Jesus said: "Let the little children come to me!"

Cherith went on to pursue a career at Boeing in Everett. Chad and Cherith bought a house in Lake Stevens on a cul-de-sac, where they have reached out to their neighbors and friends. They have at times "laid down their lives for their friends," reaching out in love to meet a need and provide shelter or a sense of community during a rough patch in the road. When we attended our grandson Preston's baptism, we watched Chad place his own son under the water as Pastor Daniel of The Bridge Church said the words, "We baptize Preston in the name of the Father, Son, and Holy Spirit." As I looked around the congregation, I saw many of their precious friends whom they had introduced to Jesus.

In 2015, the Warm Beach Camp staff had their annual retreat at The Firs Conference Center. When I saw the dormitory where the five of us ladies had spent that blessed weekend, it awakened warm memories and a deep joy within.

We know **THE COMMISSIONER**, the Spirit of God, who woos us into service for Jesus and fills us with HIS transforming grace to do the Kingdom work he calls us to do. He commissions us just as we are, knowing how He has uniquely fashioned us as conduits of HIS grace to others.

40: THE CONSPIRATOR

During the early 1980's I was excited to be part of a small group of camping professionals to hear Tom Sine speak at The Firs Camp in Bellingham. His new book, *The Mustard Seed Conspiracy* (Word Books, 1981) was hot off the press.

Dr. Sine began to challenge the group because we were only providing camp for middle to upper class white kids; what about the rest? As a food service director struggling to manage on a shoe-string budget, I was miffed: what could I do?! Even if we eliminated all the whip cream roses from the desserts for the year, it would not fund one poor kid to camp. Anger set in. I had wasted a day at this conference only to return with a wheelbarrow full of guilt that I couldn't unload. It left me agitated because deep inside I knew Dr. Sine was right!

Fast forward to 2005. Midway through a lunch with Susan Ho, one of the Camp's amazing supporters, I had just mustered up enough courage to ask if she would be willing to participate in the feasibility study for the Embracing the Vision campaign which was about to taxi down the runway. Her immediate answer was, "NO!" Little did I realize what she was about to suggest in the next few moments.

Just as I was wishing I could disappear and pretend this meeting never happened, Susan surprised me by outlining a carefully-crafted plan. "Here's what Larry and I want to do: we want to help the poorest-of-the-poor children get to Camp, and we are willing to put money behind this!" Then she went on to explain that they wanted these kids to be followed up all year-long. While finishing the rest of my salad, I told her I would have to check with our director, Ed McDowell, to see if with our limited staff we could meet the conditions of the gift she had just offered.

After that lunch, a heaviness overcame me. I felt like I was slipping into depression. Thoughts of inadequacy whirled through my mind; victories that had been preciously won as I tackled the development job were vanishing. But after a few hours, I came to my senses and realized what Susan had just offered. Within three days Larry and Susan Ho were scheduled to meet with Director Ed McDowell and Rod Brown, the Camp's program director.

During that meeting the mustard seed took hold as plans for the Camp's existing Kids2Camp program took on a new partnership twist. Warm Beach Camp would seek churches and organizations that would bring the "poorest-of-the-poor" kids to Camp and agree to provide the year-round discipling. A holy anticipation was in the air as the delighted couple laid the first big check on the table in Ed's office. A no-nonsense business woman, Susan said, "Great, let's see what you can do with this investment. If the results are good, there will be more where this came from!"

It was springtime, just months away from the busy summer season. Cowboy Rod, clad in his western boots and hat, took to the road, visiting churches and organizations serving the inner-city poor. With no takers on the radar screen, I thought we might have to give the money back. We continued to pray.

In May, I attended the M.J. Murdock Trust's "Women in Ministry" conference in Vancouver, WA. It was before the days of keynote speakers, and our meeting consisted mainly of fellowship and prayer. We went around the room and everyone shared about their ministries and personal lives, giving ideas for prayer to our group. I wrote down all of the prayer requests on the contact list provided.

Barreling back up the I-5 freeway, I felt the familiar heaviness set in again. I had hoped at the conference to receive inspiration. Instead I was saddled with tons of legitimate needs for prayer from thirty women leaders who were all on the edge of Kingdom advancement. I told the Lord in so many words that this wasn't what I expected, and questioned Him about the wisdom of loading me up with so many prayer needs. There weren't enough hours in the day to cover these women in prayer and still do my own job.

While I was still stewing over the long list in the wee hours the next day, the Lord interrupted my thoughts and simply instructed, "Just pray for one woman each day." That began the amazing adventure of praying through the list, like swallowing a one-a-day vitamin each day as a prayer went up. After praying for one Christian leader a day, I would send her a quick email with a carefully chosen Bible verse as an encouragement.

About half way through the list I prayed for Jean Millikan, a pastor on staff at Grace Community Church (GCC) in Auburn. My email also informed her of the Camp's free program for pastors of any denomination to come for a personal retreat to rest and pray. Before pushing the "send" button, at the last minute I added, "And we have money to send the poorest-of-the-poor children to Camp."

Within hours Jean was on the phone so excited she could hardly talk! Their church was located in the heart of Auburn's Hispanic Community. They had reached out to their neighbors by starting a meals program, a tutoring squad for the children, English as a Second Language classes, and a worship service in Spanish. A year before, one of their men came with the dream of gathering up all the neighborhood kids playing in the streets and sending them to camp. The idea was a big one for an already financially-strapped inner-city church, so they wrapped this vision in prayer and asked God to help bring it to pass. Somehow, in the spiritual realm God connected their prayer request to ours and the rest became history!

With only several weeks until camp was to begin, Rod quickly made his way to GCC and outlined the steps for a successful partnership. GCC would be responsible for transportation, store card money, a sleeping bag, and a Bible for each child. With the help of generous donors, WBC would provide a full-ride campership for each child.

In his strategic planning, the Lord had moved a family from the Auburn Free Methodist church to GCC a few years before. Having grown up attending Warm Beach Camp in her early days, this mom had sent her own children to our W-Bar-B camps. She led the charge in the Auburn neighborhood convincing other moms to send their kids to Warm Beach, about one and a half hours away. With the language barrier, it was a momentous task to help parents fill out the required forms, including the health history document.

In the late summer two groups of GCC kids arrived for W-Bar-B camps— one busload for junior camp, and the following week, a busload for junior high camp. We used every dollar of the Ho's gift. Without our realizing it at the time, the pilot program for the partnership element required by Larry and Susan Ho had successfully occurred.

Today, the Camp has 20 partnerships with organizations and churches around the Puget Sound area using over $200,000 each year for Kids2Camp camperships. An audacious seed of faith, planted in the GCC fellowship and watered by the prayers of many, has now mushroomed into a huge program. God was indeed embracing His vision at WBC. We humans can at best see 20/20. God's vision is infinity/infinity. He had been conspiring behind the scenes before any of us knew what HE was planning.

God is **THE CONSPIRATOR**, the CEC, the Chief Executive Conspirator of the Mustard Seed Conspiracy!

41: THE CONQUEROR

Spring was in the air, and that has always meant it's time for Women's Retreat at Warm Beach Camp. The 2005 retreat planning committee was lining up seminar presenters for the break-out sessions that would follow the keynote speaker. Final plans were also underway for the Camp's second major fund-raising campaign, Embracing the Vision (ETV), which had passed the feasibility stage. One thing I knew for certain: we would have an organized prayer team around this campaign before any of the particulars were determined.

When I caught wind that the Women's Retreat planning committee wanted to include a session on "intercessory prayer" I felt a nudge in my heart, a desire that leaped from deep in my spirit, to teach this seminar. The unexpected journey into intercessory prayer had begun when I stepped into my new role as development director. As I connected with donors they began to pour out concerns, and not knowing what to do, I promised to pray for them.

A few months earlier, after presenting a ten-minute talk for the Camano Chapel prayer team led by Joanie Yonker, I yearned for more opportunities to encourage people to pray. The retreat committee already had someone well-known in mind to teach the prayer session. After the "nudge," I secretly told the Lord I'd be willing if they asked me to do it. A few weeks later I received an email from a committee member requesting me to consider teaching. Apparently, when the experienced presenter said, "No," Joanie had suggested me. I didn't need time to consider; I responded, "Yes!" immediately.

In the months preceding the retreat, the Lord had revealed who HE wanted to be on the prayer team for the ETV Campaign. I had asked God to give us "warriors," not "wimps"—people who would follow through and stand in the gap interceding for the Kingdom's work. Relying on the Holy Spirit to act as the conductor, this group would be producing a symphony of prayer from their individual locations. I assured the willing "pray-ers" who signed up for this adventure that there would only be one kick-off meeting to attend. The rest of the time, the Spirit would harmonize the symphonic notes in the spiritual realm. Intercessors love to be left in their closets to pray! Since some of these warriors would be at Women's Retreat, we set the kick-off meeting for Saturday afternoon, after I finished teaching the two identical morning sessions on intercessory prayer

Nothing could have prepared me for the battle about to rage in the spiritual realm over encouraging people to pray! At the beginning of the week of the April Women's Retreat, I felt the Spirit's warning to pray for protection for my family. By Tuesday, our little grandson, Preston, was very sick and put on the wrong antibiotic. He continued to get desperately ill until the doctor switched to a different antibiotic and he began to recover.

But there was more. Calls in the middle of the night are never good news; the best you can hope for is a wrong number. So in the wee hours of Thursday morning, when we were awakened out of deep sleep by our daughter, Cherith, I knew it had to be serious. She wanted to talk to her dad because he had been a volunteer EMT with the local fire department. Stan quickly advised Cherith to get her husband, Chad, to the emergency room immediately, as he was in excruciating pain. Fortunately, Preston, still too sick for daycare, was at his other grandparents' house (Bill and Lauri Lee) as both Chad and Cherith were due at work in the morning. After waiting hours at the Everett Providence Hospital emergency room, Chad was rushed in for an emergency appendectomy Thursday morning before his appendix burst.

I was up early on Saturday morning to pray, and as the laundry whirled in the dryer the Lord impressed in my spirit, "It's not over yet!" A few minutes later, around 4:45 a.m., the phone rang. I heard Cherith screaming, "I am going to die!" Quickly Stan took the phone while I began to get dressed. Since the clothes I was planning to wear were still in the dryer, with adrenaline at an all-time peak I threw on a shirt from the dirty clothes basket and grabbed my curling iron, brush, and make-up on the way out the door.

Stan was scheduled to lead a group of volunteers in a few hours at Camp, so as we left we took two vehicles: I followed his black hunting Jeep with our famous old "Tank," the Oldsmobile. As we raced at break-neck speed to Cherith's home twenty minutes away, I felt as if we were cutting through thick darkness—not the kind caused by a lack of daylight. I began to cry out to God, asking Him to cover us with the blood of Jesus and to save Cherith. I also began to inform the Enemy at the top of my lungs that he was not going to have our family, that we were covered with the blood of the Lamb. I felt a force rise up from within me and I began to use the name of Jesus, praying with HIS authority, not mine.

When we entered Cherith's bedroom, the seriousness began to sink in as we were met with her shrieks caused by intense pain. Stan quickly called "911" while I dialed the Everett Clinic's on-call number. Both the emergency responders and the Clinic's physician-on-call agreed that Cherith's symptoms indicated she was probably passing a kidney stone. Since aid car attendants cannot give pain medication, in order to save medical expenses they advised that we drive her to a hospital emergency room. Cherith then wailed, "Don't take me to the same hospital where my husband is! I will die waiting that long!" So after Stan laid Cherith on the huge back seat of the old Oldsmobile, we headed up Highway 9 to the Arlington Hospital, fifteen minutes away.

It was raining so hard that I could barely see to trail behind Stan's Jeep. Sprawled across the back seat, Cherith lay screaming as I held her hand through the gap between the bucket seats. As we sped through the darkness she cried, "This is worse than having a baby!" When we pulled up to the emergency room entrance, Stan was already waiting with a wheel chair. He wheeled Cherith into the small-town hospital ER where there was no wait. A CAT scan soon revealed that Cherith was indeed passing a kidney stone, and she was sedated. After her pain medication took effect, I slipped into the ER restroom to put on my make-up and curl my hair. While my education in spiritual warfare was just beginning, I determined that that this would not deter me from participating in the prayer-filled events planned for the day.

Cherith's in-laws could hardly believe that both of little Preston's parents were in two separate hospitals. Bill agreed to stay with the baby and Lauri headed off to meet us at the Arlington Hospital to be with Cherith. Just as they were taking the IV out of Cherith's arm, Chad called me on his cell phone from the hospital in Everett. After I assured him that his wife was okay, Chad said, "Just a minute; they are taking the IV out of my arm." In amazing timing, both were released from their two separate hospitals within minutes of each other. Lauri met me at the freeway and we transferred Cherith to her car. Friends picked up Chad and brought him to the Lees' log home on Camano Island, where his folks cared for the little recovering family.

I got to Camp with just enough time to take my shirt off and iron it in the laundry. About five minutes before the first scheduled seminar, I was at the podium, ready to face a room full of ladies in the Maple Center to teach on intercessory prayer. While it felt like I'd been hit by a Mack truck, there was bright light in the room and the horrific feeling of darkness had dissipated. With grace given by the Spirit, I was able to stay focused and share what the Lord had helped me to prepare. After two teaching sessions back to back, and with no time for lunch, I made my way to The Pines near the Camp's entrance to meet with the ETV Campaign prayer team at 1 p.m. There aren't words to describe the wave of sheer pure grace that engulfed me as I joined the circle of these experienced prayer warriors!

That Saturday afternoon we began to pray for the Lord's direction and provision for the upcoming campaign. This group of mighty warriors, under the direction of Art and Martha Smelser, prayer chairmen, also began praying for my family. The Lord really does "cause ALL things to work together for good." Like all medical facilities, the Everett hospital had a Samaritan fund to cover those who could not pay for treatment, but often that type of fund is exhausted in the latter part of the year. Because Chad's surgery happened in the first quarter, even though he had no medical insurance the hospital's Samaritan fund covered his total hospital bill. Thankfully, Cherith's employer supplied her with insurance that covered most of her expenses. Through fellow Christians, the Lord provided for the remaining medical expenses surrounding both of Chad and Cherith's episodes. There's little doubt that these physical problems would have manifested eventually, but this strange experience made me wonder if the enemy can use weaknesses in our bodies (physical, emotional, and mental) and cause them to intensify at strategic times.

Weeks later, while meeting with Dr. Alvin Vandergriend, author of *Love to Pray* and an experienced leader who has taught with Harvest Prayer Ministries around the world for over twenty-five years, I shared the story of that prayer-filled day. I asked Alvin if he thought this had been spiritual warfare. This humble, Christian Reformed preacher cleared his throat and said, "Probably!" Alvin went on to explain, "The Enemy isn't too worried when we work real hard for the Lord, but he is terrified when we encourage others to pray, as he knows that this is what moves the hands of God! He will go to great extremes to stop it!"

Now I haven't a clue as to how these battles occur in the heavens. But I do know that we are more than conquerors! The theme song Stan and I learned in Thompson, Iowa, before our evangelism team launched that summer of 1968 has proved ever so true:

"We are more than conquerors through him who loved us so. The Christ who dwells within us is the greatest power we know. He will fight beside us, though the Enemy is brave. Who can stand against us? He's the captain of our fate. And we will conquer, never fear, so let the battle rage. He has promised to be near, unto the end of the Age …"

We know **THE CONQUEROR**, the Lord Jesus Christ. He doesn't leave us alone to fight our battles. Jesus is the Mighty Warrior, and He fights for us. "Greater is HE who is in us, than he who is of this world." Jesus is the Victor, and he gives victory over the darkness.

42: THE DELIVERER

After a memorable day of prayer in April, 2005, with an array of events that tried to interfere, I began to investigate spiritual warfare. My knowledge was quite limited so I asked the Lord to direct me to someone with a lot of experience. Immediately, Dr. Mike Henry's name popped into my mind. Mike serves as a pastor in central Washington, and is a former missionary. I later learned that Mike had done his doctoral work at Fuller Seminary on healing prayer and spiritual warfare. We had visited Mike and his family when we were in Hermosillo, Mexico in 1994 when our team worked at Rancho Betania Camp over Christmas vacation. Our daughter, Cherith, had spent hours playing with Mike and Shelly's children using their fancy dress-up clothes.

I quickly called Mike and he listened attentively as I described our family's recent experiences leading up to my teaching on prayer followed by the afternoon meeting with the Embracing the Vision campaign's prayer team. It didn't seem like mere coincidence that our daughter, Cherith, and son-in-law, Chad, had ended up in two separate hospitals on that day while their baby, Preston, was recovering from an infection. Mike promised to pray for my family's protection and recommended several introductory books on spiritual warfare, including Francis Frangipane's book, *The Three Battlegrounds* (Arrow Publications, 1996). My copy is now tattered and torn from multiple readings.

In Chapter fifteen, entitled, "The War Over Reality," Frangipane describes how to stand upon the Word of God to pull down strongholds that Paul talks about in II Corinthians 10:3-5. One of his introductory paragraphs states: "To be successful in battle, we must know the Word of God. If you are in need of deliverance, or if you are being used in the ministry of deliverance, the following verses will be helpful in establishing victory. It is not wise to engage in any kind of spiritual warfare without knowing these scriptures perfectly from memory" (page 100). Frangipane goes on to list nine well-known verses, with an explanation of each one regarding their significance.

While scripture memorization has never been easy for me, upon realizing its importance I quickly wrote down these nine verses on small index cards that I could hold in my hands while I jogged through our house for one-half hour a day. My doctor had advised thirty minutes of daily exercise; I decided that multi-tasking would make good use of that time. I turned the scriptures into personal prayers and prayed them out loud every day until I no longer needed the cue cards. One of my prayers, based on II Timothy 1:7 was, "Thank you Lord that you have not given me a spirit of fear, but of power and love and a sound mind. Every time I am afraid, will you remind me that this isn't from you?"

About the same time, I came across a copy of Dutch Sheets' *Watchmen on the Wall* (Gospel Light Publications, 2000) when I followed our grandson into our church's library after the morning service. Little one-year-old Preston sat down right by the book shelf labeled, "Prayer." The majority of Sheets' book is about how to stand as watchmen for our loved ones, but he also talks about guarding ourselves. Sheets gives a great explanation about how to destroy strongholds in the mind. It is similar to Frangipane's but goes into greater detail, outlining what the Word of God can do as it is active, alive, and able to cut away things that should not be in our minds.

As a triple confirmation, someone advised that I read Beth Moore's *Praying God's Word, Breaking Free from Spiritual Strongholds* (B&H Publishing Group, 2009). Moore states that "God has handed us two sticks of dynamite with which to demolish our strongholds: His Word and prayer. What are more powerful than two sticks of dynamite placed in separate locations? Two strapped together" (page 6). Moore also claims that praying scripture out loud is like planting dynamite throughout the stronghold and at a designated time, like a building to be demolished, when the dynamite is detonated, the stronghold implodes.

Most people did not realize that at one time I carried two very huge fortresses of fear in my life. One was a fear of flying, which developed when I was five years old and a Navy jet crashed into houses in the next block over from our home in Minneapolis. In my mind's eye I can still see the huge billow of smoke, as if a bomb had been dropped on that block. Thirteen people were killed in the crash, mostly children who had been playing in the nearby field. My little friend, Butch, came running home on fire and I saw his dad use a rug to try to extinguish the flames. My father was relieved when Butch died two days later at the V.A. Hospital because he was so badly burned.

It was months before I would cross the street because it would place me closer to where the crash had left four homes burned to a crisp. I remember every detail of my friend Roxanne's sixth birthday party because it was on the other side of the street. We were in her basement and when the lovely cake, shaped like a rabbit, was delivered, all I could think about was how long it would be before the party would be over so I could retreat to the safety of my home.

In addition to the fear of flying, another fear gripped me the day my mom told me, at age twenty-five, that I had had cancer surgery when I was six months old. I had always known about the surgery itself because of the huge scar under my left arm, but the news that it was the result of a cancer diagnosis left me paralyzed with fear. It didn't help that I was working in a Veteran's Administration cancer ward at the time, watching veterans die from cancer. Our family doctor had pronounced me cancer-free five years after my operation. But when my mom broke the entire story to me over the phone, it was as if the surgery had occurred yesterday. The news sent me into a two-year depression that the medical profession labeled "a severe anxiety reaction."

In 1976, after working hard at Hartland Christian Camp for a few months, the deep depression finally lifted, but the roots of fear were still there. Keeping extremely busy, I did everything to deny that this fear had a stronghold on me. I did all right until I encountered any reminder of cancer. For example, for many years I could not abbreviate California with "CA," as that is the medical term for cancer used in patients' charts. It was also extremely hard for me to visit people with cancer or even pray for their healing.

When my sister, Peggy, was diagnosed with breast cancer at thirty-three years of age, I was expecting our first child. Peggy made my parents promise not to tell me about her diagnosis until after Thad was born. A diabetic, my sister had lost a baby that died in her womb at seven months. Knowing my horrific fear of cancer, she did not want me to receive news of her cancer until Thad was two weeks old. I remember the shock of disbelief when my mom and dad told me Peggy's surgery had happened two months before Thad was born. Peggy was now partway through chemotherapy that I had known nothing about until that dreadful moment. At age thirty-five, Peggy died after a long, hard, courageous battle with the disease.

The fear of cancer surfaced again twenty years later when my mom had a breast lumpectomy to remove a cancerous tumor in her seventies. Now, I feared I was next in line; surely the DNA was stacked against me. I kept pushing the fear down under, using a lot of energy to keep it from resurfacing to paralyze my life.

I had lived with these fears for so long that I refused even to acknowledge them, worried that they would take center stage again. While I wasn't even aware of my own need for deliverance, one day, after jogging through the house for months praying the nine verses recommended in Frangipane's book, I realized that my fear of cancer was gone. When it had left, I didn't know. It was completely gone. I could sit with people who had cancer and lay hands on them to pray. Once, when Cherith had a biopsy, if the diagnosis had come back "cancer," I was prepared to take her place if by any chance the Lord would have allowed such an exchange. That's when I realized that I had been set free from the spirit of fear regarding cancer.

A few months later, when I was flying to speak at a convention for Christian Camping International, I realized that I simply had no fear of flying. I was reading a book during take-off, usually a white-knuckle time that I simply endured in order to get from point "A" to "B." But I was relaxed, and I have never been concerned about flying again. The fear of flying was completely gone—forever! I have made countless flights since that one, and the Lord has given me perfect peace each time. Granted, I still love it when the landing gear comes down and the brakes bring us safely to a stop on the runway, but I am no longer terrified when I fly.

God is **THE DELIVERER**. And when we pray HIS Word that is "sharper than any double-edged sword" it can clear a path through the lies that the enemy uses to keep us in his strongholds. When we re-wallpaper our minds by praying the truth of the Word of God, the enemy can't woo us back into a stronghold that is composed of nothing but his lies.

43: THE CULTURE CHANGER

It started with a simple request made by Max's mom, Leah Merklinghaus, while she was watching one of her children loping on a horse around the arena down by the Camp's stables with Shelly Rubatino, the Life Skills director at Stanwood High School. It was the spring of 2006 when Leah put the question to Director Ed McDowell, "Would you ever consider having a camp for children with special needs?" Actually, the Lord had already paved the way as Leah's wonderment was an answer to a prayer unfolding.

This mom knew all too well the challenges that faced special needs kids. Max, then a teenager, was autistic, and together with other moms, Leah was experienced at charting the waters, making a way for these precious children. Ed couldn't resist jumping on this new wave of God's activity that would soon engulf the Camp.

Leah was amazed that Ed's response was a resounding, "YES! We have a heart to do this. We would need some help to learn the 'how' for doing camps for the special needs population." Ed went on to tell Leah that Laurie Fertello, the Camp's program director, had been approached about doing such a program, but needed partners with experience. We had been praying about it, but we just couldn't figure out how to get our arms wrapped around this population. With both feet barely on the ground due to her excitement, Leah took a huge leap of faith and responsibility and promised to bring everyone needed to launch that first pilot "Special Friends" Day Camp program. Fortunately, in God's divine planning, there was one week open in the day camp schedule at the very beginning of summer.

With only four months to prepare, Leah rounded up volunteers from the Stanwood/Camano School District and Seattle Children's Hospital to begin working with Laurie. The pilot program would be for those who were fifteen years and older, a population that was even more underserved than younger children. There wasn't time to market the program with a fancy brochure, but that didn't deter Leah. She became the marketing specialist, a walking advertisement for the program. In no time at all, the word had permeated the local area.

That first year, twenty-two Special Friends enjoyed camp, where they were plunged into a grace-filled "YES environment." The goal was to say "YES" as often as possible. After that first week of Special Friends Day Camp, Leah and her husband produced a video letting us all take a peek at what "YES" looked like. It didn't matter if kids were confined to wheelchairs; they could be put in a harness and hoisted to the top of the fifty foot climbing tower, shouting with glee as they conquered something they had never imagined possible! A special needs camper could ride a horse even if it took three people to make it safe. And the screams of delight could be heard throughout Camp as these special needs campers flew through the air riding the zip-lines!

Eleven years later, the program has expanded to include six weeks of Special Friends Day Camp along with five weeks of overnight camp serving 250 special needs campers. This is no small feat, as each week of forty campers requires not only college-age counselors, but at least forty "buddies," many of whom are in high school. This is an excellent discipleship opportunity for teens as they learn how to interface with this special population, many who are older than they are. It is love in action. When these teens return to school in the fall, they will not allow bullying, for they have experienced first-hand that everyone is special in God's sight.

Three years ago, the Special Friends Program took over Warm Beach's old Chinook Village Camp. At last they had their own home! At the same time, Laurie Fertello narrowed her summer responsibilities, dedicating her time solely to be director of the Special Friends Camps. Private foundations have helped provide for needed renovations so that Chinook is more American Disability Act friendly. Volunteers built a brand new amphitheater that would accommodate wheel chairs along with remodeled bathrooms large enough for easy use. Thanks to generous donors, colorful features have been added to bring out the best in this population. Huge sand piles have provided hours of fun for those who enjoy playing at the beach. My favorite activity is watching the special friends beat on the huge wooden drums, filling the woods with the rhythms of grace.

Through the last eleven years, a mysterious wave of God's grace has changed the culture of camp, so slowly that we hardly noticed. People with special needs started requesting to volunteer. Big Jake worked with Stan for years helping take care of the grounds. Samuel came regularly to clean the prayer chapel. Quinten often sat in his wheelchair and did things like testing lights in preparation for *The Lights of Christmas* in December. Cody has helped clean stalls at the stables. Bruce faithfully comes each week to deep clean the staff dining room. Taran started as a volunteer and is now a paid food service staff member. And until Max moved to Idaho, he cleaned the pine cones off the sidewalks.

In addition, families are participating in working weekends, bringing their special needs kids along with them. People no longer keep at a distance; these special people are woven into the fabric of the Camp. Our volunteers with special needs are invited to attend the Partner-in-Ministry Appreciation Dinner in May, right along with the other 2000+ donors.

To be honest, I didn't realize that the culture was changing until I had an experience at McDonald's a few years ago while watching my grandson, Eli, at the playground. A special needs teenage guy, perched in his huge stroller and clinging to his Happy Meal toy, was watching the young children play. His attendant was close by. I was eager to tell them about the Special Friends Camp. When I laid my hand on his shoulder to make a physical connection, the teen grabbed my wrist, almost crushing it. I kept talking, eager to finish telling them about camp. His caregiver calmly advised me that when I could get my wrist free, I should step back and talk to him from a distance as this teen with Angelman's syndrome could break my arm. It didn't faze me; I just kept talking and stepped back a bit when he let loose of my wrist. On the drive home I realized that a few years ago I wouldn't have even approached this teen. I would have looked away in awkwardness and fear.

The Special Friends story is still unfolding. After the first over-night pilot camp in the summer of 2014, it became obvious that new cabins with ADA compliant restrooms were needed right away. The cabins were part of the program's long-range vision, and after much research, a local architect drew up plans for the new ADA cabins, using suggestions from Camp Barnabas in Missouri which had been ministering to the special needs populations for years. We had plans for the future, but the needs were immediate.

When God initiates a stream of activity, He is orchestrating what is needed behind the scenes before we are even aware of it. The Camp's main contractor, Jim Seaton, had just retired when he heard of our dream. Amazingly, Jim stepped forward to be the volunteer contractor! Business people jumped in to donate building supplies. Foundations helped to provide the needed cash to make these cabins a reality. Other craftsmen volunteered their time. The wave of God's activity is so strong that attempting to stop it would be like trying to roll back the tide.

In October of 2014, funding was complete for the first cabin. The Camp's board, in their wisdom, made it clear that the second cabin also had to be fully funded before it could be built. December was almost over; only $9,500 was needed to meet the total project goal of $427,000 which would allow both cabins to be built in January. I kept reminding God that He had created these precious children, male and female, and that both cabins were required for the overnight program. Thanks to generous donors responding to Laurie's Facebook plea, all the funds were committed in time to receive the board's approval at the 2015 January meeting.

Laurie's dreams, soaked in prayer, include year-round respite care weekends for Special Friends so their families can have a much needed break. Some day, not only will all the old Chinook A-frame cabins be replaced with ADA friendly cabins, but the old longhouse used for a meeting room will be replaced with a winterized multi-purpose room. And the best part: when the music starts on Sundays, Special Friends will be singing worship songs while dancing before the Lord. The Camp has a tiger by the tail when it comes to Special Friends. Or should I say, the Lion of Judah has these Special Friends fully in his sight!

A few years ago I was out at Chinook Village taking photos to show donors that the two Special Friends cabins were almost complete. I thought back to the spring of 2014, when four old A-frame Chinook cabins were taken down and cement foundations were poured for the two new cabins. While watching the new walls going up for these cabins, I realized then that the old walls of fear that separate us from people with disabilities were continuing to come crashing down.

Max and his family have moved to Idaho. But Max and I are Facebook friends so I still get a peek into what's happening in his world. And Max's mom, Leah, constantly reminds us that our Special Friends bring out the "special" in all of us!

God is **THE CULTURE CHANGER**. He is rather sneaky, slowly injecting HIS sheer, pure grace into all of us, making a way for beauty and joy to grace our environment.

44: COMMANDER OF THE ANGEL ARMIES

It was a mad rush to get my passport in time for the upcoming trip to Burundi, Africa that was scheduled for the end of August, 2007. While approaching the window at City Hall in Stanwood, I wondered how in the world I had ended up on the team going to this little heart-shaped country bordering Rwanda in central Africa to help start their camping program. Denise Patch, former director of Sister Connection, an organization that ministers to widows and children in Burundi, had saved me a ticket for the flight before the Lord revealed to me that I would be going!

Originally, I had been interested in visiting Hope Africa University in Bujumbura, Burundi's capital city, as I had volunteered to help write a grant proposal to the Gates Foundation for the university's new medical school. But there was a quickening in my spirit to go with the team of younger staff who would be helping the Burundian church leadership develop their camping program for 300 teens. Still, I was afraid. The theme song going through my head was, "Lord, please don't send me to Africa."

A few weeks before, at a prayer conference held in Lynden, Washington, I had bought a book by Don Nori entitled, *The Prayer God Loves to Answer* (Destiny Image, 2006). Eager to know what that was, I devoured the book in record time. I found out that the prayer God loves to answer is, "YES, LORD!" One morning as I was sitting in my big prayer chair at home, the Lord impressed a question into my spirit: "When are you going to say, 'Yes, Lord, I will go to Africa'?" A quick call to Denise confirmed my flight reservation that she had saved for me without my knowledge.

I had never been on an international flight before, nor to another country that didn't border the U.S. Beside the required passport and visa, I would need to be up to date on every vaccination imaginable, including yellow fever. Some shots had to be given at the Snohomish County Health Department in Everett. While I was awaiting the dreaded needles, the nurse looked up Burundi, and, in addition to outlining all the shots that I would need, she proceeded to tell me the risks of going to Burundi at this time.

Because the Hutu-Tutsi genocide that had occurred there was not too far in the past, the infrastructure of the country was devastated. Roads were in terrible shape. Rebel forces were still active throughout the country, and what little sanitation there was before the war was greatly compromised. Diseases were spreading rapidly. It was this nurse's duty to warn me of the dangers that lay ahead, which she summed up by saying, "Are you sure you want to go to Burundi?" Upon my saying, "Yes," she proceeded to give me six of the required vaccinations.

I left the Health Department with not only bandaged arms and sheets of paper detailing the possible side-effects of all these shots, but with a bucket full of fear. My name was already on the airplane ticket; it was too late to back out. Before I had entered the nurse's office, I was afraid of snakes and giant bugs, but I came home with concerns that I never dreamed would be awaiting me in Africa!

To be honest, I was a little miffed at God! The next morning in prayer I begin to read Psalm 91, a place I often turned to when afraid. I had just finished reading a small booklet by Graham Cooke, *Crafted Prayer* (Swiftfire Ministries, 2004), which encouraged me to make a text of scripture personal and pray it many times until it was integrated into my being. Thus began my earnest praying of Psalm 91, beginning with writing it out in my prayer journal for several days. I then began to pray it out loud, over and over again, in both *The Message* and the NIV. "Thank you, Lord, that I am dwelling in your shelter, and resting in your shadow...Lord, I am making you, Most High God, my dwelling...then no harm will befall me, no disaster will come near my tent...thank you, Lord, that you command your angels concerning me to guard me in all my ways..."

By the time the team boarded the plane, I had prayed Psalm 91 hundreds of times. Faith does come from hearing! These words were wound down into my spirit and were needed as soon as we got off the plane in Bujumbura. We learned that our itinerary had been revised because twenty people had just been slaughtered by rebel forces near where we were scheduled to visit some of the Sister Connection widows' homes.

After spending a couple of days at a fancy hotel in Bujumbura, we were scheduled to leave for the up-country with Burundian women and their teenage children from Hope Africa University. We met in the yard of the university, behind the heavy metal gates which guard the school. I was amazed how many Burundians can fit into a van! Excitement was in the air as the women, adorned in their colorful dresses, were at last on their way. Some had never ridden in a car before. Over 150 widows would be gathering at the retreat site in the province of Gitega, along with 300 teens. While the women's retreat was happening, the teens would experience their first camp.

Fortunately, the temperature was cooler in the up-country where we spent three days at the retreat center. At night, our team loaded into three vehicles and headed down the horrible road with potholes large enough to swallow a van to a motel in Gitega, Burundi's second-largest city. We had been warned not to travel after dark, but there was no alternative since the camp programming went late into the evening. No one wanted to leave when the Lord was moving so mightily throughout the camps. Each night we trusted that the Lord would protect the team as we journeyed back to the motel.

One of the things we learned during the team's orientation was that if we were ever stopped and things were demanded from us Americans, to give the men what they wanted, and not risk our lives. What an immersion in high risk overseas touring! Furthermore, the president of Burundi had been scheduled to appear at the kick-off of the camps to honor Sister Connection as a newly established non-profit, but because of the latest rebel uprising, he sent the governor of Gitega Province in his place. A sense of danger permeated our entire experience.

I was part of the team that taught seminars at the women's retreat, which used the theme of "The Armor of God" from Ephesians 6. David, Shelly and Audra Goodnight, David Smetters, Randy Cloes, Denise Patch, and a lady named Toni Sloan were all assigned topics that went along with the theme. Music was provided and oh! How the women loved to worship and dance before the Lord in their colorful wraparound "pagne"!

With the help of an interpreter, my task was to teach the effectiveness of using the Word of God in prayer as a weapon. Because the country's genocide was so fresh, I was warned not to refer to the Word as "the Sword" of the Spirit. Instead, the Lord gave me the imagery of sowing the Word into our lives like the widows used their hoes to plant their seeds for crops. What a symbol of hope! In my enthusiasm, I used the word, "WOW" in my teaching. The interpreter looked at me in surprise and, after much thought, said something that made the women laugh!

At the same time, our younger team from Camp (Pat Patterson, Emily and Matt Lambert, and Stephanie Harris, along with Daniel Cloes) had the awesome privilege of working alongside Burundian church leaders to host their first teen camp. Pat was the keynote speaker. Using bracelet craft with colored beads representing the "wordless Bible," he invited the teens into a relationship with Jesus, and to experience His transforming grace. The others led the teens in group games like Rock, Scissors, Paper. Once inflated, the soccer balls we brought in our suitcases also got a real workout.

The final night of the retreat, as we were creeping along in the van on high alert for gigantic potholes that could swallow our vehicle, we came upon a huge mass of barbed-wire spread across the road. It was circular in nature, and like a spool that had been unwound, the black wire stood about three feet high. When we stopped, several police officers with machine guns approached the car. With loud voices, they conversed with our driver in the native language. Fear crept in at an alarming rate; my heart began beating faster and faster. Suddenly, from deep in my spirit arose the words of Psalm 91:11, "He has commanded His angels concerning you to guard you in all your ways." I immediately relaxed and imagined angels all around our van.

At last the officers removed the barbed wire across the road and signaled the two vans of Americans to pass by. The Toyota Land Rover carrying Sister Connection's national director, Joy, was not so fortunate. They held Joy for several hours, no doubt hoping to extort money from her. Joy is a tough leader, and at last they let her and the chauffeur pass through the road block.

Not only did I have a once-in-a-lifetime, unforgettable experience as part of the most unique Spirit-led retreat, but I also got to meet and receive a hug from widow #87 whom Stan and I sponsor with thirty dollars a month. This widow's picture is taped to our bathroom mirror as a reminder that she prays for us every day. She is standing in front of the house that Stan and I had built for her. She requested a long room be added to the house as she hosts prayer meetings for the other widows.

Several of us on the team were invited to join the President of Burundi, who is a Christian, for dinner and worship with his family and his soldiers on the front steps of the palace. When the president, clad in blue jeans, heard that I would be approaching the Gates Foundation for Hope Africa's new medical school, he promised to write a letter of recommendation and even gave me a hug!

Warm Beach Camp participated in the youth retreats for three years until the Burundians were prepared to fully lead them on their own. Our daughter-in-law, Pastor Abby, was the keynote speaker for the retreat camp for two years. She is beloved by the Burundian teens and has had an amazing ministry among them. Abby has also returned to teach Christian education seminars throughout the country.

The 600-plus Sister Connection widows look forward to the women's retreats each year as a time of spiritual renewal and fellowship. Last summer, over 1,500 children and teens attended the youth camps. These future leaders of Burundi are some of the most traumatized teens in the world. With the grace given by their Master, Jesus, they are learning to forgive those who killed their grandfathers, fathers, uncles, and brothers. From The Word sown in their lives, the seeds of hope are beginning to bear fruit in these young men and women.

The Lord is true to HIS promises, for I did not get sick nor did the team experience harm at any time during our visit. God is **THE COMMANDER OF THE ANGEL ARMIES**. Our team and the camp participants were protected and provided for in every way. When we store HIS word in our hearts, HE retrieves it at strategic times and reminds us of HIS abilities and how HE can command HIS forces to counteract evil.

45: THE REDEEMER

Little did my assistant, Theresa Smiley, and I realize when we jumped into the old Oldsmobile one day in 2006 that within minutes we would both be strapped to backboards en route to the Emergency Room. On our way to Stanwood for lunch, Theresa saw that the big brown delivery truck waiting at a stop sign to our right had begun moving toward our grey "tank." Theresa shrieked, "He's coming at us!" I slammed on the brakes so hard that my ankle was instantly on fire with pain. Thankfully, we stopped in time to witness one giant truck crushing through the car's hood. A split-second later and it would have come right through the passenger's side. Within moments, the advertising slogan, "See what brown can do for you" took on a whole new meaning!

After $20,000+ worth of x-rays in the ER, I learned that while I had bruised ribs and a badly sprained ankle, the Lord had miraculously spared me from further injuries. Theresa couldn't believe that I didn't have brain trauma, for she had watched the upper part of my body being hurled back and forth into the steering wheel.

Actually, Theresa was in worse condition, as she had braced herself with her right hand on the dash; the impact of the truck had broken bones in her hand. In the twinkle of an eye, two-thirds of our Development Department had been put out of commission, leaving Gary Kocher, Annual Fund director, to oversee the Kids 2 Camp fund-raising breakfast less than twenty-four hours away. Not feeling well himself, Gary had just returned from the doctor's office when he heard of our accident.

The whole incident left me wondering again whether this was strategically placed spiritual warfare. I had just begun teaching our adult Sunday School class at church using Alvin Vandergriend's *Love to Pray* video series (PrayerShop Publishing, 2009). In addition, I had joined a friend in praying for her husband to be released from a stronghold of bitterness that was holding him captive. This accident had shades of similarities to our experience with Chad and Cherith's hospitalizations right before a day committed to intercessory prayer at a Camp women's retreat in 2005. I remembered Alvin's words: "…The enemy is terrified when we encourage people to pray because he knows prayer is what moves the hands of God and he will go to extremes to stop it."

A few days after the accident, early on Easter Sunday, I awoke and couldn't breathe. The discharge instructions said that if this should occur to get to the ER immediately, as it might be signs of a punctured lung. Once again I was in an aid car speeding down I-5 to Providence Hospital attended by EMT's who at one time had washed dishes at Camp when they were in high school. Thankfully, it turned out that I just needed more medication because my bruised ribs made it too painful to breathe. Chock full of more meds, I went home with Stan just in time to attend Easter service at Camp. Later I found out from my friend that her husband had been set free from his stronghold of bitterness and he had reconnected with his estranged parents just hours before I returned to the ER on Easter morning.

A couple of weeks after the accident, while still on regular doses of narcotics, I went to a conference with the Camp's management team. The guys took turns pushing my wheelchair through the airports in order to make all the connections to get to a conference center in North Carolina. For weeks I couldn't wear a shoe on my swollen right foot. After various treatments, my foot still wouldn't return to normal size, which would allow me to wear shoes with backs on them. Even an ice-bucket regime didn't produce results: at the request of the physical therapist I had soaked my foot in ice water for ten minutes, three times a day!

My doctor did not allow me to drive for quite a while, since it would put pressure on my foot. Little by little, however, Dr. Andrews lifted the driving restriction. I felt like a teenager when at last I was given permission to drive further than the few miles to Stanwood! For about eight months, due to my pain issues and lack of energy, we stopped entertaining at our home on the lake, a loss I grieved. After a year of seeing various doctors, a chiropractor, a physical therapist, and a massage therapist, my foot was as good as it was going to get.

At last I could get a tennis shoe on, even though it was a half size larger than before the accident. I began to jog slowly around the house, working up to my pre-accident thirty minutes a day. As was my practice, I prayed scriptures out loud, making them personal. For months one of the verses I personalized was Romans 8:28: "Lord, you promised that ALL things work together for good, even when a big truck totals my car. I don't know how you are going to cause all this to work together for good, but you promised, and your Word is true!"

To be honest, after a few months I quit asking how God would work all the pain and inconvenience together for good and forgot all about it. But God doesn't forget. Our prayers never die! God doesn't have a speck of dementia: His memory is perfectly infinite, even if we quit reminding Him!

Two years after the accident, in the summer of 2008, I received a settlement from the truck's insurance company. Because Stan had doctored me back to health, taking on most of the home responsibilities for months, I had told him he could donate a portion of the settlement to something he wanted to fund.

Secretly, I regretted granting him that latitude because Denise Patch, Sister Connection's director at the time, had just notified the Camp prayer team that there were many teens still needing assistance in order to attend camp sessions in Burundi, which were then just a month away. The first year Warm Beach Camp had raised all the necessary funds. This second year was the transitional year: Sister Connection was to be responsible for the entire cost of the camps this coming season, but they were still facing a significant shortfall. In our conversation, Denise also shared that a woman had felt the Lord nudging her to give five dollars so that the prayer team could ask the Lord to multiply her small gift given in obedience. What followed was miraculous.

Stan had decided that he would take his share from the insurance settlement and purchase a huge attachment for the tractor at Camp that would vacuum up leaves in the fall. Having it would save hours of labor and was something that, without a designated donation, would never be possible. In eager anticipation, he headed out to meet with the implement dealer but soon returned with a look I'd never seen on his face. When the dealer found out that Stan was ordering the giant lawn vacuum for Warm Beach Camp, he insisted on donating it!

It took me only a couple of seconds to tell Stan of my overwhelming desire to fund 200 camperships for teens in Burundi. Stan agreed, and we hurried to notify Dan Kurtz, Sister Connection's treasurer, of the gift so that they wouldn't turn kids away or cancel the camp altogether. When the national Sister Connection director, Joy, received the Camp's check created from our donation and gifts from many other folks, she held it in the air and asked the Lord to multiply it, just as He had done with the fish and loaves to feed the 5,000. In the end, Sister Connection dispersed the funds widely, and mysteriously, our gift actually sent 300 kids to camp!

Recently, while at a board training session on development, the consultant, John Pearson, asked each of us to share a time when a gift we had given brought joy. I instantly thought of the once-in-a-lifetime gift that had made it possible for those kids to attend camp in Burundi. I remember laughing on and off for days after serving as the conduit the Lord used to provide for those kids. Never in my wildest dreams…that joy made the pain and crutches worth it! But trust me: I can spot a big brown truck a mile away! Even our grandson, Preston, is on the lookout so we can be extra cautious.

Life has gone on with a right ankle slightly bigger than my left one. As long as I exercise regularly, I do not have pain. A week without jogging and my right foot is stiff. Due to the effects of the accident, it is harder to find shoes that fit properly, and often the right shoe will curl to the outside after few months.

My friend, Rita Nussli, said she wrestled with Romans 8:28 for years. How could she, who was then the executive director of New Horizons, look street kids in the face and tell them that "all things work together for good" when some had suffered unbelievable abuse at home? After studying Romans 8:28 in the Greek, Rita came to the conclusion that another translation is "all things are redeemable."

We know **THE REDEEMER**, who by HIS sheer pure grace can redeem anything, even a big brown truck T-boning an old Oldsmobile. Whether or not it was spiritual warfare waged against us didn't matter. What mattered was that it was redeemed, providing a way for teens, some of the most traumatized in the world, to be able to come to camp. Why? Because they mattered to God and HE keeps His Word!

46: THE DOG CATCHER

Having a pet was not an option during our seventeen years of living in Camp housing, except for a brief year-long trial period which didn't work out too well. Secretly, I was relieved not to have the additional burden of caring for a pet. So nothing in our family's experience prepared me for the phone call from our son Thad Johan in May, 2007. He and Abby were set to head west from Kentucky in a couple of days to live in the apartment in the lower level of our home while they transitioned back into Washington.

The voice at the other end of the line said, "Mom, a dog wandered into the Oakdale School yard last week and we are going to bring her home with us. Can we keep her in the downstairs apartment?" It was amazing that Thad would even ask, for he knew my stance on pets. Even when we moved off the campgrounds into to the first house we purchased on 81st Street, with brand new carpets and an empty nest in sight, I had made it clear that it didn't make sense to get a pet.

While tightly gripping the phone, over the next several minutes I reviewed with Thad all the reasons why it wouldn't be practical to keep a dog at the lake. For example, we had recently encountered neighbors upset over local dogs being left to bark and wander all through the day, with the resulting messes deposited in their yards. But Thad was determined. He firmly let me know that Abby and he would be bringing their new-found companion, Latte, a chocolate lab, with them, even if they had to board her somewhere other than our home while they looked for a different, more "pet-friendly" place to live.

After throwing up a quick prayer, I talked to Stan when he got home that night. Stan loves dogs, and the kids had often heard tales of his beloved Scout and Peanut while falling asleep at bedtime listening to Dad's childhood adventures. Stan posed a simple question: "Why not allow them to bring their dog home?" There was something in Stan's tone that made me realize that the Lord was concocting something, and quick surrender was my best option. Even though this scenario seemed impractical and crazy, God had a track record of revealing that HIS ways aren't like our ways!

I have to admit that when Latte entered our lake home it was love at first sight. No wonder this dog had quickly moved into their hearts! She was skinny from lack of nutrition, and her brown coat had dull gray spots on it. But Latte's energy, along with her love of Thad and Abby, showed through her bouncing eyes and body. With no record of her birthday, we guessed that she was a teenager. It wasn't long before Latte was spending the days on our big glassed-in deck, soaking in the sun or rain while keeping her eye on the beach front and guarding our fleet of boats and canoes.

Not only did Thad and Abby love their companion with the waggly tail, but our two year old grandson, Preston, and Latte quickly became fast friends too.

Whenever the two of them landed in our living room at the same time, Preston would get a biscuit from Grandma's supply in the hall closet for Latte. Outside, Latte would play for hours, fetching anything Thad or Preston would toss into the lake.

With all the fun we were having with our new family member, none of us was prepared for that fateful weekend when Latte disappeared in the woods near Lake Cavanagh. She wandered off while Thad and Stan were zeroing in their rifles to be ready for the October "black-powder" hunting season. They searched the woods for hours before returning home without Latte.

We were all in grief over losing Latte. We posted signs all over the Lake Cavanagh area announcing a "LOST DOG" with a picture of Latte wearing a little hat that she had worn at Preston's third birthday party several weeks before. Stan and Preston returned to Lake Cavanagh for a full day, searching the woods and calling out, "LATTE!" until their voices were hoarse.

A few months before Latte's disappearance, I had dreamt the strangest dream, and it had become forever "fast-frozen" in my brain. It was a vivid dream—not like the kind one gets from eating too much pizza before going to bed. In it, Preston was hiding under our big dining room table, hovering by the big pedestal legs. He looked afraid. For months I had tried to figure out what this dream meant, applying all kinds of interpretations from my human imagination but coming up with nothing of certainty. And so I moved on.

A week after she went missing, reality was setting in that Latte would probably not ever be coming back. There was a deep sense of loss; even little Preston felt it. We were coming down the stairs mid-morning on the following Saturday when Preston inquired, "Grandma, will Latte ever come home?" Out of desperation, I said, "Preston, why don't we ask God to help Latte find her way back?" Right there on the stairway we both bowed our heads and I prayed a very simple prayer that a three-year old could comprehend, asking God to bring Latte home. Afterward, I began to fret, wondering if I had just set Preston up for a huge disappointment with the Almighty.

Around lunchtime there was a knock on the door. Preston disappeared while I answered the door. There stood a stranger asking if we had lost a brown dog the previous weekend near Lake Cavanagh. She and her husband had been driving by and were afraid the dog they saw would get hit on the busy road, and so they stopped. When they opened their car door, Latte had just jumped in. Her dog tag provided our address in Stanwood, but no phone number. The rescuer went on to apologize, saying that their busy work schedules had prevented the couple from returning the dog until the weekend.

The stage was immediately set for a grand reunion of epic proportions when Thad and Abby came running up the stairway to be greeted by Latte, jumping and licking their faces. But where was Preston? Scanning the room, my eyes found him hovering, afraid, hiding under the table, clutching the pedestal legs. It was the exact picture embedded in my memory from the dream months earlier! With a little coaxing, Preston emerged from under the table and embraced Latte.

When I first received that phone call from Kentucky, none of us realized how important Latte would be in Thad and Abby's life. Even when Latte found her way back home that glorious Saturday, we still didn't know the long journey ahead. Thad and Abby would wait until they had been married eleven years for the gift of their first child, Julie Laele, whose middle name in Hebrew means, "belonging to God." Latte stayed with them and remained their ever-faithful and loving family member during all that time, comforting them during the long period of waiting and praying for a child.

When precious "Jules" arrived, we wondered how Latte would adjust to the junior member of the household. A quick look at their Facebook photo album will reveal a picture of Julie, just a few months old, nestled safely with Latte's body curled around her. In the photo, Latte has a contented motherly look on her face. After five years, they are close buddies, romping around the yard together. "Latte" was one of the first words "Miss Julie" learned! Then two years ago, Baby Clara JoAnn joined the family and Latte tends to her with that same care and protection.

Latte is now one of our two GRANDdogs! A couple of years ago, at the insistence of Preston, a Plott Hound, "EZ," was rescued from going to the pound by the Lees and joined our extended family. Grandma still keeps treats in the closet for the grandkids to feed both EZ and Latte, the dog who now has a shiny chocolate-brown coat and a weight problem! And Latte now sports an identification tag that has both Thad's and Abby's cell phone numbers engraved on it. When Thad and Abby turn onto Lakewood Road, Latte knows she is on her way to the lake! They can let her out at the beginning of Olive Avenue and she automatically returns to her first home in Washington.

For months the grandkids had a cardboard playhouse that Papa and Preston made out of a huge box retrieved from the Camp. Throughout the time it sat in our living room, Preston added features to his brown abode which was also colorfully decorated and autographed by his playmates, the Schreiber triplets, Trip, Georgia, and Ashley. It was even equipped with cardboard furniture, pillows, and a mail slot so the kids could drop letters into the house. Just when we thought there was nothing left that Preston could add, he stapled a sign on the house which read, "LOST DOG, call the Nelsons!"

It's been eight years since Preston and Papa searched the woods, but Preston still remembers the day God answered prayer and returned Latte. The Sovereign God of the Universe, not bound by our time or space, had already orchestrated the answer to our prayer before we stopped on the stairway to pray.

God is **THE DOG CATCHER**, and HE appointed several "angels" to protect Latte from the dangers ahead and bring her safely home. God has spoken truth to us through this beloved chocolate lab, just like HE used a donkey to speak to the prophet Balaam in Numbers 22:30!

47: THE SHADOW CASTER

It was December of 2010, and I had just officially joined the faculty of the M.J. Murdock Trust's Essentials of Development, the same training program that had launched me into the field in 1998. This program, designed to teach the "four essentials of development," is offered by the Trust for smaller nonprofits who are just learning how to raise resources. Each nonprofit chosen to participate must send their executive director, a board member or two, and the person in charge of development.

After several sessions, Dr. Jay Barber, the Director of the Essentials training at that time, sent me back to his suite at the Vancouver Hilton Hotel with the team from Clydehurst Camp in Montana. Jay could sense this group needed a little coaching to get themselves on the same page. The training provided an excellent environment for this to occur between members. I remember when Roger Hancuff, Frank Cranston, and I boarded a small plane to participate in the Essentials of Development training in Roseburg, Oregon in 1998. Not only did we come away with the same basics of understanding for raising resources, but we were allowed quality time with one another. Something mysteriously happened, knitting us together as a team, right before the Journey of Faith Campaign was about to launch.

I was praying all the way as I walked down that hallway in the Hilton with the Clydehurst team in tow. Hopefully, they wouldn't realize how green I was. This was my first experience at coaching. Somehow, the Lord would have to give me the wisdom to get this team together in one accord for the awesome task ahead of them.

The team was a mix of ages and experience. Development Director Scott Brownson, in his thirties, was brand new to his role. After the training Scott would be moving his family from Nashville to Clydehurst. He was certainly not new to Clydehurst, as his dad had been the camp director for over forty years. Scott had grown up at the camp and knew the ministry like the back of his hand. His father, still serving as the executive director, was leading this team. Kelly Fried, a consultant for the Trust in Christian Education, was the chairman of the board. And another long-standing board member had come along for the training.

As is often the case, the team had different opinions on how to raise money, varying from just praying to boldly asking, with some variations in between. After hearing all their concerns, I felt led to share my experience of my first twelve years as development director at Warm Beach Camp. We had watched the Lord work with a combination of our best efforts and a lot of prayer. Our team certainly depended on God as the provider, and watched how HE took our work and blessed it as we prayed our way through.

Somehow, mysteriously, the Spirit bonded this Clydehurst team together in a mighty way. When they left that Hilton suite they were expectant and in one accord. I was very impressed with the newly hired development director, Scott.

For a few years, as a professional musician he had traveled the U.S. until it became too hard on his family life. Scott and his wife had varied ministry experiences, including planting a church. Like most of the younger generation, he was not about to "play church." Scott wanted the real thing.

While Scott showed respect and honor for those who had gone before him at Clydehurst, I sensed this rebel would be innovative. Like the four men who brought their paralyzed friend to Jesus (Mark 1:1-12), Scott would be dreaming up out-of-the-box methods like chopping holes in roofs! There was something so genuine in my encounter with Scott. I admired his passion for the Lord and "smelled the Kingdom" during that brief time around this young man.

God is the initiator and is always on the hunt for those who will jump into the streams that He is opening. Scott was about to take another leap, and it wouldn't be easy. I secretly committed myself to be praying for this new development director who would soon be leaning on the Lord in a new arena, trusting Him to turn mountains into molehills.

On the way home from our second training session in May, 2011, Scott gave me a CD that he had just produced as a "thank-you" gift for donors. Drawing on his extensive background, Scott had put together an album, including tracks from a band that played back-up for well-known Christian artists Rebecca St. James, Hillsong United, One Sonic Society, and others. During the four-hour trek back to Stanwood I listened to Scott's CD many times. Two of his numbers, "Faithful" and "Your Reign," registered deep within my heart.

Scott would keep in touch from time to time through email. Just as I had imagined, he was connecting with all generations and thinking outside the box. One of the development events he organized was "An Evening with C.S. Lewis," at which he brought in a person to impersonate the cherished saint. It was a smashing success with all ages. Scott's big challenge was to oversee the $700,000 campaign for a new chapel at Clydehurst, a huge stretch for such a small camp which operated mainly in the summer time. I continued to pray for him whenever the Lord brought him to my mind.

At the December, 2011 Leadership Advance hosted by the Trust, I ran into the Clydehurst's board chair, Kelly. He was impressed with Scott's progress and wondered if I would let Scott job-shadow me for a couple of days if they flew him out to Washington. In the past I had always turned down job-shadowing requests. It would be awkward to take a stranger on donor calls, which often ended up with deep sharing that ventured well beyond the bounds of raising resources. But, I had learned from past experiences that when you pray, you need to be willing to be a part of the answer. After responding, "Yes," to Kelly, I chuckled. The Lord had sneakily cornered me again!

Several weeks before Scott was to arrive, I contacted five amazing donors and one prospect, requesting their participation in the up-coming job-shadowing experience. They all graciously accepted the invitation to be a part of this new development director's training. There was excitement in the air as I laid out the purpose of each visit with them. Some would be "thank-you" visits. Others knew that I was coming to ask for either money or volunteer service. All would be prepared to answer why they supported Warm Beach Camp and to indicate how they liked to be thanked. There were varying generations and both male and female donors represented.

Scott and I began the journey by attending the weekly Stanwood/Camano Rotary meeting where I introduced him as my guest. Then we were off to have coffee with a local business man, Wade Starkenburg from Stanwood Self Storage, who regularly sponsors events. He was willing to again sponsor the up-coming Partner-in-Ministry event. Upon wrapping up the visit, we sailed down Marine Drive to the Warm Beach Senior Community to have coffee with the former president of Seattle Pacific University, Dr. Curtis Martin, who had been primed to tell "Mr. Montana" what he felt was important for a new development director to know. Curtis did an excellent job of honoring Scott and sharing in his journey.

The following morning we had breakfast with Warm Beach Camp Director, Ed McDowell. I knew this would be an encouraging time as Ed had also grown up at Camp and followed in his father's footsteps. Both Scott and Ed were men of vision, and a voice to their respective generations. Mid-morning we had coffee with a former staff member, Noel Culbertson, who together with her husband, Stan, has a real heart for the Kids2Camp ministry. As we left I handed Noel a thank-you gift of the Camp's famous granola.

At lunchtime we met John Overton at the local Chinese restaurant. John knew that I would be asking his company, Vital Soft, to help put up the match for the up-coming Kids2Camp auction. In addition, while no arm-twisting was needed, John agreed to again be the on-site coordinator for the auction in August. Minutes away, Eilene Zachry, one of the Camp's gracious donors, was waiting for afternoon coffee at an Arlington restaurant. In addition to agreeing to provide me with shopping money for the Kids2Camp auction, Eilene spoke from her heart describing what being connected to the ministry of the Camp had meant on her own journey towards wholeness in Jesus.

The last visit was with Chuck Anderson, a former trustee of the Stewardship Foundation, and director of his own family's foundation. Both of these foundations have blessed the Camp over the years. Chuck was primed to share with Scott from his years of foundation work. As we leaned forward around the little booth at Jimmy's Italian Restaurant in Stanwood, I learned more about the foundation world of which Chuck had been a part for years. Chuck also shared with us the reasons why it is so difficult for many people of wealth to part with their money. At Scott's request, Chuck went home and put the list of reasons in writing so that I could send it to him in an email. And of course, Chuck smiled when I gave him a treasured tub of Camp granola!

There's no doubt that I learned just as much, if not more, than "Mr. Montana" from our two-day trip on the donor trail. These supporters' reasons for investing in Warm Beach Camp were amazing, as were their tales of what God had done in their lives while supporting the Camp's ministry. Through the years, God had been multi-tasking in ways of which I was not totally aware until visiting with these donors.

I didn't know Curtis Martin all that well at the time of our mentoring visit with Scott. But Curtis believes in the camping ministry and dived right in to organize two fund-raising dinners for the Kids2Camp program, opening up his email list of friends in order to raise around $10,000. When his wife, Carol, died, Curtis designated the memorial gifts to go to the Kids2Camp program.

Two years ago in December, I was thrilled to hear from "Mr. Montana" that they had tripled their budget at Clydehurst in the last three years, and that they had raised $700,000 for the new chapel, which was nearly finished. They had received a $150,000 grant from the M.J. Murdock Trust to help with this project. In addition, Scott is now directly involved with the Christian Camps and Conference Association, eager to network with his peers as the next generation of leadership fills the ranks.

This past January Scott returned as the keynote speaker and worship leader at our Camp staff's annual retreat which was held at Black Lake Camp near Olympia. The songs he's written can be heard coming from the kitchen and offices throughout the Camp as we are all humming along to Scott's latest CD. My all-time favorite song, "Grace upon Grace," is found at the end of this book.

When we finished those two days of job-shadowing in 2012, Scott dropped me off before returning to the airport. I was wondering what his thoughts were. He only had one word to describe our job-shadowing experience: "WORSHIP." That was it, in total. He thanked me, backed the rental car out of our driveway at the lake, and headed home.

The next morning during prayer time, I sat pondering what Scott had meant by his response to my question. Perhaps it was just because he was a musician, gifted at bringing people into the presence of God with worship music. Like a breeze out of nowhere it hit me. I grabbed my Bible and turned once again to Psalm 91, with which I was so familiar and which I had prayed so often...

> "He who dwells in the shelter of the Most High
> will rest in the shadow of the Almighty.
> I will say of the Lord, He is my refuge and my fortress,
> my God, in whom I trust."

Laughing out loud, I realized how the Lord had continued to answer my prayer over and over again: "...Lord I want to work with you, I want to watch how you do it. Teach me the unforced rhythms of grace..." (*The Message*, Matthew 11)

God is **THE SHADOW CASTER**. Mr. Montana wasn't job-shadowing me; we were sitting in the shadow of the Almighty, working with Him, watching how HE did it! Once again the Lord had to kidnap me, His child, to let me in on what HE was doing. Scott hit the nail on the head. There was no better way to describe it than "WORSHIP," being in the presence of God and acknowledging who HE is!

48: THE ARRANGER

Everyone was talking about Facebook. I was the last in our office to hop on this latest social media craze in 2010. The very first person's name I plunked into the search engine was Gary Alfson, my long-lost youth pastor who would then be in his late sixties. Via the grapevine I had heard that Gary had disappeared into the corporate world.

Much to my surprise, I was delighted when up popped Gary's picture. While looking a bit older, there was no doubt that this was THE Gary Alfson, former youth director at Trinity Lutheran Church of Minnehaha Falls in Minneapolis. I sent a "friend request" along with a message, hoping that Gary would remember me, the daughter of the bus driver who used to cart the youth group around to every imaginable event. Gary's acceptance of my "friend request" soon became the beginning of many emails.

Besides catching up on the last forty years of life, I got swept into reviewing the history of the Lutheran Evangelistic Youth Movement (LEM) that Gary, as the first LEM national youth director, was writing for Jonathan Anderson's book, *Our Father Saw His Mighty Works: The LEM and Forgotten Mid-20th Century Revival.* Tears came to my eyes when I read about the LEM Board's request to have the young men on the last team Gary was supervising cut their hair. While there are likes and dislikes in every generation, how could something so unimportant as hair length threaten to drive a wedge between generations and possibly dampen the desire to advance the Gospel? I asked God to remind me of this as the next generation of leaders was emerging at Camp with differing tastes than mine.

A few months later, our Camp's general manager, Pat Patterson, sent an email asking program managers to review the current policy in the staff manual regarding tattoos and piercings, in order to make recommendations for any needed changes. The Lord quickly reminded me of Gary's account from the chapter he had written for Jonathan's book. As the oldest member of our management team, my response to Pat was that I would pray for wisdom, and trust whatever the team decided best during these changing times.

Stan and I had gone through tattoos and piercings with our daughter, Cherith. She sports several darling small tattoos, including the Christian symbol of the fish, on her back. A few years earlier my friend, Rita Nussli, had prayed me through this phase of Cherith's life. Rather than freak out over Cherith's desire to have her belly button pierced, under Rita's tutelage we had prayed for God to pierce her heart. Rita, who was directing a ministry to kids living on the streets of Seattle, also reminded me that God has our names tattooed on His hands.

So that morning in May of 2013, I typed Gary a quick email telling him that his chapter in the LEM history book had helped me to greet any style changes in the emerging leaders of tomorrow with acceptance. I informed him that after the journey with our precious daughter, if I weren't such a wimp, I might be ready to get a small hidden tattoo myself! He sent a quick email back teasing that he considered researching the internet for tattoo ideas to suggest to me, but he was getting ready to fly out the next day from Florida to visit his sister, Cindy, in Minneapolis.

What a wonder! Within a couple of days I too would be flying into Minneapolis to visit one of the Camp's supporters who had become a dear friend! Gary and I checked schedules and we were both free on the coming Thursday morning—just days away. God had divinely arranged this cross-over in Minneapolis for the two of us living on opposite corners of the country.

Excitement filled my soul as the plane approached the Minneapolis/St. Paul Airport. As we started our descent, I had an overwhelming desire to see my dear friend, Patty, who had prayed with me so often at California Lutheran Bible School, where I attended after graduating from high school. Patty lived only minutes from the airport. But I quickly extinguished the thought as the friend I had actually come to visit had graciously planned my short stay. The full schedule included a trip to Balsaam Lake to visit my dad's and sister's graves after lunch with my aunts and uncles at the Thirsty Otter's Tavern next to my folks' former lake home. There was no time to visit Patty on this trip.

My eighty-three-year-old host, Eileen Voth, was waiting at the airport in her cute, sporty red Honda. She whisked me away to a concert at a huge church in Minneapolis where five choirs would be performing. Her friends were saving us seats near the front. As the orchestra was warming up, I slipped into the pew and Eileen's friends directed me to sit next to a couple. To my amazement, it was Patty and her husband, Carlie! I had not seen them for over twenty years! My host could not believe that I was suddenly involved in a big group hug with these seemingly total strangers! The three of us tried not to scream too loudly with sheer delight! I also knew Carlie well as we had traveled together for a year in southern California in the second group of Coruscation Singers.

When Patty heard that I would be seeing Gary Alfson in a couple of days, she sent this message: "Tell Gary that the Crusade team on which we traveled the summer of 1968 totally changed my life. I had always marveled at the Trinity kids at CLBS. I didn't have the opportunity to be involved in a youth group like Trinity had. The kids from Trinity really knew how to pray and believed that God would answer. The summer on Crusades gave me a chance to experience that kind of trusting relationship with Jesus."

On Thursday, Gary picked me up for a three-hour trip down memory lane. We went back to Trinity and toured the rooms where the youth group had hosted the Campus Club meetings. We peeked at the "holy" ground outside where the volleyball tournaments happened. These games were followed by times of serious prayer together.

We traveled on to Lake Nokomis where our gang often hung out, having times of fun and singing. Gary took my picture on the famous park bench where he often sat during summer evenings to receive inspiration from the Holy Spirit regarding what to share with the Trinity kids during the many devotional and prayer times we had together. After snapping my picture, Gary mentioned how, during some of those times on that bench, he had wondered whether God was confirming what he had earlier felt as a call—to do the work of an evangelist. He surprised me by suggesting that, during the forty years since leaving the evangelistic youth ministry at the LEM to pursue a successful business career, he had often wondered whether he had frustrated the Lord's will and let Him down by changing life's direction.

I began to tell Gary that he had spent the most significant years of his life—seven years to be exact—discipling emerging leaders at the point when they had their entire lives before them. If he added together all the lives that were impacted with the youth group and the LEM teams alone, well, that number of souls would be far greater than most pastors could hope to influence during a lifetime of shepherding a flock—not to mention the ripple effect of working with youth who were serious about spreading the Gospel. I passed on the comment that Patty had given me a couple days before during our glorious reunion. There was a holy excitement in the air!

Gary drove me through the neighborhood around Trinity, pointing out where all of us teens used to live. He remembered because he had carted us around and visited most of our families. Gary started asking about different people as we passed their houses. I had kept in touch with some, but was sure that through Facebook we could find all of them. After a wonderful day with Gary, we parted with my promise to look up as many former youth group members as I could.

Upon returning to Washington, I jumped on Facebook and began to tell former youth group members about my time with Gary, encouraging them to connect with him on Facebook and to wish him a happy seventieth birthday. It was like a fire igniting, pulling us all back around the campfire at Camp Patmos. Within a few days, an idea started floating around Facebook to plan a youth group reunion. A month later, in June, due to some hard work by Gary's sister, Cindy, and several others, we came from around the United States to gather at Trinity for a youth group reunion. Some of us hadn't seen each other for forty-six years, including my next door neighbor, Brian Barnes, who had been like a brother to me!

Gary led the reunion in the new upper fellowship room as if we were back in the old Campus Club days! Paul Nye, now an accomplished musician, played some of the old-time favorites on his guitar. Gary went around the group and had each of us share the highpoint of our last forty-six years since high school. The Kingdom ripple effects we discovered that day are still ringing in our ears; the total impact only God can really know.

Out of that group of about thirty adults, there were teachers, social workers, foster parents, a pastor, a pastor's wife, and missionaries who had helped Brother Andrew smuggle Bibles behind the Iron Curtain. Most had families and had trained up their children in the faith. That experience in the upper room at Trinity gave me a slight whiff of another upper room where Jesus' disciples had gathered after his resurrection. Little did they realize that, through the power of the Holy Spirit, they would send waves of grace throughout the world.

A year later, in June of 2014, many of us reassembled at Trinity Lutheran Church for another reunion. LEM Crusader teams gathered there for a fiftieth anniversary reunion concert. It was put on by the Scandinavian team on which Gary had traveled shortly before he became our youth director and later the LEM national youth director. Because Stan had not been able to come the year before, Gary wanted to give him a big hug at the airport when we arrived. Conveniently, without planning the day or time, our flights landed one minute apart! To make the trip affordable, Patty and Carlie picked us up at the airport, loaned us a car, and provided a place to stay. After the concert, Stan and I had the opportunity to meet with three other members of our Crusade team, including Dick, Patty and Marlene.

Spurred by the excitement generated by these two events, Gary organized a team of us to plan an "All Teams Reunion" at Trinity Lutheran Church that was held in Minneapolis in June, 2017. It was a blessed time of reunion for those who traveled with the Lutheran Evangelistic Movement during that period of the organization's history.

There's no doubt in my mind that God is **THE ARRANGER**. He is able to arrange for whatever HE wants done...down to the day, flight, and yes, even the placement of people in a pew!

49: THE HEART READER

It was my birthday, October 17, and I was on my way to the Abundant Living Care Home to visit the woman who labored to bring me into the world sixty-six years prior in a Minneapolis hospital. Just after crossing the railroad tracks near Lakewood, a big Toyota Tundra truck in front of me came to a screeching halt. I stopped too, but the driver behind me, a little seventeen-year-old decked out in her homecoming dress and driving her mom's huge SUV, rear-ended my burgundy 2002 Malibu that I had inherited from my mom when she had to cease driving. The impact thrust my car into the truck ahead of me.

The force of the crash tossed me back and forth between the steering wheel and seat. All of a sudden I realized that my car was wedged between two other vehicles. Thankfully, my seatbelt, while it bruised me, saved me from more serious damage. I was able to climb out of the car, and found that my legs were working even though my entire body was trembling from head to toe. Soon we drivers were snapping pictures of the wreck on our cell phones. Because the traffic was backing up, we decided to pull the vehicles into a nearby empty lot and call the police. Fortunately, while the trunk of my car was smashed in and I had no tail lights, my car was still drivable.

While waiting for the police to arrive, I realized that none of us were strapped to backboards on the way to an emergency room, as was the case in my accident involving a big brown delivery truck a few years prior. An incredible sense of peace filled my body and I stopped shaking. My car had the most damage of the three vehicles, but I found myself calming down the other two drivers along with the teen's mom, who arrived shortly after her daughter notified her. Stan was just leaving work at Camp, fifteen minutes from the accident, when he got my call to come quickly. After we drivers gave our statements, the police officer who had arrived let me drive my car home on the condition that Stan follow me closely and that we arrive before dark. I didn't get to see my mom that day, but the family went ahead with their plans to take me to a restaurant for my birthday celebration. It was quite a party, as we were all grateful I was alive to participate!

The next morning was Sunday and I posted a message on Facebook thanking everyone who had sent birthday greetings from around the country. Before I hit the "enter" key I added: "I had a birthday surprise. On my way to see my mom I was rear-ended and my car is probably totaled…my dream car is a mini-Lexus SUV with low mileage." Now, I would never ask God for a car such as that as it seemed rather excessive. After hearing widows in Burundi, Africa, exclaim that "there really must be a God" because they were getting to ride in an old beat-up van to the Sister Connection retreat, I doubted whether God would consider my dream car a need.

As is my practice, every Sunday I lead the prayer time in the adult Soul Crafter's Sunday School class at my church. That morning I shared that I was thankful for God's protection and that since the Malibu was my work car, I would need another road-worthy vehicle. And of course, to add some levity, I shared the vision of my dream car with the class. That day, Leigh Wilson, a retired school principal and college English professor, started a three-Sunday series on prayer. What made it so remarkable was that Leigh had already volunteered to edit my book and I had no knowledge of his passion for prayer and his Biblical basis for believing in prayer. I was swept away in sheer delight during the class; I couldn't quit smiling and nodding my head in agreement with everything he shared.

When Leigh came to the part on "persisting in prayer," he looked at me and said in fun, "Nancy, you will need to ask more than once for that little Lexus SUV." I laughed because I hadn't dared ask the Lord for such a dream car. Everyone else laughed too. Then someone in the class hollered out, "I wonder what the license plate will say on the little Lexus SUV when it arrives?" The class was used to seeing the "PRAZ HM" plate that I often held up as a template for beginning prayer. They knew the story behind the plate and the order that our son, Thad, had placed while praying for a car. The Lord had arranged for that car, right down to my son's specifications as to the make, its four doors, a standard transmission, and the burgundy color that he wanted.

Little did any of us realize what God was planning behind the scenes. When my dear friend, Rita, was getting into her car in Sumas, Washington, her husband, Ron, read her my Facebook post. She wanted to call me right away to express her sympathy, but they were on their way to church. After the service they decided to attend the church potluck fellowship, which they had never done before. They sat next to Elmer Radke, the gentleman who sold them their first car when they were newlyweds years before. Rita asked Elmer if he was finally retired, to which this eighty-something man exclaimed, "No, I'm still selling cars, one or two at a time from my front yard, when I can help people find what they need or need to sell." Without giving them a chance to respond he stated, "You should see what a friend brought over last night…a little Lexus SUV with low mileage."

Rita could hardly believe her ears. She excitedly said, "My friend's car just got totaled yesterday and that is exactly her dream car!" Rita wanted to know if she could call me and inform me of the car. Elmer said she had better do it quickly as his son was about to post the Lexus SUV on Craigslist and that it wouldn't last long. The little SUV was in mint condition and he was selling it for his friend at $3,000 below book price. With that information, Rita called me right away.

Stan was working at Camp that Sunday but said that I should drive up to Ferndale, about one and a quarter hours away, and check out the car, as it sounded like a "God-thing." Within twenty-four hours of the accident, I was test driving my dream car, a little burgundy 2009 Lexus SUV with 90,000 miles on it. Elmer graciously gave us the rest of the day to pray about purchasing the car, but asked for an answer by 8 a.m. the next morning. He promised not to call any of the other inquirers back until he heard from us.

Within forty-eight hours of the accident, after Stan test drove the Lexus, we were pulling out of Elmer's driveway with my dream car, sporting a license plate that read, "AMY5410." After registering the car at the DMV, Stan returned home with the old plates. I propped the plates up so I could see them from my big prayer chair and started pondering if there was any significance. They made me smile, as Amy was Stan's mom's name. Three years earlier she had stepped into heaven. Amy was a prayer warrior and for years had prayed for us. Because she had left a small inheritance for her family, we had enough money to purchase the car without taking out a loan.

The next morning I was still wondering about the "5410" part of the old license plate. Was it related to Stan's mom's birthday or his folks' anniversary? When I could not come up with any dates that matched those numbers, the Lord prompted me in my spirit to check for "54:10" in the Bible. I quickly scanned the scriptures and found that there was only one passage: Isaiah 54:10. "Though the mountains be shaken and the hills be removed, yet my unfailing love for you will not be shaken nor my covenant of peace be removed says the Lord, who has compassion on you." I was stunned! It was as if Stan's mom had delivered a message to us from Heaven!

The next Sunday we drove to the upper parking lot by the Wesley Center at the Warm Beach Free Methodist Church in the little burgundy-colored mini-SUV with low mileage. I started prayer time by holding up the license plate and reading Isaiah 54:10, giving praise to God for His unfailing love and supplying us with the dream car that I dared not request from Him. After pondering that all three cars (Thad's little Toyota, "Prazmobile," the 2002 Malibu, and the little Lexus SUV) were the same burgundy color, I realized that they symbolized the blood of Jesus! We were driving cars that were covered with the blood of Jesus.

Since the accident was the fault of the little gal who plowed into me, her insurance company gave me a fair settlement for my wrecked car and also for the six months of pain and suffering I endured while I underwent chiropractic and massage therapy for the effects of the whiplash. Without having to hire a lawyer, we received a settlement that was almost the same amount as what we paid for the Lexus!

We know **THE HEART READER**. He not only can point out when sins like selfishness, bitterness, envy, and jockeying for position need to be confessed and forgiven, but He also knows the desires of our hearts and delights in surprising us!

50: THE PROMISER KEEPER

In the book of Psalms, there are fifteen individual songs of thanksgiving scattered throughout King David's marvelous work, and he thanks God repeatedly for deliverance from the perils of life such as scheming enemies, poor health, and dangers of many kinds. Psalm 34 is one of those songs of rejoicing, and early in our marriage Stan and I adopted it as a key passage of scripture in our lives. While we love this entire psalm of King David, there are parts and phrases that have special meaning to us and have thus become central in our daily living.

First and foremost, Psalm 34 begins by telling us that real living starts with "extolling the Lord at ALL times and having HIS praise on our lips" (verse 1). Stan and I have found that when we praise God, not only does He delight in the praises of HIS people, but we are somehow swept into a deeper knowledge of HIS presence, even in the difficult times. And like all healthy relationships, it's a two-way interchange. Mysteriously, we become delighted in the process of delighting HIM. In our later years, I have discovered that having grandchildren makes this "delighting" concept more real to us. We are all made in God's image, so it doesn't surprise me that when we observe delight in our grandchildren, we reap even more delight ourselves. Stan and I are constantly dreaming up exciting outings for our grandkids. We find great joy in our family's delight, as God does when we delight in Him.

In verse four, David tells us, "I sought the Lord, and he answered me; he delivered me from all my fears." Through the years we have found that praying the Word of God, especially HIS promises, is effective and powerful. God has infinite memory, and certainly doesn't need reminding, but it must give him pleasure to realize we are aware of HIS promises to us as children of the King. Perhaps reminding God of HIS promises is all for our benefit, but I don't think that's entirely the case. We were created for HIS purposes and HE craves relationship with us. And, after all, it lets HIM know that we are trusting in HIS credibility and HIS character. I can't help but imagine that God enjoyed the raw honesty, the questions, and the reminders as David wrote his way through real life. David certainly wasn't perfect, but he was intimately close to God. As I tackle journaling my prayers every morning, I also wonder how God keeps track of us all. When Thad and Cherith were young, I could hardly handle two kids talking to me at the same time!

I love that David includes verse five: "Those who look to him are radiant; their faces are never covered with shame!" Some of my heroes are the "Trueface" guys who make this verse come alive: Bruce McNicol, Bill Thrall, and John Lynch. I first heard Bruce at an M.J. Murdock leadership conference in 2007, at a very strategic time in our family's life. The Lord had specifically placed me in Bruce's seminar to begin the journey of understanding how we all try to cover our shame; it goes back to the Garden of Eden when our first parents used fig leaves. Over time, we human beings have gotten much more sophisticated in using various addictions, including the behavioral narcotics of people-pleasing, performance, perfectionism, and workaholism. Thankfully, in an environment of grace, we can come just as we are to the Father and our faces will reflect HIS glory because of the grace of Jesus (II Corinthians 3:18). And, according to McNicol, Thrall, and Lynch, as written in *The Cure,* it's love, usually applied by others, that is the solvent that helps us remove our masks so that our faces can become radiant.

Psalm 34 also states in verse eight: "O taste and see that the Lord is good." It's always been one of my favorite parts of the psalm, probably because my first love in camping was, and will always be, the food services. I love praying, "Oh, Lord, I am tasting, and YOU promised that you are good!"

The all-time favorite portion of Psalm 34 for Stan and me is found in verse ten: "... but those who seek the Lord lack no good thing." This promise from God has rung true throughout our lives. It proved true for us even before tying the knot in holy matrimony, though our life has not been without challenges. After a 2,000-mile separation during our two-year romance, I could hardly believe that when Stan's student deferment ran out he received his draft notice just months after we were married. Thankfully, the draft law expired and Stan was able to join the reserves, sparing him from the probability that he would have been sent to Vietnam, where a lot of army draftees fought in the early seventies. Then again, in 1978, we found ourselves humming the all-too-familiar song, "Leaving on a Jet Plane," when Fresno State University demanded that Stan return to California to take his three-month internship there if he wanted a degree from their institution. In each case, the Lord kept his promise and turned each situation into good.

Furthermore, from day one in our marriage incredible things have happened which could only be because of the grace of God. When Stan and I went into camping ministry, we were well aware that people serving in camping would not make the money that they could in other careers. Thankfully, we both obtained all our degrees with no debt. And, while there wouldn't be a lot of income, we were from very frugal, blue-collar families who knew how to stretch every nickel beyond belief. We had both grown up with love in abundance and didn't lack any good thing! Besides, most of the good things in life can't be bought, and God has granted us the opportunity to live in beautiful places with stunning scenery all around. For example, after spending only a couple of months in our first apartment on Marconi Street in Sacramento (we affectionately called it Macaroni Street), through wonderful circumstances we met a couple who not only wanted a gardener but who needed a couple to live on their estate in a cute little honeymoon cottage. They trusted us and gave us free rein of their place when they were gone.

Our first home in the camping ministry was the little cottage by the creek at Hartland Christian Camp in the Sierras in central California. Moving to Warm Beach Camp (WBC) in Washington, we were placed in the top apartment of the McMillin house overlooking Puget Sound at a time before the trees grew up; we reveled in the panoramic view and savored beautiful sunrises and sunsets. After playing "musical houses" a couple of times at WBC, we spent thirteen years in the camp house located in the woods across from the Camp's main entrance. Our children grew up in safety and with all the recreation that kids could ever imagine including horses, swimming pools, mini-golf, tennis courts, and woods with trees to climb and places to build forts. With relatives far away, we were delighted that we belonged to a loving staff and church family. And after a few years on 81st Street, with a back yard facing the beauty of nature bordering the Camp, the Lord arranged for us to live in our current home with a fantastic, peaceful view of Lake Howard. My early morning prayer time often begins with the request, "Here I am, Abba; lead me by the still waters of Lake Howard."

The Lord even provided an excellent dentist in Seattle, Dr. Perry Jones III, to take care of all the year-round, full-time, Warm Beach Camp staff's and their families' teeth, almost free of charge, for thirty years! In addition, God provided a group of three chiropractors, Dr. Avery Martin and his sons, Nick and Nathan, who for years have come to camp each month to keep our spines in tip-top shape.

And it doesn't end there. During our years in camping, the Lord has provided a way for us to travel and attend conferences throughout the U.S. and Canada. For years I have taught seminars at Christian Camping International (now named CCCA) conferences. During an eight-year stretch (1988-1996), Stan and I were on the advance team of volunteers that went to the city where the national CCI conference would be held. Stan was in charge of the set-up and take-down crew and I became the lead registrar, training the other volunteers. This enabled us to take our vacation after each conference was over and sightsee in different parts of the country. Once someone asked me, "Don't you want to retire so you can do all the things you've dreamed about doing?" My response was, "Wow, we have already done way more than we could have ever asked or imagined in our wildest dreams," as the Lord has filled our lives with purpose and involvement in Kingdom work.

More than anything, the Lord has been good to us in the gift beyond measure of our two amazing children, Thad and Cherith, and their wonderful spouses, Abby and Chad. Just the other day our daughter-in-law, Abby, made a comment that blessed me: "Isn't it good that even though we are aware of shortcomings, we can all love each other, just as we are!" What she was describing was an environment of grace, a place to belong, to be loved— something we all crave, even if we can't name it. And God has granted that to us in our family.

And finally there are our grandchildren, as I mentioned in the beginning of this story. There are no words to describe the joy they bring into our lives. In little-bite-sized bits, grandchildren give us a chance to do it all over again, without being so concerned about whether they are on schedule in learning to walk and talk, getting potty trained, not sucking their thumbs or a binky, and so forth.

While each grandchild is so special, I often remind Preston William that God sent him at the right time, for he was the only one who got to meet G.G.'s (Great Grandma's) husband, my dad, because Preston's first year of life overlapped my dad's last year before going home to the Lord. And then there's Preston's little brother, Eli Ennis, who keeps us on the lookout for trains and reminds me of my dad: he is very mechanical and has my dad's shape and hands. Eli tags along after Papa everywhere. The two of them are like two peas in a pod. They can lie on the floor for hours putting puzzles together, reading books, and designing creations out of Legos.

It was also a delight to find out that we would be welcoming a little grand-daughter, Julie Laele, into the world five years ago! This grandma took to shopping the sales so that Julie would be dressed in grand style, differently than the boys! "Jules" brings more happiness into our lives than can be put into words. And two years ago last October baby Clara JoAnn entered the world. What a joy to take Julie to the hospital to meet her new baby sister, who is now affectionately known as "ClareBear"! Come December, another grandchild will be added to the tribe as Thad and Abby are preparing for their third baby, Johan, to arrive.

In our home, there's a little wooden sign perched on the ledge above our wood-burning stove that says TGIF (Thank God It's Friday). And Friday certainly is the best day of the week for us. Since Preston was born thirteen years ago, we have set Fridays aside as our special day to delight in our grandchildren. Before retiring, Stan was blessed by being allowed to work Saturdays in order to have Friday reserved for our little people. As for me, if I am not scheduled to work a weekend day, then I have spread my vacation and holidays throughout the year to cover the remaining Fridays to be with our little ones. Trust me: we have been blessed far more than the grandkids!

As David so beautifully exclaims in Psalm 34, we are to praise the Lord and to seek Him at all times—even when in distress. As we look to Him our faces are radiant and never covered with shame. When we seek Him, we lack no good thing. He invites us to taste and see that He is good. God is indeed great and He has been ever-faithful as we have reached out to Him in prayer. We know that God is **THE PROMISE KEEPER** and His word is true. He can be counted on to keep His promises, both now and forever.

AFTERWORD

It is our prayer that all of you reading these stories will know GOD intimately and embrace HIS promises, in order to experience HIS transforming power and HIS sheer pure grace offered through Jesus. It is also our prayer that in each generation the Lord will raise up serious intercessors to pray for their families and the generations to come.

"Goodbye, friends. Love mixed with faith be yours from God the Father
and from the Master Jesus Christ.
PURE GRACE and nothing but GRACE
be with all who love the Master, Jesus Christ."
Ephesians 6:24 in The Message

GRACE UPON GRACE

VERSE 1

Jesus, I believe in You, and everything You say is true;
Sometimes I turn my back to You, but oh, how You forgive me!
For all the wrong I've ever done, and all the times I choose to run,
You paid the price of death for us, and we are truly free.
Oh, oh, oh...

CHORUS

We receive the fullness of Your grace upon grace;
    it covers all of us,
And we will boast in You alone:
    Your grace upon grace it covers all of us.

VERSE 2

Lord, You sent the glory of the Father in the Only Son,
The Word becoming flesh for us, full of grace and truth;
I can't see the height of it, and I don't know the depth of it,
So what am I to do with this, but surrender all to You.
Oh, oh, oh...

BRIDGE

We forever sing to the Gracious One;
Love has overcome, and it covers all of us.

NOTES

NOTES

NOTES

Made in the USA
San Bernardino, CA
04 January 2019